49 Butler Road
CROWTHORNE
Berks
RG45 6QZ
Tel. 01344 773917

My Memories of Crowthorne Yesteryear ...
(an autobiography)
and other accounts

(An autobiographical account of life in Crowthorne, Berkshire with other contributions by past and present residents of the village.)

Shirley E. Peckham
(née Woodason)

Shirpec
ew Milton
Hampshire

PUBLISHED BY

ShirPec
7 VINCENT ROAD
NEW MILTON
HAMPSHIRE
BH25 6SN

© Shirley E. Peckham   1996

All rights reserved; no part of this publication may be reproduced, stored in a retrieval system, or transmitted in any form or by any means, electronic, mechanical, photocopying, recording, or otherwise, without the prior written permission of the publishers.

FIRST PUBLISHED   1996

ISBN 0 9524215 1 8

Printed by
antony Rowe Ltd
Bumper's Farm
Chippenham
Wiltshire.
SN14 6LH
England.

DEDICATION

I dedicate this book to Peter, Beryl, Margaret and Lily.

ACKNOWLEDGEMENTS

My very grateful thanks are extended to the following for their very valued support in the making of this book, without whose assistance, collectively, the enterprise would not have reached fruition. The names are listed alphabetically and not in order of merit:-

Michael Abbott; Barclays (Bank PLC) Record Services (Senior Archivist); Peter Bhagwat; Bracknell Forest Borough Council; The British Film Institute; Sue Boyce; Revd. Peter Burtwell; Alan Butcher; the late Lily Cambage; Catford Copy Centre; Crowthorne C. of E. School (Secretary); George Daniel; Beryl Day; Dixon Stewart Webb, Solicitors; Brian Down; Edwin (Ted) Dray; Peter Elliott; Virginia Fairless; Bernard Fourness; Joan Franklin; Margaret Franklin; Jeff Gibson, Edward Jones (Crowthorne) Ltd.; Nicholas Gossip, photographic; Frida Harris; Laura Hill; Les Howard, Crowthorne Fire Service; Josephine Hurdle; Michael Ifould; Mary Lane, Broadmoor Hospital; Maidenhead Citizens' Advice Bureau (Manager); New Milton Citizens' Advice Bureau; Derek Marder; Michael Mason; Colin McQueen, G. M. (Crowthorne) Ltd.; Clare Mundy; Martha Oram; Ken Over; Cyril Owen; Ken Parker; Susan Parkinson; Maureen Pearmain; Bill Peckham; Tom Pepper; Joan Peters; Glennis Priest; John Priest; Public Library, New Milton (Librarian and Assistant Librarian); Public Library, Reference, Bournemouth (assistants); Peter Ratcliffe; Stuart Rayner; the Reading Evening Post; Brian Richens, Royal British Legion, Crowthorne; Winifred Rixon; Melanie Robson; Janet Rowe; Joyce Simpson; Gerald Smith; Pamela Smith; Michael Taylor, Taylor & Whitlock; Peter Tickner; National Westminster Bank PLC, R. B. Tucker; Wellington College (The Archivist); Joy Webb; Jackie Watson; the Wokingham & Bracknell Times Group; Doris Woodage; Malcolm Woodage; Elizabeth Woodason; Maurice Woodason.

I apologise for any inadvertent omissions.

Photographs. Most photo's in this book are individually acknowledged, indicating their source. Those that were taken by the author are indicated by the mention 'Photo - Shirley E. Woodason, Robson, or Peckham'. The pictures bearing no acknowledgement are from the author's own personal, family collection accumulated over many years, or their source has not been established despite efforts to achieve this end.

I gratefully acknowledge the contributions from Michael Taylor, Taylor & Whitlock, Jewellers, of 170 Dukes Ride, Crowthorne, and Jeff Gibson (Managing Director), Edward Jones (Crowthorne) Ltd., Pinewood Avenue, in the village, towards the cost of this book.

Shirley E. Peckham.

Shirley Woodason, aged eighteen. (Photo - Ron Francis.)

MY MEMORIES OF CROWTHORNE YESTERYEAR AND OTHER ACCOUNTS

CONTENTS

	Page No.
Acknowledgements	(iv)
Memory, autobiography	(x)
Foreword	(xi)

CHAPTER ONE
Shirley E. Peckham (née Woodason)
My family history — 1

CHAPTER TWO
Childhood continued — 11

CHAPTER THREE
Other childhood memories — 21

CHAPTER FOUR
School and other childhood experiences — 27

CHAPTER FIVE
More school and other stories — 33

CHAPTER SIX
Further school incidents — 41

CHAPTER SEVEN
My eleven-plus experience — 47

CHAPTER EIGHT
More childhood memories — 51

CHAPTER NINE
My Wellington College grounds experiences — 63

CHAPTER TEN
Religious aspects — 71

CHAPTER ELEVEN
Christmas, domestic, and more childhood memories — 75

CHAPTER TWELVE
My parents — 81

CHAPTER THIRTEEN
The Second World War — 87

My growing up	CHAPTER FOURTEEN	105
The in-between	CHAPTER FIFTEEN	113
My first and only job in Crowthorne (at Talmage's)	CHAPTER SIXTEEN	121
Dorothy and Des Reay	CHAPTER SEVENTEEN	131
Continuing my Talmage years	CHAPTER EIGHTEEN	133
Final on Talmage's	CHAPTER NINETEEN	143
A dire emergency over my mother	CHAPTER TWENTY	155
In young womanhood	CHAPTER TWENTY-ONE	159
My serious boyfriend relationships	CHAPTER TWENTY-TWO	163
My dancing continues	CHAPTER TWENTY-THREE	167
The Sandhurst Cadet	CHAPTER TWENTY-FOUR	171
Gordon, my future husband	CHAPTER TWENTY-FIVE	175
My sisters' and my weddings	CHAPTER TWENTY-SIX	183
Our honeymoon and first home	CHAPTER TWENTY-SEVEN	197
Changes	CHAPTER TWENTY-EIGHT	199
My memories of various Crowthorne shops	CHAPTER TWENTY-NINE	203
Some Crowthorne traders of 1948	CHAPTER THIRTY	208

OTHER ACCOUNTS

	Page No.
TAYLOR WHITLOCK, JEWELLERS	210
MICHAEL IFOULD	213
ALAN BUTCHER	242
CYRIL OWEN	243
PETER RATCLIFFE	244
LILY CAMBAGE (née REASON)	246
LAURA (BABS) HILL (née BENNELLICK)	253
MARTHA ORAM (née FLOODGATE)	268
J. H. LECKENBY	271
JONES' SAWMILLS	276
CLARE MUNDY (née PRICE)	284
THE WOODAGE FAMILY BUSINESS IN CROWTHORNE	289
REVD. PETER BURTWELL	294
PAMELA SMITH (née GANGE)	297
WINIFRED (WIN) RIXON (née ELLIS)	306
DEREK MARDER	309
KEN PARKER	315
PETER TICKNER	321
MICHAEL ABBOTT	326
E. C. (TED) DRAY	329
TOM PEPPER	331
Gymkhana fancy dress group photo	333
Charabanc outing photo	334
Crowthorne C. of E. School class group photo	335
Her Majesty the Queen in royal car photo	336
Broadmoor Hospital entrance-exit photo	337
Peter Tickner in retirement photo	337
MY MEMORIES OF TYPHOID FEVER – Shirley E. Peckham	338
SKETCH MAPS OF CROWTHORNE in the 1930's	339

Many other photographs appear throughout the book, also, and there are some sketches.

MEMORY

'The time within which a person may remember what is past' - *The Concise English Dictionary*. 'The faculty of the mind by which it retains and can recall previous ideas and impressions' - *Nuttall's Standard Dictionary of the English Language*.

This book is based on the personal reminiscences of all those people, myself included of course, whose accounts lie within its covers. As far as possible we have tried to be accurate, but the long passage of time may have unwittingly caused some flaws to arise. Please allow for this, reader, as you absorb the text and illustrations, hopefully with the maximum of interest and enjoyment as I have received in writing the volume.

Shirley E. Peckham.

AUTOBIOGRAPHY

'It is not what a man is, nor what he does, that makes a good autobiography; it is his attitude towards life and his power of absorbing and communicating experience. Humour, perception and the capacity to assimilate experience are the best gifts an autobiographer can possess; without them adventure and achievement are as nothing'.
Kathleen Betterton, B. A. *(source Teach Yourself to Write, English Universities Press Ltd., London, Chapter IX Autobiography and Biography)*.

FOREWORD

I am very happy in bringing before you the sequel to my original volume on Crowthorne, *Our Memories of Crowthorne Yesteryear*, published in November 1994 and now sold out.

The sequel, to a comparatively large extent, is autobiographical, based on my life in the village from my birth in 1934, through wartime, to 1960, when I moved with my new first husband, Gordon Robson, to live in North Wales; and the accounts of twenty other contributors dear to Crowthorne, some of whom still live there.

The books, labours of love for me, took five and a half years to produce, from the germ of an idea sprouting, through forests of research to the writing and publishing.

The extremely time-consuming commitment necessitated many sacrifices - family, friends, domestic, leisure, financial and possibly health ones. I have needed to neglect other duties; often I have not even known what has been growing in my garden (other than weeds), that my, also far from work-shy, husband Bill has never neglected, putting in many hours of work there on his own.

All has been worthwhile though, *I* think. (*He's* not commenting.) Many Crowthorne residents (and some who, like me, are no longer so) have been in touch with me for interesting, pleasurable, stimulating chats on their well-satisfied views on my first book on this unique Berkshire village. In some cases we were at the Church of England school together, and some were educated there with my late father.

Now that the work is all over for me, except for the marketing of this volume, I can sit back (I don't think I've ever done *that* for more than a few minutes in my life) and reflect on my fulfilling time spent on the books. This, gladly, is bound to happily occupy my thoughts on many occasions for probably the rest of my life.

I now pay my special tribute to all-her-life-Crowthornian, Beryl Day, for being so magnificent, concerning both books, in helping me over query-hurdles on the fairly frequent occasions I have stumbled against her with them. Her on-the-spot situation, against my distant one, and her ever-willingness to oblige me at all times, however inconvenient some of them might have been in her busy life, have been like a third leg, or arm, to me. And she has certainly helped my brain! Very well done, Beryl, and my extremely grateful thanks to you.

Some of the many messages, in letters, I received from appreciative readers in praise of *Our Memories of Crowthorne Yesteryear* follow (many others were expressed to me verbally, constituting too lengthy a list to include here):-

"I was absolutely thrilled with it, and think it is a marvellous achievement for you to have recorded so many interesting accounts - after all, people are what make a village come alive" - D. S.

"I congratulate you on finally completing your project, and am finding it very interesting to read the memories of the various contributors, particularly as I remember many of them from my early days in Crowthorne. Previous publications, whilst very good in dealing with the history of the village, have missed out because they had little to say about the people who made up the community, and by getting individuals to recall their own memories of the events that occurred in village life and the people involved, you have covered the gap. The book will, I am sure, revive memories for many of the older people of Crowthorne" - J. L.

"I have found it very interesting; it brings back lots of memories" - G. S.

"I have had a lot of late nights reading it. It's very good reading, of course, to one who lived through it all" - E. W.

"Well done! You have achieved an excellent effort in publishing *Our Memories of Crowthorne Yesteryear*. Many congratulations. The memories you have recorded would have been lost and you have created a lasting record" - J. H-C.

"I can't put it down. Very well done - *how* it's done!" - A. R.

"*Thank you*, for bringing pleasure to the people of Crowthorne" - T. E.

"I have been enjoying your book very much. It has certainly brought the memories flooding back. As many in the book said, 'Happy Times'" - B. S.

"I have just finished reading your compilation of recollections of life in Crowthorne, and found it enjoyable and interesting, bringing back names and many thoughts of the past" - R. B.

"Congratulations on your book! What a feather in your cap!" - J. D.

"Congratulations on your *Our Memories of Crowthorne Yesteryear*. I found it very interesting and absorbing" - E. W.

"I very much enjoyed the book. A first class publication that, with each person's memories, you have captured the moment, taking us back to those happy years of childhood. I am totally absorbed and will continue to 'dip in' to the contents. You must be very pleased with this achievement" - D. M.

"My husband and I were very pleased with your very readable book. There is usually a fight over whose side of the bed it should be

left! I'm quite sure that everyone who has a copy is as pleased as we are with ours" - J. L.
"A really great effort" - J. S.
"I have very much enjoyed your book. It brings back very happy memories" - J. E.
"I have found it of interest. Photographs always enhance the text" - M. C.
"I want to thank you for the hard work and commitment you've made to produce this book - about a unique community before it was almost swamped and swallowed by its present day form. Thank God some of the life of the old village still plays a significant part in its life today" - P. B.
"I am enjoying reading *Our Memories of Crowthorne Yesteryear*. Thank you for all the hard work put into this publication by your good self. You can be proud that your book has undoubtedly brought great pleasure to so many people who, like you, started life in Crowthorne" - K. O.
"I am enjoying your book, but just want to remember Crowthorne as it was" - S. K. (who lives in the north-east of the country, but was in service in Crowthorne in the late 1920s).
"I have read every word in your wonderful anthology on the village of Crowthorne. Even though I have been in America for over forty years, I still appreciate my early formative years in the Crowthorne area. The recollections of the people you interviewed showed that Crowthorne was a "fun" place in which to live. People helped each other. I spent several hours scanning your book. It brings back many memories! So much so that, as I have a good memory, I send you mine of the village." - J. H. L. (See pages 271– 275.)

The items above and on page (xii) represent a very small proportion of the many glowing messages I received in letters over twelve months, following the publication of *Our Memories of Crowthorne Yesteryear*. The other, verbal, messages were on very similar lines. In total they gave me ample encouragement to produce the sequel without undue delay. This has come to be just over one year from the publication of the original book.

Shirley E. Peckham.

Shirley Peckham (née Woodason), left and Joan Franklin (née Burton) in 1993 who, as classmates, sat together at a desk in teacher Gladys Burton's (Joan's aunt) class, at Crowthorne C. of E. School.
(Photo - Ruth Page.)

CROWTHORNE

Every so often I step again
Into my home village and
All about me are the once-upon-a-time residents
And the church school with yesteryear pupils
Running around its playground,
And the shops have back-in-time smells
And long-since customers
Being served by bygone assistants.

About the roads, some gravel and dust
I ride my thirties bicycle
Wearing my forties clothes,
See soldiers 'mong the villagers
And say to myself
One day I will be married with a family
And have a home somewhere of my own,
But will never forget this.

Shirley E. Peckham

My Memories of Crowthorne Yesteryear and other accounts

CHAPTER ONE
SHIRLEY E. PECKHAM (née WOODASON)
MY FAMILY HISTORY

BORN IN PINEWOOD AVENUE. I was born on the 18th June, 1934 in the bungalow home that my father, Dudley Alphonso (Syd) Woodason, built at the far end of Pinewood Avenue. Two doors from Crowthorne Farm, it is now known as No.4.

Dad was the fourth child of Ada Mary and James (Jim/Jimmy) Woodason of 'St. Leonard's', still standing in Old Wokingham Road. Mum, Sarah Ellen (Helene), was one of six children from High Spen, Newcastle upon Tyne. Her father, John Laybourne, died of yellow fever in India during wartime service, in about 1917. With my father's family being mainly bricklayers and my mother's chiefly colliery workers we were very much working-class, in which I have only pride. My sister Glennis was born in January 1936 and Virginia (Virgy) was born in December 1938.

MY PARENTS. In service as a parlourmaid in The Lodge, Wellington College, to Mr F. B. Malim, the Headmaster, and his wife Amy, my mother came to meet my father. They spent their courtship in Crowthorne, much of the time in the company of other courting couple friends of theirs. For their wedding, on August 29th 1931 in St. John the Baptist Church in the village, Mum travelled from The Lodge. Although she never gave me the details, she always showed pride in telling me, several times, "I was married from The Lodge." Mum was in white for her wedding and her four bridesmaids were in apple-green. The reception was held in Crowthorne Social Club (now The Parish Hall) in Heath Hill Road, where exactly 28 years later I also held my own wedding reception. They honeymooned at Whitley Bay, then spent the first year of their marriage in a flat above what was the wool shop in the High Street opposite the Crowthorne Inn. I believe the flat was owned by Morrison's, the dairy family, who traded from their other premises, now Bob's DIY shop, on the corner of the High Street/Napier Road. In 1932 my parents moved into the bungalow Dad had built, near Crowthorne Farm, and named their home 'Sydellen' after themselves.

MY EARLIEST RECOLLECTIONS. I was born nearly three years after my parents' wedding. My earliest recollection is of lying on my back in my pram looking up to the blue sky through leaves of a tree. It was a silver birch by our drive that Mum had put me under.

1

I also recall being put into leg braces, while in the pram only and of an age I sat in it. They were restrictive, with straps which held my legs together. When I was about 8, and asked her about it, my mother explained that a girl in my father's family had had serious problems with walking, so she and my Dad had tried to safeguard me from any such thing. I feel that they had no real cause for concern.

TODDLERHOOD, I LEARN TO GARDEN. At 2-3 years old I played in our garden. When I wet myself Dad would sometimes smack me and with Mum's agreement I was sent to bed with "there'll be no tea for you" ringing in my ears. Lying in bed, I would turn my head and look at my stinging red bottom. Probably I cried, but was soon asleep.

I 'helped' Dad in the garden from the age of 3. My parents came to keep poultry in a run, chickens – Rhode Island Reds and White Leghorns – and Khaki Campbell ducks. Vegetables and fruit occupied the rest of the garden. Dad taught me to make drills in the soil and sow seeds. It thrilled me to see the first green shoots out of the ground and Mum was also pleased for me. I helped Dad protect the plants with small leafless twigs. In warm, wet and sunny springtimes Dad would say "this is just what plants like, it makes them grow well." Unfortunately, so did the weeds. I hated weeding the rockery, because I grazed my knuckles on the stones, although I never minded my hands getting dirty. As well as the rockery there were ordinary 'straightforward' flowerbeds, from where Dad would pick a flower for his suit jacket buttonhole each Sunday morning. I was sometimes responsible for keeping filled the round brick bird-bath, later with its two cement birds on the rim, which Dad had made. This was surrounded by crazy-paving. To stop weeds growing between it, that were difficult to get out, Dad came to put cement of various colours between the slabs.

VISITS TO GRAN. Regularly on Sunday mornings, while Mum cooked our roast dinner of the week, Dad, looking very smart in his suit, with flower buttonhole, took my sisters and me to visit his mother in Old Wokingham Road. Like us, Gran had a bird-bath in her front garden, where there were beds of various low-growing flower plants: marigolds, asters, and others. She also grew a profusion of perennials: antirrhinums, cornflowers, phlox, stocks, delphiniums and many more, in a garden at the side of her house, whose pretty blooms, with lovely scents, were level with my eyes when I was very young. Michaelmas daisies were another regular feature there.

My Memories of Crowthorne Yesteryear and other accounts

GRAN'S WELL. This was at the side of her detached house and supplied all her water. It was of great interest to me. Nobody else we knew had a well and my cousin Denis Evans, who lived next door in 'Denvale', pulled up buckets of water for Gran. (His younger sister, my cousin Valerie, is deceased while Denis still lives in New Wokingham Road in the village, with his wife Diane, née White).

When I asked for a drink of water Gran sent me to the large bowl, covered with a white cloth, which stood on her kitchen table, near her old black cooking range: "Help yourself and make sure you cover the bowl again!" she would say. The water was clear and sparkling and thinking of it recently I penned these lines:-

> My Granny's well was grannyish
> Its young days long since gone.
> "How can you drink that water from the ground, Gran"
> I asked, "It must be dirty, surely?"
> "There's nothing dirty about well water" she replied
> "Its cleaner than yours from the tap."
> Well, I suppose Gran was right! I settled for it
> As there wasn't a quizmaster in sight.

Gran's large back garden was worked by a local man who, in lieu of paying her rent, supplied her with vegetables he grew there and also had some for himself. The tomatoes from Gran's greenhouse were especially good. She grew them herself and would give my sisters and me some of the small ones, to eat like sweets, on our visits to her.

GRAN'S OUTSIDE LAVATORY. Another novelty for me was the small wooden and corrugated iron structure at the back of Gran's house. I did not like the unavoidable nasty smell of the bucket lavatory there and the paper was either newspaper squares or shiny Izal 'squares' in a box. When I asked Dad about the emptying of the bucket I was told it happened "up the garden" and the subject was abruptly changed.

I WAS INQUISITIVE. Gran wore long voluminous black or navy skirts well down her calves, nearly to her ankles, and a blouse covered by a dark-coloured cardigan. Sleeveless aprons completed the outfit and she wore flat, strapped and buttoned, shoes. One day, when about 9 and alone with Gran, I showed myself to be sufficiently inquisitive about the bandages she wore on her legs (not satisfied with Dad's explanation of her having "bad legs"), that Gran offered to show me the seat of her problem.

My Memories of Crowthorne Yesteryear and other accounts

She turned down her stocking and started to unroll the bandage on one leg. I felt uneasy. Suddenly all the bandage was off, followed by the dressing beneath it, leaving me to gasp at the dreadful ulcer near Gran's ankle. "It's not nice, is it?" she said.

"No," I whispered, still upset by what I had seen.

"Now you know why I have to wear bandages," she continued, replacing the dressing and bandage. The incident taught me what open inquisitiveness can do!

GRAN'S ACTIVITIES. Gran Woodason, who had a round face and regular big beaming smile, was a keen needle-woman with the help of a treadle sewing-machine. I never saw her using this, and neither did I see her knit. She was also a good laundress and washed, starched and ironed the district nurse's white collars and cuffs. Gran had a large mantle clock in her living-room, which fascinated me by chiming every quarter-of-an-hour. Sort of musical, I liked that. And she kept a tall, round tin containing boiled sweets in a high cupboard. We knew the rule at home: "Askers don't get," so we didn't, but always waited till Gran gave us one sweet each (never more). One day, aged about 7, I swallowed mine whole. Would I die? I waited somehow till we were back home, then confided the incident in Mum, who replied, "You'll be alright, I expect, it should dissolve naturally."

Sometimes we children swallowed farthing coins. Mum would reprimand us for putting them in our mouths, then add, "It will come out of you naturally tomorrow or the next day when you go to the lavatory." We smiled when this happened and the dull copper coins appeared clean and bright and shiny!

GRAN'S FRONT ROOM. This was an only-used-for-special-occasions room, in which Gran kept her healthy-looking, well looked after, mainly fern-type, pot plants. They were all large ones, in choice, colourful, porcelain containers, that stood on tables and plant stands. Otherwise the room was modestly furnished and always in apple-pie order. We were usually taken in there briefly on each visit, when at least Dad and I enjoyed seeing the plants.

MY MATERNAL GRAN. Clara Laybourne visited us only about three times, in my memory, from her home in the North East. When, originally, my mother led me before this fairly short woman, Gran looked me up and down and then squeezed my breasts gently, before, "She's developing well!" I was shocked and indignant, later voicing my feelings to Mum, who said, "There was nothing wrong

My Memories of Crowthorne Yesteryear and other accounts

with it. She's interested in you, that's all." Taken by my Aunty Blanche (Mum's sister, of Farnborough) to see Gran at her home in Newcastle, later, I was relieved that she paid no more attention to my anatomy!

Sarah Ellen (Helene) Laybourne (later Woodason), in her late teens, when in service at Wellington College. (Circa 1930.)

Dudley (Syd) and Sarah Ellen (Helene) Woodason's wedding group, 1931. Back, l. to r. Len Clacey, of Green Lane, best man; Ada Mary Woodason (mother of the groom), Greta Evans (née Woodason, sister of the groom); bridesmaids facing camera, l. to r. Evelyn Laybourne (bride's sister), Jenny Laybourne (bride's sister), Christine Jennant (who became the wife of Dudley's youngest brother, Maurice Woodason.) The children, Denis (left) and Valerie Evans.

My Memories of Crowthorne Yesteryear and other accounts

Above, The very first photo of Shirley Woodason, aged 5 months.

Left, Shirley Woodason aged about 3, in the back garden of her home 'Sydellen'. A field of Crowthorne Farm (now part of Crowthorne Farm Estate) lay to the far right-hand-side of the garden.

My Memories of Crowthorne Yesteryear and other accounts

Ada Mary Woodason (centre), with two of her sisters (names unknown), mother of Dudley (Syd) and grandmother of Shirley, in the front garden of her Old Wokingham Road home 'St. Leonards' (her bed of annuals is seen on the right).

My Memories of Crowthorne Yesteryear and other accounts

Left, Ada Mary Woodason, Gran of Shirley, in her front garden, holding her granddaughter Valerie Evans; in front, Valerie's brother Denis (cousins of Shirley). (Circa 1930.)

Right, Ada Mary Woodason, Gran of Shirley, holding baby Mary Woodason, her granddaughter, at the rear of her home, 'St. Leonards', Old Wokingham Road. Behind Gran, on the left, is Gran's corrugated iron outside toilet (or earth closet). (Circa 1940.)

My Memories of Crowthorne Yesteryear and other accounts

Above, 'Gran' Woodason's mantle clock, which was "sort of musical" when it chimed, to the young Shirley Woodason. Below, a modern-day picture of 'St. Leonards', Old Wokingham Road (right), one-time home of James (Jimmy) Woodason, who may have built it (he died in 1936), and his wife Ada Mary 'Gran' Woodason (who died circa 1958). The house next door to 'St. Leonards', in the picture, is 'Denvale', the one-time home of Greta Evans, later Partner (née Woodason), her first husband Sid Evans, and their children, Denis and Valerie. (Photo's – Shirley E. Peckham.)

CHAPTER TWO
CHILDHOOD CONTINUED

MY FIFTH BIRTHDAY PARTY. In a green organdie dress, I celebrated my 5th birthday in our garden with friends including Pat Butcher, her brother Ken and Joan Watt. My Gran Woodason was there and loved it. As a special treat from him, for the occasion, all we children rode in Mr V. Burgoyne's miniature train at Crowthorne Farm (where my mother worked for a while). My sister Glennis (3 1/2) fell asleep in one of the little carriages and wasn't missed until the rest of us were back at the house. Mum went and collected her.

MY FIRST ACCIDENT! In the months following my birthday I had my first notable accident, when I seriously injured my left leg. I was on my way home from school, walking alone, one afternoon. By the grocer's shop in Pinewood Avenue, Marder's, I decided to walk in a roadside ditch, where bladed grass cut deep into the front of my leg, just below the knee. Dr Chapman, of 'Quatre Bras', New Wokingham Road, was summoned to my home by my mother, after I limped there with blood running from my wound down my leg to my white sock and sandal. He stitched the deep, horizontal, bow-shaped cut below my knee, at my home. I still have the scar he told me I would have for life. The doctor congratulated me for being "a good girl and not crying" while he did it. "I will tell all my other patients that," he said. When I returned to school with my leg heavily bandaged I was treated by the teachers and children with compassion, and the latter were 'all questions' while literally giving me and my leg space.

OUR NEIGHBOURS. The Wheeler family lived next door to us, on the south side, their semi-detached house (now No.10, Pinewood Avenue) being across a little wood that came between our two homes. I remember old Mr and Mrs Wheeler, but not their other names, who had three sons, Walt, Ernest (Shan) and Tom (however I do not recall anything of Walt). Shan came to marry Daisy, a Londoner, who worked in the Waterloo Hotel for a time. Shan and Daisy lived in the Wheeler family home and had two children, Diane and Barry. Much later, Tom married Jessie (née Maynard). They lived in what is now No.76 Pinewood Avenue, and had twin sons.

Blonde Diane Wheeler was a popular friend of my sisters and me. All our family were very shocked one morning to hear of the sudden death of her mother Daisy in a road accident (maybe a hit-and-run

My Memories of Crowthorne Yesteryear and other accounts

affair) late one evening while cycling home from working at the Waterloo Hotel. She was found by her bike in Duke's Ride. Eventually, I believe, Shan and Barry emigrated to South Africa.

In the next house (a semi-detached one adjoining that of the Wheelers, now No. 12) lived an unassuming elderly couple, Mr and Mrs Ballard. My friends and I sometimes played pranks on them because their quiet, private lifestyle seemed unnatural to us.

On adjoining scrubland we played games of all kinds and loved every moment, except when we occasionally squabbled. The Parker family – Margaret, Dennis, Ken, Ann, Kathy and Sylvia – were among our playmates and lived in a semi-detached house (now No.14) alongside another piece of scrubland we played on, where we also had bonfires on Guy Fawkes nights. Opposite them lived Lillian and Bert Butcher with their children: Pat, Ken, Pearl, Jill, Maureen, Terry and Nicholas (Nicky). Bert is now deceased, but Lillian and some of her family now live in their purpose-built (by the family, I believe) house (No.3) opposite my one-time family home 'Sydellen'.

Next-door to us on the north side (between our bungalow and Crowthorne Farm, now No.2 Pinewood Avenue) lived, alone, Miss Ada Frances Churchill, a retired schoolmistress. Mum and Dad worked for her sometimes in her home. She came to feature quite a lot in my young life.

ROUGH ROADS. Until some time in my teens the roads round us were rough (not made-up); gravel and dust in the summer and 'seas' of mud and stones in the winter. We children regularly 'came a cropper', often from our bikes, in the pot-holes of the unadopted roads, and Vaseline and plasters helped mend our cuts and grazes. When the roads were made up, some Polish men were among the labourers.

WILD FRUIT AND WILD ROSES. Opposite our home was a wild raspberry 'plantation' where we picked and ate the fruit, writhing maggots and all! We also ate the fruit by the dishful, with 'top of the milk', at home. Blackberries grew on scrubland next to the Ballards house, corner of Pinewood Avenue/Ellis Road, where the bungalows are now. We would pick and eat these straightaway too. They also contained many maggots which, as far as we could, we picked out and squashed between our fingers. But at home more maggots surfaced when the fruit was cooked. In a field off Pinewood Avenue and Ellis Road, to the west, grew wild pink roses and in the autumn the bushes were ablaze with hips.

ROSEHIPS. When I had reached my early teens, the Crowthorne branch of the British Red Cross Society organised a collection of hips for making syrup. As a junior member (a cadet) I set out on cold, foggy November mornings to collect them, there having been promise of a prize for the greatest amount handed in by anyone. I grew more and more excited as the weight of my harvest mounted. My friend Pat Butcher, who had also been collecting them (along with a number of other cadets), finally had to give up doing so, as she couldn't spend any more time on it, and gave me her share. I subsequently won the prize with about fifty pounds of hips.

OUR GAMES. The boys kicked tennis balls about and girls played rounders in the road and netball at school. We were not angel children. I 'stole' spoonfuls of condensed milk from a tin of it in someone's house, with the encouragement of some of my friends who lived there who did the same. We played wild in the woods and on the scrubland about our home, often at Cowboys and Indians, with our home-made bows and arrows. Also we played war games, that involved stone throwing, which occasionally resulted in us injuring ourselves and others.

One evening, when aged 9, I was in trouble after firing an arrow, from my self-made bow, which broke our kitchen window. Dad thundered: "You will go and get a glazier to replace the window and pay for it yourself!" I stood stunned, had expected a good telling-off or a smacked bottom.

"Where is the glazier and how can I pay for it myself?" I murmured, disconsolately.

"In Pinehill Road," he replied. "You will go there now and find out when he can do the job. And you must pay for it out of your pocket money!" I dragged myself to the distant, 'world away' for us, Pinehill Road. My friends, who had observed my reprimand, watched me go and said nothing. I think the cost of having the window replaced (which Dad could have dealt with himself) was six shillings (30p) which took 4 weeks of my pocket money. It was an effective punishment. So, full marks to Dad!

HERO. Our hero was an older boy, Derek Archbald, known as Dedge who had a sister, Jacqueline, some years older than him. Their mother was killed, sadly, in an accident while cycling in Old Wokingham Road when Dedge was about fifteen. Dedge organised our games fairly and well, and with others built a tree-house, made underground cubbies, etc., for himself and other children who were

My Memories of Crowthorne Yesteryear and other accounts happy to make use of them. I never ventured there!

DICK BARTON / COMICS / ENID BLYTON. All the children listened to 'Dick Barton, Special Agent', with its compelling signature tune, Charles Williams's 'Devil's Gallop', on the wireless every weekday evening 6.45 - 7.00. This coloured our subsequent games. We bought comics – Beano, Dandy and Film Fun, and later Radio Fun and others, at about 2d each and loved reading them. I particularly recall Desperate Dan and Pansy Potter, two of the characters featured in one or two of the comics. I became greatly absorbed also in Enid Blyton's 'Fives' books, reading them from cover to cover.

WOKINGHAM WITHOUT. Pinewood Avenue children did not play much with Hatch Ride ones, despite living quite near to each other. Both areas are in the parish of Wokingham Without, not Crowthorne. Our postal district though was Crowthorne, where we always considered we lived. Complaining about council services our parents would say, "It's Wokingham Without anything where we live!"

TROUBLE AT THE FARM. At Crowthorne Farm, a Mr Bennett (Jack, possibly) of Pinewood Avenue, who carried out various farming activities there, but lived near the shop in the avenue, was livid once on finding about five of us children on one of the haystacks. He threatened us with a pitchfork and we fled. Some of us rolled off the stack, others used the ladder; my heart was thumping as we charged through fields to a five-barred gate, hurt ourselves a little falling over its top bar, and dashed home. Mr Bennett rapidly followed us, yelling and cursing, but did not catch us or tell our parents.

One summer Dad was compensated for cows escaping from the farm and eating the cabbages in our garden, leaving only their stumps.

SCRUMPING. The boys climbed other people's trees and helped themselves to the fruit. Sometimes I was given some of the pickings. One day I joined in the actual scrumping for some small, hard, almost tasteless pears. The tree was at the side of Jones' Sawmills, near the top of Pinewood Avenue, and was easy to get into from standing on a pile of sawdust. Then, from the branches of the tree, a boy suddenly shouted, "Old Hookey's seen us and is coming!" 'Old Hookey' was a Mr. Cotterell, a watchman of sorts at the mills, who wore black greasy-looking clothes and had a steel hook in place of a hand, affixed to a wooden arm. Waving the hook at us menacingly, while hurrying towards us, he shouted "Clear off, the lot of you!" We scrambled down the tree (with pears in our pockets) and ran away, up

My Memories of Crowthorne Yesteryear and other accounts

to the High Street, very frightened. I did not go scrumping any more after that!

OUR PARTIES. My birthday being in June, meant I didn't usually have parties after my fifth one as to me they weren't the same in the summer as at other times of the year. But in December my forever-lively mother laid on parties for my sisters' birthdays (Virgy's on December 8th and Glennis's on January 2nd), that were also loosely connected with Christmas. We invited up to eight children. Among the guests were Jim and Peter Clarke, both 'a scream', humorous to the core, Peter's being a very special dry kind. Indeed, they both created laughs, almost by the minute, and would be back at our home the next day, reliving the party and making our sides ache again.

At the parties we played numerous party games – 'dead men arise', 'blind man's buff', musical chairs, musical parcel, musical bumps, charades, consequences, ones involving the use of a torch and the boys and girls kissing each other, with all the lights out, etc. – and we had a good array of food and drink. No-one wanted to leave at nine o'clock. Such super times, never to be forgotten! And where was Dad throughout? Well, not at home!

BONFIRE NIGHTS. During the weeks leading up to every 5th November we built a big bonfire on the scrubland by Ellis Road (next to the Parkers house), and our parents helped us children make a 6-foot guy. On the evening the event 'got cracking' soon after six o'clock and our faces were soon aglow from excitement, the blazing fire and the active fireworks. When the guy was burning we all cheered, then baked spuds (produced by our parents) for our supper, in the hot embers. Next morning we returned to find the spent firework cases and sadly reflected on how long it was to the next bonfire night.

SWEETS. The war did not affect my sisters, friends and myself directly at first, but our meagre sweet-ration (2oz a week for children, 4oz for adults) did not go far. We patronized the Misses Stokes (sisters, Elsie and 'Sis') shop in the High Street. They were patient with our choices, sometimes allowing slight overweight, on other occasions cutting confectionery with a knife or toffee hammer to get the weight spot on! We children often had yellow tongues from the lemonade powder we literally lapped up. Sweets and Lyons ice-creams (cornets or wafers, 2d each) could be bought from Townsend's shop adjoining their garage, also in the High Street, but they often only had one half-jar of soft-centred boiled sweets in the whole shop in those war-ridden days. The array of empty jars beside it emptied one's heart.

I RAFFLED MY PET. When aged seven I made extra pocket money by raffling my white mouse, Snowy, in his cage. This was because I had tired of having to clean out the cage and we had found him rather smelly at home where – at Mum's direction – I had kept him in the kitchen on a high shelf. The raffle took place solely at school, with my teacher, Miss Burton's, permission. The winner was a boy I hardly knew, who was very pleased and excited at his success, and I was richer to the tune of eleven shillings and threepence (56p) from the exercise. A pocket-money boost indeed!

MY SECOND ACCIDENT. About this time, when aged 7, I had my second notable accident. I broke my right leg. While wearing wellington boots I was playing about in the gutter fronting Manhattan Place one Saturday afternoon, with my sisters. This was from boredom while Dad, who had taken us out, was nearby talking at length to a friend. I was in much pain, couldn't stand on the leg, and Dad had to carry me home. Dr Chapman came to attend me, before I ended up in the Royal Berkshire Hospital, Reading. My very painful time continued before arriving there, not helped when one of the ambulancemen dropped the foot end of the stretcher I was on, by our garden gate!

From X-ray, plaster of Paris was applied by an old-looking, impatient, miserable doctor. "Stop whimpering or I'll take it all off and start again!" he blasted. What a contrast to the Adonis who had carried me from the ambulance into the hospital!

I had to use a walking-stick and sometimes a wheelchair while the fibula knitted. It was not, however, straightforward. After weeks of wearing one plaster cast, the leg was immediately put in another, as I presume the bone had not healed sufficiently. Altogether I was in plaster for about 4 months, after which my leg was thin, purple-mottled, and the skin was peeling. I then limped for a long time and the leg would collapse suddenly, causing me to fall without warning. Mum, in her concern, would be agitated with me about my limping and tell me to try and stop it, "Or you may come to always do it." Her 'advice' was a waste, for I had no control over this.

After some enforced time off school because of my problem, while in plaster and with my stick, I walked there carefully one morning to surprise Miss Burton and my classmates with my visit. Both she and the pupils enjoyed my visit and made a fuss of me. Miss Burton, radiant-faced, said, "Thank you, Shirley, for coming along, we're pleased to see you."

CHAPTER THREE
OTHER CHILDHOOD MEMORIES

THE COUNTRYSIDE AND OUR 'PICKINGS'. As children we wandered happily along familiar routes near home, occasionally venturing along unknown roads – a little way, or sometimes for what seemed miles (especially when in tiring warm weather). Caesar's Camp turned out, disappointingly, to be just a clearing in the trees. We found **bilberries** (**whortleberries**) on the Walter Recreation Ground and ate them, and munched and devoured leaves from the **'bread-and-cheese'** shrubs there.

With my friends I would cycle to Big Wood, near Easthampstead Park's main gate, where we were greeted by an enormous heart-stopping, strongly-scented carpet of **bluebells** under the trees. We would pick them to our sheer delight, and take enormous bunches of the flowers home to our mothers and for our teachers at school the next day – in each case to their joy.

And we would go and pick **primroses** from the railway bank off Nine Mile Ride, where they grew in profusion.

We sometimes picked **dandelions**, despite the revolting, slimy milky juice oozing from their stems, and played the age-old game of 'What's the time?' When all the fluff had left the seed pods, the number of blows or puffs we had carried out told us the time!

Buttercups and **cowslips** growing in fields attracted us girls. We would pick buttercups and hold them under each other's chins to see who liked butter. If a deep yellow glow showed on the person's skin, she liked butter. If a pale yellow glow showed there, she did not like butter.

Also, we girls would pick wild **daisies** and make daisy-chains with them, which we used in a circlet to decorate our hair, or on our wrists as a bracelet. Neither however served to impress the boys, who barely took notice!

In the autumn I went with Dad to collect dead leaves in a wood near the East Berks Golf course. We put handfuls of them into sacks that we balanced on our bicycles to take home, Dad said they would do the garden "a power of good."

There were **snowdrops** early in the year, and later **violets**, in the wood between New Wokingham Road and the course of the East Berks Golf Club. Sometimes we would walk to the course. Green and spacious, I liked it there but wondered if I would get hit by any golf balls. Gladly, I wasn't!

One **May** night (the 6th, I think) there was an unexpected

My Memories of Crowthorne Yesteryear and other accounts

snowfall! Dad was cross that it broke off a large bough from our plum tree.

ICE-CREAM VAN. Some summer afternoons an ice-cream van would park on the scrubland on the corner of Pinewood Avenue and Ellis Road. One day the driver lowered his head, so that his face was a foot from mine, from serving me with some cones, and said, "Look into my eyes and tell me what you see there!" When I told Mum, at home, she flew up the road, minutes later returning home triumphantly, "There, I've told him off and that we will buy no more ice-creams from him!" Oh dear, we missed them!

PEDLARS. As mentioned in my volume *Our Memories of Crowthorne Yesteryear*, rag-a'-bone men, muffin men and onion sellers used to come to Crowthorne. Householders were probably paid small amounts for the rags, bones, jam jars, etc., that they gave the rag-a'-bone men. The muffin men rang large handbells in the road to attract customers, who went to them and bought muffins and crumpets from the trays they had had balanced on their heads. The onion men, who I think wore distinguishable close-fitting black caps on their heads, came from France with strings of onions hanging from their bicycles for sale at favourable prices. Mum gave the muffin and crumpet men and the onion men business.

GIPSIES. These colourful characters (women usually) sold their wares door-to-door from big-handled, arm-carrying wicker baskets. For many years in the old days they lived in nearby Owlsmoor and sold small cloth items and 'dolly' clothes pegs, both of which Mum bought, in moderation.

"LAVENDER JIM". This was the name we in our family gave to our cesspit (or cesspool) emptying vehicle and its crew, that used to call at ours and our neighbours' homes. When in operation, with its snake-like tubing extending from the vehicle by our front gate to the cesspit half-way down our back garden, the awful smell was strong enough for us to need to hold our noses!

MY HAIR. During childhood I wore plaits, neat and tidy but a temptation to the boys to pull from behind. Sometimes Mum would curl my hair with curling tongs heated on our gas cooker and I was afraid that she would burn my ears off! My hair *was* singed on occasions, filling the air with smoke and the smell of singed hair, even though Mum had tested the heat of the tongs on newspaper before using them on me. I was not sorry to be old enough to have a perm when I was fifteen! (We fed our gas meter with shilling, 5p, coins.)

HORTICULTURAL SHOWS. My Grandad Woodason (a bricklayer, who unfortunately died when I was 2 and whom, sadly, I never knew) had been an enthusiastic entrant to the local horticultural shows and a number of the family also put their hearts and souls into participation – my Uncle Maurice and his wife, my Aunty Chris, my Aunty Greta, and, to a lesser degree, my Dad. At the events (the family entered both their flowers and vegetables) there were also dog shows and bonny-baby contests, as well as games and competitions for the children. These took place on the Derby Field by Crowthorne Station, and on Broadmoor Cricket Ground. Sometimes, I believe, St. Sebastian's Hall housed purely the shows. We cheered on the tug-o'-war teams and had exciting, good fun throughout. The slow bicycle races I found enjoyable to watch, but they looked too difficult for me and I did not enter. Men won them, mostly.

OUR OWN FUN-FAIR. In a clearing in the woods we children set up our own fun-fair. An old pram body, we'd hung by ropes from a tree, served as a swing-boat, until we found it unsafe. We threw mop-heads at stacks of old tins and charged 1d a time to anyone who wanted a go on any of our several rides and games.

'MOTHERS AND FATHERS'. Another outdoor occupation popular with the girls was cooking sausages and little cakes on a small stove in the woods. Again, we made coppers from selling some of the cakes and used our dolls as 'children' for the game of Mothers and Fathers. The boys usually did not want to play this and so most of the time girls had to be dads as well as mums! However, happy days!

DOLLS' HOSPITAL. Somewhere in Reading there was a dolls' hospital, where parents sometimes took their chidlren's dolls and teddies for replacement limbs, eyes, etc. I went there once with Mum, for my doll to have a new leg, and was very pleased with the result when we collected her the following week.

MAT MAKING. My family made cloth mats, worked on hessian held taut in a purpose-built wooden frame Dad had made. Four of us at a time, two each side, sat at this contraption, and with metal prodders pushed 3-inch x ¾-inch strips of rag of various colours, clippings we'd spent days cutting out, in and out of the holes. Sometimes Dad drew a design on the hessian to make the working on the mat and

My Memories of Crowthorne Yesteryear and other accounts

the finished product itself more interesting, and we held many family conversations, or would listen to the wireless, while mat-making.

Our fingers and thumbs became sore from *all* the work concerned (the cutting out and prodder activity), but we were jubilant when a mat was finished and again when we saw it on the floor. The mats were placed, on the lino, in all our rooms and hall. Admittedly in use they collected a lot of dust and dirt, but they served a good purpose. Mum would throw them outside to beat or shake, when clouds of dust left them, some of it possibly falling on her *and* us when we were there!

OUR SCOOTER AND TRIKE. Besides my sisters and I having successive bikes each through most of our childhood (from about the age of five) and beyond, we also, as young children, had a very popular large scooter and a trike, that we rode on very regularly for years. We often squabbled over them, as to whose turn it was to use them. All of our big toys (bikes and dolls prams, beside those mentioned here) were acquired secondhand – new to us though!

MY LITTLE PIECE OF CROWTHORNE! I jump ahead in time now to relate that I always consider, cosily, I have a little piece of Crowthorne in my New Milton garden. My father, you see, was very fond of digging up apple saplings that he found growing in the little wood adjacent to our home 'Sydellen', through my childhood and teens. He then planted them (only ever one at a time) in our garden, and some 'took' and came to bear fruit, and some didn't. But he enjoyed doing it.

Sometime after moving into my New Milton home, on a visit to my parents with my second husband Bill, Dad asked me if I would like one of the saplings he had dug up in the wood some time previously. It had grown to five feet tall. He needed the room it was taking up in his garden, he said.

I gladly accepted and Bill and I drove home with the small tree in our car boot. The tree, near the back of our house, is now some sixteen feet tall and twelve feet broad. It took about five years to bear fruit, and now gives us some three dozen apples a year. We cannot identify them, that are predominantly green with a trace of red and have a sharpish taste.

What I like best about the tree is its lovely show of blossom each spring. Seeing it through my dining-room window, or when outside, gives me the impression that it represents my Dad smiling at me, and of course it lasts for a week or two.

My Memories of Crowthorne Yesteryear and other accounts

I WITNESSED A MULTIBIRTH. Aged about 9, I called on my friend Daphne Robertson, to come out and play. While she finished her tea, I waited in their garden. There came a sudden, heavy spring shower and I sheltered under a chestnut tree by her front gate, near her neighbour's (coalman Mr George Donnelly's) smallholding. Then I heard a loud squealing sound. Looking over the fence, from where it had come, I saw a large sow lying in the long damp grass, panting and in distress. Amazed, I observed a piglet emerging from the sow! Then, enthralled, I watched four more of the births before Daphne joined me. "Just look!" I said, pointing.

"Gosh!" Daphne exclaimed, "Look at those little pigs!" We went to tell Mr Donnelly the exciting news, who expressed gratitude to us and said the sow should not have been anywhere near where it was. Feeling special that I had been sole witness of the incident, my playing with Daphne after that seemed, in comparison, very mundane.

CATERPILLAR PLAGUE. One summer there was a plague of yellow and black striped caterpillars in Crowthorne, and I have always had an aversion to caterpillars – the way they look coupled with the way they move along! The creatures covered all the cabbages and every patch of grass. The crops and grass growing in the Crowthorne Farm fields were smothered in them, while all green areas in the village had their share. I had to stop visiting my friends the Robertsons, in Pinewood Avenue, because the caterpillars from their cabbage patch, immediately at the back of the house, were regularly travelling into the nearby kitchen itself, via the windows and back door. From the back doorstep I saw them on the walls, furniture and ceiling, and one fell off the latter into a cooking pot of boiling food on the stove too!

POOR. Many families in our area were often short of money – including us! With payments for a mortgage and other necessities, things were 'tight'. My parents managed a few extras for themselves and us, and we were used to the situation. Some neighbours would borrow or scrounge items, especially foodstuffs; they (or their children with notes from them) arrived on our doorstep with a dish, bowl or plate, when tea-leaves (we had no tea-bags then), sugar, salt, flour, bread, and soap-powder were requested, among other things. On weekly pay-days the loans were often returned, but not always. When my parents could not afford something we usually went without it, but some mothers sold household goods (often without their husbands' knowledge) when they were hard up. Some housewives funded their smoking and other habits in this way – or bought essential items for their homes and family with the proceeds.

My Memories of Crowthorne Yesteryear and other accounts

GATHERING CHESTNUTS IN BROADMOOR WOODS.
A number of sweet chestnut trees grew on the Broadmoor Estate and each autumn we children could not get enough of the nuts. We removed the prickly casings with our fingers and back home roasted them on the fender, or on a toasting fork, by the living-room fire, and ate them with a little salt. If we forgot to prick them with a fork first they exploded and shot across the room, sometimes hitting us in our faces!

OTHER BROADMOOR VISITS.
From a good vantage point in the woods at the back of the asylum, later hospital (see pictures on Pages 265 and 337), we could see over the high wall and enthralled by the unique spectacle would watch warders (now called nurses) and inmates (now patients) in the grounds for some time.

To ensure we were not disappointed my mother always obtained tickets, weeks in advance, for us to go to the variety concerts held inside Broadmoor. The twice yearly Broadhumourists amateur productions (which to us seemed professional) were staged by the patients and a collection was always made during the interval for various charities. We were always told at the end of the show what amount of money had been given by us for the named charity. Sometimes, besides many, the Patients' Benevolent Fund benefited. They also staged fine choral concerts in the Central Hall, but I preferred the variety ones. Patients served us refreshments in the interval.

BROADMOOR PATIENTS' WORKING PARTIES.
On the Broadmoor Estate, I used to see parties of up to twenty male inmates working on the shrubbery and undergrowth, at the side of roads, and sometimes quite a way from the roads themselves. Under supervision, they were clearing the greenery back, or thinning it out. They were always accompanied by one or two Broadmoor attendants.

I kept my distance on seeing them, so cannot say what they wore exactly, but distinctive, near-identical, lightweight working clothes (probably overalls of a kind) that easily distinguished them from anyone else.

Sometimes the attendant (or attendants) with them couldn't be seen at first, and I was nervous while in their vicinity on these occasions in case the inmates were on their own. But voicing of my concern to Mum later, brought the reply, "Of course, they *always* have attendants with them. Don't worry about it any more. They are the trusted ones anyway, or they wouldn't be outside like that." This in itself didn't ease my mind though.

My Memories of Crowthorne Yesteryear and other accounts

Above, Shirley (left) and Glennis Woodason, aged 3 and 1 years.
Below, Shirley (left) and Glennis, aged 4 and 2 years.

My Memories of Crowthorne Yesteryear and other accounts

Above, Maurice Woodason, aged 3, and Shirley Woodason aged 4, cousins, in the front garden of Shirley's home 'Sydellen'. (Circa 1939.) Below, Shirley, Glennis and Virginia (Virgy), when the sisters were aged about 6, 4, and 2.

in those times, but those and snowy ones did not mean we had to refrain from playing in the playground.

Snowballing was not allowed in the playground though (but some of us cheated a little), because of all the windows about. This was a problem too when playing with balls. We all had to be careful and mishaps involving damage were usually caused by the boys. As most of the girls' playground was adjacent to the vicarage woods and garden, the vegetable area particularly, we would regularly hear the cry from Mr Goodband of, "Keep all balls from going into the vicarage garden." Mostly, this was obeyed. When it wasn't and my group and I were concerned, I looked the other way while some brave soul opened the vicarage side gate, nipped light-footed to where the ball was – sometimes on a bed of freshly sown seeds – retrieved the item and darted back to us wearing a cheeky grin. There was a gardener at the vicarage and if a ball went over the iron fence (that was previously a high hedge) when he was there, he would treat the event light-heartedly whether it had upset any of his work or not; usually, too, he threw it back to us.

HULA HOOPS, HOPSCOTCH. There were always play-time games (which we also played away from the school) 'in fashion'. These were played by just about every child, some, girls only and others boys only, till those games were 'out' and others were 'in'. They involved jumping in and out of hula hoops, also having them about our waists and gyrating our bodies to keep the hoops moving round us and not falling to the ground. And there was hopscotch, when we drew a pattern of squares on the tarmacked ground, using chalk, before taking our turns throwing a small piece of slate into each square successively, and then hop, without ever putting our other foot down, gradually into all the squares that did not have the slate in. In turn the members of the team playing would make a mistake and be 'out'. Doubtless it was good exercise for us!

MARBLES, FAG CARDS. We also played with marbles, the big coloured ones being called 'alleys'. In these games we would win marbles from our friends (an alley was a very good win and to lose one was almost tearful) and they would win some from us, depending on one's skill or, more often, luck!

Cigarette cards ("fag cards") we also played with a lot, by way of a flicking process. Again, we would win and lose each others. It was a very bad day always when we had lost all we had. We came to acquire more by (if not winning) swopping something for them, or getting

My Memories of Crowthorne Yesteryear and other accounts

more from our parents', or other adults', cigarette packets.*

SKIPPING. Many girls, including me, did much skipping. I preferred individual participation with a short rope from the group activity, the kind where three or more of us were involved with a long one. Some girls were very good skippers, me excluded. I did not take it as seriously as they seemed to. A clever way of doing it concerned very fast skipping, involving what was termed 'bumps'. This I mostly failed to get right, particularly alongside those who were superb at it.

TOPS AND WHIPS. I used to like playing with tops and whips. Sometimes I was hopeless at it, while on other occasions I surprised myself with my success. This was often a very popular activity with the girls, boys only rarely participating.

DIRNDL SKIRTS AND SEERSUCKER. You will read on Page 44 of our school wear. Here, though, I mention of my particular memories of girls – at school and elsewhere – wearing for a time, while in fashion, dirndl skirts. These were brightly coloured, cotton ones, that were full, gathered, and had a close-fitting waistband. I had one.

A new type of material, at least to us, that came 'in' when I was past my mid-childhood, was seersucker. This was a thin cotton one, that had a puckered surface. I had a dress and a blouse made of it. These I wore on very warm days, which gave the required cool effect.

---

* In our home was a wooden, varnished, special cigarette container (free standing) whose place was on the very top of a writing-desk cabinet in our livingroom well away from little hands. The container held two sections that each held packets of 20 cigarettes stacked one on top of the other. At the bottom of each stack was a drawer (in fact the lowest packet on each side 'sat' in the drawer). Dad was a regular, quite committed smoker (who often 'rolled his own') and Mum was a light, irregular smoker; the cigarette container therefore was principally for his use.

A man would come to our house about once fortnightly to restock the container and take the money from it that had accrued. The device was otherwise kept locked. The packets of cigarettes were released by the drawer (or drawers) being pulled out to obtain a packet of them at a time, once coins for the appropriate cost had been inserted in a slot at the side of the container. After each packet was taken from the drawer and this was closed, another packet fell into the drawer. Mum and Dad liked Players Weights and Wills Woodbines.

Crowning ceremony of the May Queen, at Crowthorne C. of E. School (year unknown). Mr A. C. Goodband, Headmaster, is in the left in the foreground. The Vicarage lay behind the tall beech hedge at the rear. (Photo courtesy of Joan Franklin.)

My Memories of Crowthorne Yesteryear and other accounts

Crowthorne C. of E. School playground May Day occasion (year unknown). The Queen and attendants are walking away from the stage after the ceremony. Miss G. Burton stands to the right of the stage, a male teacher (unidentified) stands nearby, backs of parents' heads are in the foreground.
(Photo courtesy of Joan Franklin.)

My Memories of Crowthorne Yesteryear and other accounts

'Sydellen', No.4 Pinewood Avenue, in recent times, the one-time home of Dudley (Syd) and Sarah Ellen (Helene) Woodason, and their daughters, Shirley, Glennis and Virginia. (Syd built the bungalow 1931-'32.) (Photo - Shirley E. Peckham.)

Shirley Woodason at home, making daisy-chains, aged about 5.

My Memories of Crowthorne Yesteryear and other accounts

A group of Pinewood Avenue playmates with their dolls in the wood that was between the Woodason family home 'Sydellen' (in the background of the picture) and the Wheeler family home, now No.10. The bungalows now occupying what was the wood plot are No's 6 and 8. L. to r. Daphne Robertson* (now Mrs Johnson); Diane Wheeler; Pearl Butcher; Pamela Eckett; Virginia (Virgy) Woodason; at back, Glennis Woodason. (Photo - Shirley E. Woodason.)

(*Daphne Robertson's younger brother, Ian, and eldest sister, Heather, were also regular playmates of the Woodason sisters. Their youngest sister, Jennifer, was born when Shirley was about 12 years old. The parents of the Robertson children were Mabel and George.)

My Memories of Crowthorne Yesteryear and other accounts
CHAPTER FOUR
SCHOOL AND OTHER CHILDHOOD EXPERIENCES

STARTING SCHOOL. In April 1939 I began my time at Crowthorne Church of England School, the first of my family to take this step. I was shy and nervous in my early days in the Infants' School. Under the kind eye of Mrs Edith Hallett and then Miss Badger, we sat at little tables on cast-iron and canvas chairs and played with bead-frames, made necklaces and so on. One morning I mistakenly went home at playtime instead of dinner time and Mum, cleaning our bathroom, was flabbergasted – "What are you doing here?" – and said indignantly that I should go straight back there. I told her I did not want to, for I might get told off. She allowed me to stay at home till after lunch, when I returned to school with a note of explanation from her. Gladly, no one commented on my embarrassment. But wasn't I missed?

MY FIRST BOYFRIEND. My first ever boyfriend, when we were 5, was Michael Sims. We would have little chats and kisses by the dustbins in a quiet area alongside an Infants' School wall. What a sweet little romance that was! Michael was the classic 'tall, dark and handsome'.

I LEARN TO CYCLE. When I was aged 6, my uncle Maurice Woodason finally taught me to ride my bike. Mum's and Dad's teaching had been good, but had failed to get me over the final hurdle. Uncle Maurice held on to the saddle while, full of confidence, I set off down our back garden path. Then he let go of the machine and I did not know at first. The bike gathered speed, until I fell off it, into the shrubbery at the end of the path. I rode a lot after that and cycled regularly to school. I have ridden a bike practically daily ever since, other than when pregnant and when I spent some time abroad.

THE OTHER INFANT TEACHERS. Mrs Coulstock 'took' me in the second class of the 'Infants'. She was a tall, quiet and demure lady, akin in temperament to both Mrs Hallett (who was a supply teacher at the time I started school and was only my teacher for one week) and Miss Badger. I very much liked all three ladies.

In the final class of the Infants', Mrs Harrington taught me. She was probably specially selected for the post because her methods of control, in contrast with the other teachers mentioned, prepared us for main school life. I liked her too, though felt the need to be on my

My Memories of Crowthorne Yesteryear and other accounts

guard in her company, who was alert to slothfulness and misbehaviour!

JUNIOR SCHOOL. Mrs Daisy Luckock's class was my first in the junior or "big" school, where I first experienced mental arithmetic. This I enjoyed and did quite well. She also taught us to knit, sometimes picking up our dropped stitches. Or she would make us unpick the whole 'scarf' and start again, which I thought very unreasonable and it put me off her! The boys learned to sew with us, when we all had to work straight lines of tacking stitches on pieces of shiny lavatory paper.

MISS BURTON'S CLASS. This followed from Mrs Luckock's. For some of my time there, at least, I sat at a desk in the front of the classroom with Miss Burton's niece, Joan Burton (now Mrs Franklin). We were more-or-less equal academically. Some children in the class wondered if Miss Burton wore a wig – her short, curly hair loaded with hairpins looked like it! I once saw a boy pupil, constantly very naughty in class, swiped on the hand with a blackboard pointer, which seemed to work wonders. I liked Miss Burton's quiet style when all was going well for her and her teaching was not hindered by the disruptive boy pupils we had in the class, who once put carbide powder in the inkwells to cause a sticky mess and a stink.

MAY DAYS. Miss Burton and Miss Mohr (a more senior teacher who taught me later) were responsible for the success of the annual May Days at the school. They taught us songs and dances, dressed the Queen and her attendants and oversaw the erecting of the wooden stage decorated with flowers and leafy sections of branches, in the playground. Parents came to watch the proceedings. I do not remember playing a major role, but enjoyed dancing round the maypole and singing. The successive May Queens and their attendants, also the boy heralds, were selected by vote from the other pupils before each day arrived. And every year the previous year's May Queen returned, by invitation, to the school to crown the new one.

PLAYTIMES. There were a number of playtime activities we carried out at school, mostly in the playground of course. We only stayed in our classrooms then if feeling unwell (but not to the extent to have to go home), or in wet weather, when we would read, or if enough of us (especially the girls), played consequences. There were many foggy days, as well as nights, particularly in the autumn months

MY FINAL CLASSROOM. An elderly male teacher, tall, always grey-suit-clad, Mr John Hayward, taught my final class in a purpose-built prefabricated building close to the main school. At the beginning I found him fair and reasonable in his teaching methods, but he became far from what a teacher should be! For instance, during scripture lessons he discussed football with the boys (being a subject he himself obviously liked) after the girls had been invited to read comics, etc., that were always in the classroom for wet playtimes. Not many of us did this, but read our bibles instead.

Outrageously disrespectful, he would say (referring to through the windows), "If you see Goodband (the Head) coming, get everything away quick and we'll get back to talking about Jesus Christ." His attitude, often deplorable and sometimes indecent – I witnessed – brought tomfoolery and disrespect from us, often en masse, when he was totally defeated! Eventually, in December 1948, after several years at the school, Mr Hayward's engagement was terminated.

OUR OTHER SPORTS ACTIVITIES. At school, we carried out sprint, three-legged, egg-and-spoon and sack races. We also did high jump and long jump. Whereas I was nervous of participating in the former, in case I caught a leg, or my legs, around the stick involved and broke a bone in one again, I was a very good long-jumper. Although I did not enjoy the races very much, and didn't do very well at them, I always carried out my successful long-jumping with enthusiasm and enjoyment.

SCHOOL INSPECTORS. When any children were away from school for an unacceptable length of time (I can't recall how long), without good reason, men who we knew as school inspectors, sent from the local education authority I expect, had to go to their homes to investigate and make efforts to get them back to school. It seemed to work well. School inspectors were mentioned with awe by some!

CHILDHOOD ILLNESSES. The most serious, scarlet fever, hit my sister Glennis badly. With a secondary (kidney) complaint, she was whisked by ambulance, sharing it with our Pinewood Avenue friend, fellow sufferer Daphne Robertson, to the then isolation hospital at Maidenhead – St. Mark's, in St. Mark's Road, now, in 1995, a local GP unit and out-patient hospital.

Men in protective clothing and masks fumigated our joint bedroom, of which Dr Chapman, on entering it once, when we were all ill at the same time, quipped, "It's like coming into a hospital ward coming in here." The men took away all our soft toys and books that were likely germ carriers. For the same reason Mum had to boil our flannels (or facecloths). Then the room had to be locked up completely for a period and Virgy and I were forced to sleep in another room.

Visitors to the hospital were not allowed inside, so, after travelling there on two buses, we could only talk to Glennis through the closed windows.

Virgy came to develop the disease – although mildly and was not hospitalized. I feared I would get it, but didn't. We both had to spend time off school and Glennis was in hospital for seven weeks.

Symptoms of mumps surfaced when I was aged eleven and spending part of my school summer holidays with my Aunty Blanche, in her Farnborough home. My uncle Les was away in the RAF at the time. My aunt was very agitated at my condition and once her doctor had diagnosed my having mumps, she packed me back home, alone, on the two-bus journey, with my swollen neck wrapped in a scarf, even though summer, and a note for Mum explaining all.

Travel sickness was always a bother to me on buses (but not on coaches), when the unbroken journey was more than a few miles, and often our journeys to Reading on family outings had to be interrupted at Woodley, so that I could get off and get fresh air. Then we would catch the next bus (half an hour later) that came along, after I had recovered. Mum's, "You'll be all right in a minute, I expect, just sit quietly and try not to think about it," during the journeys, never worked.

Children's hair at school was checked regularly for nits, by personnel who came there specially for this, and treatment was advised upon where appropriate.

A VERY SPECIAL MOVING EXPERIENCE. One day, when I was about ten, Mum herself was ill. She was having strong tummy pains at breakfast time, after Dad had gone to work and before my sisters and I had gone to school. Very concerned, I expressed this to her and asked if I should stay at home to look after her. But she said she would be all right and we should all go to school.

Later I was collected from school by the district nurse, who drove me home in her little black car. Mum had had a miscarriage and from her bed explained about it to me. At the time I had not been told about 'the birds and the bees' from her, and had only 'picked up' some things concerned from my friends.

"Where is it?" I asked of the miscarried (at over twelve weeks) baby, not knowing it as a foetus then.

"Over there," she replied, pointing to the wooden washstand with a marble top that stood in a corner of the bedroom.

"Can I see it?"

"Yes."

I went to the stand and looked about. "Where?"

"In the soapdish." Hesitatingly I lifted the porcelain lid. With it still in my hand I saw the five-inch-long form of the 'baby' lying in and nearly filling the three-sectioned dish. I was very moved by this and unable to comment at first other than say, "Oh." Then, struggling for the right thing to say next, asked if it was a boy or a girl? "A boy," she replied, "if you look carefully you will *just* see it is?"

I did this and saw for myself it was a boy, which made me very sad, for I had longed for a brother and Dad had longed for a son.

"He looks like Dad," I commented.

"I believe they all look like that," Mum responded, disappointing me. "He definitely looks like Dad," I insisted, having thrown off Mum's unwanted remark.

She said no more before I carefully put the lid back on the dish and went to her bedside again. Then she spoke further about miscarriages and told me she had had me, particularly, brought home from school "because you are the eldest and I wanted you here, you don't have to tell anyone about it." My sisters learned of the situation later in the day, when they returned from school. We had not even known Mum had been pregnant.

Mum had given birth safely at home to the three of us – the occasion of Virgy's birth, when I was 4 1/2, remains in my memory – and gradually the myth that babies were brought to mothers in the nurse's black bag was exploded for my sisters and me. As far as I personally was concerned, I never fell for the gooseberry bush and stork stories!

"COME AND SEE MY (DEAD) GRANDMA." I was about eight when a friend of mine in Pinewood Avenue said, "Come and see my grandma."

"But your grandma is dead."

"Yes, but come on, see her in her coffin, in her front room." Such was a common token of respect for the dead in those days. Curtains would be drawn across the windows (particularly at the front) of the deceased's house and close relatives and friends would go in and pay their last respects till the day immediately preceding the funeral.

Mum said I was right to refuse my friend's invitation politely (I had not liked the idea either) and added, "It is only for their adult friends to do that."

My Memories of Crowthorne Yesteryear and other accounts

The one-time domestic science (cookery) building in Cambridge Road, also used for woodwork, where girls and boys (on different days) were sent from Crowthorne C. of E. School. The building is no longer in use for the school.

(Photo - Shirley E. Peckham.)

CHAPTER FIVE
MORE SCHOOL AND OTHER STORIES

THE HEAD. Called by some 'Gubber', or 'Gaffer', our headmaster, Mr A. C. Goodband, dealt firmly with trouble-makers and also taught the senior pupils sometimes, myself included eventually. Sitting in Miss Mohr's class we could see children waiting by his door to go into the head's office to be caned, sent there by the relevant teachers. Mr Goodband took Morning Assembly, held in the top two classrooms in the main (junior) school building with the dividing screen folded back to make one big room. He played the piano for hymns, led the prayers, and issued important notices. These included a warning to be careful with our sweet-ration coupons, for some had been supposedly stolen from children's coat pockets in the cloakrooms.

We all stood for Assembly. We could not have all fitted in the room otherwise. Sometimes children fainted while the crowded session was in progress. They were then carried by teachers, or senior pupils, to near the school's outer door and laid there, on a blanket in the fresh air, till they came round. A teacher would undo any restrictive buttons and belt on their clothing to help their recovery.

MISS GOODYER. After Miss Burton, Miss Goodyer was my teacher, who was a quiet lady. I recall her having a very red neck at the front, that looked as though it had been scrubbed. As my mother used to be always telling me to "scrub your neck, I can see a tidemark on it," my eyes were often drawn to this feature of Miss Goodyer. I had no reason to doubt her teaching methods and found her to be a likeable character. A boy in the class gained permission from the teacher to stand up sometimes while doing his work at his desk. I never knew why he stood.

MISS GREEN'S MONITOR. Miss Green, my next teacher (with pince-nez hanging round her neck, or on her face, and who would send us peremptorily to wash our dirty hands), was a quite fearsome lady, who appointed monitors from us to watch the class while she was marking books. I dreaded the pupils misbehaving when I had this duty as I did not want to have to report them, but if I had failed to I would have been in trouble with her. One day I was monitor and needed to 'spend a penny'. I did not dare ask to leave the room and after a while found that I was wetting myself, which came to cause a puddle on the floor. Miss Green noticed the mess. "That must have come from one of our jars of flowers on the window sill," (nearby) she said, then ordered a boy to fetch a bucket and mop. I felt very very guilty and sorry for him as he cleaned up the 'flower water' and, my socks and sandals wet too, was very sore when I reached home.

MISS MOHR – MY 'SOFTEST' TEACHER. Very different from Miss Green, Miss Mohr, the teacher whose class I was in next, was softly spoken even when grumbling, which brought her voice a fraction of an octave higher. A needlework and French language specialist, she did not teach me, or my class, the latter. My first needlework effort there was an embroidered hessian shopping bag for my mother, and I carried out some dressmaking in her class: a blue summer dress for myself, in particular, stays vividly in my mind.

MISS AITKEN'S COOKERY CLASS. For domestic science we went to a building (for both its use and that of woodwork, for the boys) in Cambridge Road, which still stands today. In charge there (or at the "cookery centre", as we termed it) was Miss Aitken, an unsmiling Scot with a temper. Lessons began with washing small cloth articles brought from home, and later ironing them. Then we had to thoroughly clean cast-iron kitchen utensils, having been instructed to "bring them up sparkling" with steel wool – the application of which set my teeth on edge! I reported this fact to Miss Aitken, who then, to my utmost surprise (I had expected nothing like it), excused me from the job for all my time there. The other girls turned against me for a while over that, seeing me as "teacher's pet", a very uncomfortable tag to ever have to wear at school.

The first item I actually cooked at the centre (much theory was taught for a few initial weeks) was an unexciting bowl of porridge. I took it home, cold, on my bicycle in the hessian bag made in Miss Mohr's class, but found the bowl had tipped over on the way, and the porridge in entirety was spilled in the bag and finding its way through the cloth! Mum threw the whole lot, bag and all, in our dustbin!

Later, at the centre, we had to choose (a week in advance) what we would cook, sometimes taking our own ingredients or Miss Aitken gave us money to buy them from local shops. We paid her back later. Those, like me, who took the lessons seriously and did well at them, eventually could make "anything under the sun," she said. Under direction, two of us each week entertained the teacher to lunch at the centre – which rather spoilt the meal! Once Miss Aitken began choking on a piece of meat while at the table, which she released in the sink. She recovered, and maybe also took an extra dose of the Yeastvite tablets she had a penchant for and 'downed' regularly in front of us.

"PERHAPS THAT'LL TEACH YOU!" Even from greasing the cake tins three times, as instructed, my sponges stubbornly refused to leave them one day. In a rage Miss Aitken flung them 30 feet down the room. The tins shed chunks of cake and crumbs as they flew, eventually crashing under a cooker. "Perhaps that'll teach you!" she thundered. "I've told you and told you to grease the tins *three* times."

"I *did* do," I replied, though felt the plea useless. She took no notice and was shaking from wrath.

Other girls kindly offered me items of theirs to take home, but I quietly cleared up the mess and declined with thanks. This sort of unreasonable and bad treatment by Miss Aitken led us to play her up. Amongst other things, we hid at break time one morning, in an outbuilding, and so were missing when she called her "gerrels" back to lessons. After twenty minutes of giggling about it, we emerged, expecting some verbal 'stick'. But Miss Aitken surprisingly let the matter go, with simply, "It was rather silly, wasn't it?" Perhaps she was glad that we had not instead gone to higher authority with our complaints about her often grossly unfair and extreme teaching methods!

GAMES. From the age of eleven I was plump and embarrassed about it. Wearing sports gear made the matter worse, especially when the boys watched our netball matches, a situation I hated. I suffered similarly during our swimming lessons at baths in Bracknell. The energetic, young Miss Hardman, teacher at the school (but not of me in a classroom, as I recall), who lived near my home with her mother, taught PT. Frosty, foggy mornings in the playground were the worst for exercises and her "get yourselves moving" led only to the situation improving a little. Fresh air was a fetish of the staff. If we yawned in class the remedy meted by some of the teachers was, "Open the windows, fresh air is needed to stop this yawning!" We became adept at yawn stifling.

SCHOOL PHOBIA? Nearing adolescence I suddenly found that I could not face school and the thought of having to go there made me feel ill. So Mum said I could stay at home. But I felt better as soon as the school bell would have rung at 8.50 a.m., which fact Mum eventually realised. Finally, she sought advice on the situation from Duke's Ride chemist, Mr Connock (who had taken over the shop from Mr Dring), leading to her one day escorting me to school herself. Once there, time allowed me to go into 'the offices' (lavatory block), I needed to escape to. I promptly shut myself into one of the cubicles until, after Assembly, Mr Goodband himself, prompted by Mum, I later discovered, came for me.

From calling my name through the closed door, he went on, forthrightly, "Your mother has gone home. I want you to come out here, where I am waiting for you. In your classroom nobody will say anything to you and you will carry on with your work as though you have not been away. Do you understand me?" Defeated, I responded with a meek "Yes," and, my problem almost over, returned to my classroom with him, where he let me in alone and no one even looked at me, nor *ever* said anything to me about it. I wonder whether I was a victim of what is now known as school phobia?

EDUCATIONAL VISITS. The school leaving age rose from fourteen to fifteen during my school days, so there was plenty of time for outside visits with our teachers. We were taken one hot day to the gasworks at Blackwater (Camberley) – dirty and very smelly, and we sweltered! I did not like Broadmoor Farm much either, unexciting indeed, especially as I lived near a farm. Far better was a trip to the Wellington College kitchens where we saw the making of potato crisps, from 'scratch', and gleefully sampled the tasty results.

MRS COMYNS. Before my final two classrooms, teaching me for a spell in Miss Mohr's (she was away, but I do not know where), was a supply teacher, decidedly uncomfortable in my memory, named Mrs Comyns. She went hand-in-hand with Miss Aitken for exercising her wrath towards us and would go red in the face with it. One day after she had told us not to talk to other pupils in class, I took a chance and asked one at the desk behind me something. With that – while my head was turned from her – she threw the big bible she normally always kept on her desk, at my head. It missed and crashed, open, pages down, on the floor. "*Now* perhaps you'll do as I tell you!" she yelled. "Bring it here!" I did do, by which time any morsel of respect I previously had for her had winged itself through the windows and over the roof-tops.

MR HOLLEY. My penultimate teacher was the young, tall, lanky and bespectacled Mr Holley, who was fair and acceptable in his methods. For a time it was rumoured by pupils that he, whom we nicknamed "Old Prickles", and young and attractive teacher Miss Kinley, had an eye for each other. But it was never proved. Miss Kinley came to the school after I had left the class she came to teach in (Miss Green's or Miss Goodyer's).

My Memories of Crowthorne Yesteryear and other accounts

two sweet (Lincoln Cream) biscuits. Sometimes I was given a second-helping of this, highlighting my day! There came a time when the meals were cooked in the kitchen of the school canteen, after renovations and improvements, creating a much better situation all round. The prices regularly rose to match increasing costs, naturally.

FREE SCHOOL MILK. For a time all the children who wanted it had free school milk, which was delivered daily in one-third-of-a-pint bottles in metal crates. The bottles had cardboard tops, usual with all milk bottles then, whose centres pushed in to make it easy to take the tops off, or to put a wax straw through. (At home we used the tops and wool to make pom-poms.) My sisters and I had the milk, which was distributed to all the children at the start of the morning playtime. I believe at some point a charge for it was introduced when, if so, a number of children stopped having the milk. Horlicks tablets (maybe Horlicks itself too) came to be introduced at the school, which I had and enjoyed, being oblong-shaped that had to be sucked.

(Also at home, we were given – allocated by the Government – a special brand of concentrated orange juice, also cod liver oil, during, probably, some of the war years. I believe, at least in part, it was to help prevent children getting rickets, which some had suffered from, though I never heard of any Crowthorne cases.)

THE CARETAKER. Very regularly seen at the school, the caretaker, short, Fred Beauchamp had a wife Maud and four children: John, Mary, David and Janet – Mary being in my class. Nothing seemed to ruffle often smiling Fred, of whom we knew "we have a friend here." Fred was also responsible for the heating stoves that were in some of the classrooms (Mr Hayward's prefabricated one included, who used to perch his bottom on its guard rail, maybe in part explaining the redness of his face) and a coke pile at one side of the girls' playground was Fred's to watch over, as it were. Sometimes children, from running about, fell on to it, but were soon up, and running again after a dust-down. There was a cycle shed for the children's bikes, fairly near the coke pile.

Fred was also responsible for the thankless task of cleaning the lavatories in the two playgrounds. As mentioned earlier, those in the girls' brick-built block we termed "the offices". I never knew why. At one *separate* end of this were urinals for the youngest of the boys. Fred's efforts in this respect were undoubtedly short-lived. The state of 'the offices', hour-by-hour, often led me to 'hold it in' till I got home! Do some of my medical problems today spring from this, I wonder?

Crowthorne C. of E. School. Modern-day picture of what was the front part of the 'big school' (separate from the Infants' School at the rear of this), which was Miss Mohr's class, left, and Mr Holley's class, right, when Shirley Woodason was at the school. Far left was the office of Headmaster, Mr A. C. Goodband, and the house partly showing at the far right of the picture, was that of Mr Goodband and his wife.

(Photo - Shirley E. Peckham.)

CHAPTER SEVEN
MY ELEVEN-PLUS EXPERIENCE

THE EXAMINATION. Aged eleven, I sat the eleven-plus exam with my classmates, which, if successful, would lead to us going to grammar school. I was feeling anxious and soon found myself in front of the paper (our teacher Mr Holley had distributed to us in his classroom) completely stumped by the questions! They did not seem to relate to my class work, in which I had always been very successful, as my end-of-term exam results regularly showed. My problem in my isolated situation mounted, as I was aware of how the time was moving on while I had barely begun even attempting the questions.

All too soon it was over, when I felt miserable at the real possibility of failure. Perhaps I would just scrape through? Later, at home, I told my parents (from them asking) that the paper "wasn't bad" and "I did my best," feeling this sufficient for them, *then*, and if I passed I need say no more on my dreadful experience. They seemed satisfied.

SHIRE HALL. I failed the exam and my heart was in my shoes. Mum was in a state about it, while Dad was baffled though calm at the news. Mr Goodband and my teachers, present and past at the C. of E. School, also showed immense surprise that I had failed to get through. One playtime I overheard several of them in a group talking about it.

Mum, greatly concerned by the situation, asked Mr Goodband if anything could be done to help or remedy matters, considering my academic record till then had been very good. This led to him arranging for Mum and me to go to Shire Hall, a large old building in the town of Reading, to see an official of, presumably, Berkshire County Council's education department, on the subject. We duly did this, though I felt despondent from the start. Mum, however, considered there was a chance that good would come of it. We were there, with an official in his office, for less than an hour, when Mum and the man did most of the talking. The result was disappointingly that things had to stay as they were.

A SECOND CHANCE. Sometime later, however, I had another chance to win myself a place at The Holt (Wokingham), along with some others who had failed the eleven-plus with me. This involved an interview and short oral test to take place at The Holt. Mum was pleased and excited at this, while Dad, like me, remained calm, though wanted me to do well, obviously.

The day concerned was dogged by misfortune. I was to travel

My Memories of Crowthorne Yesteryear and other accounts

there early in the afternoon, while Mum was at work. This was with a friend Yvonne and her parents, in their small car. Mum had left a change of clothes on my bed for me to change into when I returned from school at lunch-time and after having a good wash. "You must look nice and tidy for this," she'd said. Alas, when I put on one of the ankle socks I saw it had a large hole as big as a penny coin in the heel. And I had insufficient time to look for a decent pair! It was a question of my doing my hair nicely or searching for decent socks. I opted for the former and hoped my sandal strap would *permanently* cover the 'spud', as a hole in a sock was widely termed.

On our journey to The Holt, Yvonne's parents, in the front of the car, argued with each other almost constantly concerning something of their own. My friend looked unhappy and embarrassed by it and I was ill at ease.

THE TRIO. At The Holt, where I was conscious of my sock 'spud' showing sometimes, a team of three women interviewed girls from various schools. We had to read passages from supplied books and answer questions on what we had read. I was given the impression that the women were not really interested in us. They were unsmiling and I felt, again, uneasy.

I failed this too, while not really believing from the outset that I would succeed. Mum saw Mr Goodband about it and asked if there was anything else I could try, hopefully to take me beyond Crowthorne C. of E. School for the rest of my school life.

GUILDFORD TECHNICAL COLLEGE. "The only option now," he told her, "is for her to take an exam, at thirteen years, for hopefully a place at Guildford Technical College." This to be sat there. Mum felt pessimistic about the journey to and from the college that would be involved for me, by train from Crowthorne Station and I think there was also a bus journey, but we came to decide I *should* sit the exam for my last chance of the sort. When the time came round I dealt with the paper well, I considered. But I failed this too! I was not disillusioned by it, nor were my parents. Deep down I did not want to go to the college, but by now instead remain at the school I knew so well and liked, where mainly I also enjoyed a good rapport with my teachers and classmates. My future was still not a consideration with me.

I CRIED BEFORE THE HEAD. A few weeks before I left school, at fifteen, Mr Goodband, the head, had all of us who

CHAPTER SIX
FURTHER SCHOOL INCIDENTS

THE DENTIST. Our teeth were regularly examined and later treated, where appropriate, by the school dentist, whom we all dreaded coming. This was in the British Legion Hall in Wellington Road. One day, when aged 9, I had a painful time in the dentist's hands and my "Ouch!" to let him know he was hurting me, produced his sharp slap on my face, and he voiced angrily, "Stop it! I've got my work to do!" This dismayed his lady assistant and astounded me.

I did not dare tell Mum of it when I joined her in the waiting-room afterwards, for she would have made a fuss on the spot which might have frightened the other children there and embarrassed me. But I told her instead on our way home, by the Crowthorne Inn. She exploded, instructed me to wait there and marched back to the Legion, as we called it. Rejoining me twenty minutes later, still flustered, she said, "There, that's it, I've told him – disgusting, smacking a child like that."

But when the dentist was to next come to look at the schoolchildren's teeth, on my treatment card handed to me by my teacher in readiness was the humiliating message in large black letters, 'Child was a nuisance in surgery – mother made a fuss.' I told Mum of it and she said, "You will not go to the school dentist ever again."

MORE PUNISHMENTS. When aged twelve, girl school bullies ill-treated me for publicly declaring I *fancied* a boy whom I was unaware was another girl's boyfriend! One winter's afternoon, after school, four or five of them stopped me in 'The Valley', the wooded, scrubland area between Crowthorne C. of E. School and Pinewood Avenue, I and other children walked through to and from school, and enticed me to go with them into the nearby, also wooded, Walter Recreation Ground on a pretext, "To show you something." In good faith, though baffled, nothing like this had happened before, I went along. There, three of them together pushed me headlong into snow-caked bushes and turned and walked away, quipping, "That's for taking someone else's boyfriend!" I'd not *taken* anyone, so was very undeserving of this, I felt.

When aged 15, just before leaving school, I received a formal punishment from Miss Mohr. At the time she was teaching me as Acting Head in place of Mr Goodband, who had been ill and was soon to retire. On my way to school on the morning concerned, I and others heard, in Pinewood Avenue, from another child, that our beloved Plaza cinema had burned down overnight. We could not believe this and decided we wanted to go there to see whatever there was to see, so as to ascertain the situation for ourselves.

We went straight to the cinema site, and saw the still smouldering ruins of the place where we had so enjoyed many film shows, as well as some live stage ones. Before us, the sight of half-burnt seats, charred-black metal, and piles of debris of various kinds, gave us a sickening feeling. We stood in animated disbelief, which soon turned to the stark impact of full realisation of what we were viewing.

Feeling the time was getting on, we turned to make our way to school, first looking back a few times to view again the stinking, smouldering wreckage. Arriving at school late, after Assembly, Miss Mohr greeted us with, "Where have you been to make you late?" We told her and why. She said we must stay in after school and do one hundred lines of 'I must not go and see a burnt-out cinema before school to make me late again'. It was almost laughable! This, such a dramatic and heart-breaking event in our young lives, and likely in the history of Crowthorne, we had felt absolutely compelled to go and see, had surprisingly, it appeared, failed to move the teacher with any compassion and understanding towards us.

THE LESSONS. I did well in English lessons, being good at composition and letter-writing of the 'thank-you, aunty, for your Christmas present' kind. Also, I was good at arithmetic, including fractions and decimals. But algebra and geometry were a different story! Most of the history and geography teaching and learning escapes me now, although I remember teacher Mr Hayward telling us of King Alfred burning the cakes, which we all in class listened to attentively. Also, in Mr Hayward's class, the first sentence in a book I read has stayed forever in my mind: 'Let's take a bird's eye look at democracy in the world at large'.

MISS CHURCHILL. When about twelve I had some private coaching, in her home, from Miss A. F. Churchill, the retired schoolmistress of a girls' school in Sherborne, Dorset, living next door to us. This was in the bungalow she had named 'Sherbornia' (now No.2 Pinewood Avenue). My mother worked a little for Miss Churchill at the time. The old lady gave me exercises in several subjects, while I sat at the dining-table in her living-room, under a ceiling gas light she lit from home-made tapers from a jarful in her fireplace.

She made the tapers from 8-inch-long pieces of white exercise book paper, she folded vertically several times. Miss Churchill would light a taper end from her hearth fire before reaching up and lighting her gas light from it. I saw the procedure as very dangerous, but apparently she always got away with it!

Whether I learned very much from the exercises beyond what I already knew, I do not know, but I much preferred them to the piano lessons in our home enforced upon me by Mum earlier in my life!

Short, bespectacled Miss Churchill, with a very neat home and corresponding garden (regularly attended by her gardener, a Mr Smith), was a devout Christian and regular churchgoer, who attended St. John the Baptist Church every Sunday morning, wearing a smart coat and brimmed hat. She was always confusing my name with that of one of her nieces she rarely saw and who lived out of the area, so calling me "Ruby". I would respectfully correct her on each occasion, but she would get it wrong again next time.

On very frosty or snowy mornings I would accompany Miss Churchill to and from St. John's church, holding her arm to prevent her from slipping on dangerous surfaces. She would be very grateful and say, "Thank you Ruby."

I would also go to Talmage the butchers' every Saturday morning for her, to get the one lamb chop (never anything different) she had ordered, which was always one shilling and sixpence (7½p), and when I handed it to Miss Churchill she would say, "Thank you Ruby, and this is for you," while handing me a nickel threepenny-piece. I was always grateful to receive the reward, boosting my pocket money.

AWARDS. I gained an impressive list of awards from Crowthorne C. of E. School over the years, although I never forgave Mum for throwing away as "clutter" my old school reports and certificates, when I was married and living in Germany in the sixties. Forgive my trumpet blowing (information as obtained from the Berkshire Record Office, Shire Hall, Reading):-

20 Dec 1944 (age 10½)	S. Woodason, Class 4, was awarded a Certificate for Proficiency and Good Conduct.
13 Jul 1945 (age 11)	S. Woodason, Class 3, was commended in Vicar's report on the school (for a written Scripture paper).
20 Dec 1945 (age 11½)	S. Woodason was awarded a Certificate for Proficiency and Good Conduct.
18 Dec 1947 (age 13½)	Miss Warren's Prize for Good Conduct and Usefulness: S. Woodason. (The same year my youngest sister, Virginia – Virgy – received a Certificate for Proficiency, at the school.)
21 Dec 1948 (age 14½)	Miss Warren's Prize for Good Conduct and Usefulness: S. Woodason.

My Memories of Crowthorne Yesteryear and other accounts

I do not remember who Miss Warren was and tried to find out recently, but to no avail! But I feel she was never a teacher at the school, so maybe a governor or similar. I benefited a lot as a pupil throughout all of my school life at Crowthorne C. of E. School and am very grateful to the teachers who guided my academic and character development, particularly, of course, the reasonable and fair ones!

SCHOOL WEAR. Girls at school mainly wore navy-blue or black gym-slips, white blouses, and varied cardigans, in the winter, and in the summer, cotton dresses, and cardigans when necessary. Boys wore grey short trousers until they were about 9, whatever the time of year, and then long ones. Some of the children's clothes were ragged (especially with elbows of garments holed), for parents could not always keep up, because of the cost, with their growing offspring's needs. With large families being quite commonplace, many children's clothes were what were termed 'hand-me-downs' (ones handed down, age-wise, naturally, from one child to the next and so on, till worn out).

Girls wore lace-up shoes in winter and buckled sandals in summer. I favoured red ones. Boys wore ankle-hugging black lace-up boots, in winter and summer. We all wore plimsolls for PT and kept the local cobblers (shoe and boot repairers) busy! For us this was Mr George Watkins, who lived in Duke's Ride, opposite the school, and had his work-shed in his garden. He was a kindly, soft-spoken man, always politely interested in the children, who I liked to watch doing his work when calling on him to take or collect shoes.

The Headmaster and staff always dressed conservatively, being well turned out and smart. The men wore suits and the ladies dresses or skirts with blouses and cardigans – sometimes twin-sets, with necklaces of pearls or beads. We addressed the Headmaster and teachers as "Sir", or "Miss", as appropriate, and they addressed us by our full names always.

THE SCHOOL DINNERS. These were introduced at the school in September 1943 at 4d each. Mum liked the idea, so Glennis, Virgy and I were participants who came to mainly enjoy the meals, that were transported to the school after being cooked in Wokingham. The boiled cabbage (pale and slimy), though, was in particular not suitable to my palate. The unrecognisable, mainly thinly sliced, meat often did not have much taste and the gravy was not a patch on Mum's! For me the best pudding (out of the chiefly milk ones we had, besides those of the steamed or baked sponge kind) was caramel custard served with would be leaving (ten or so) sitting with him in a classroom. He told us that shortly we were going into the working world, a big step in our lives, and he wished us all the best for our futures. As he spoke I felt tears in my eyes. He noticed and said, "Good gracious, you are the first child who has cried on leaving school in my experience."

I replied, "It is because I have enjoyed it."

THE ELEVEN-PLUS AND MY SISTERS. Glennis, 18 months my junior, fortunately made it to The Holt and our parents had to buy her uniform, complete with the necessary blazer and hat badges. I had some mixed feelings on her success (including being pleased for her, like Mum and Dad were), after my own abortive attempt to pass the eleven-plus, and was baffled that Glennis passed the exam, while I had failed it. When Virgy came to also fail the eleven-plus, I felt even more baffled (a feeling that has remained), since we were all successful pupils at Crowthorne C. of E. School.

Glennis took elocution lessons while at The Holt. I believe she liked her time there and did quite well. However, she left at sixteen and achieved her ambition of working in a sweet shop in Camberley.

Doris Denton, of Ellis Road (in dark coat) and her friends, L. to r. sisters, Virginia (Virgy), Shirley, and Glennis Woodason, school girls, circa 1946.

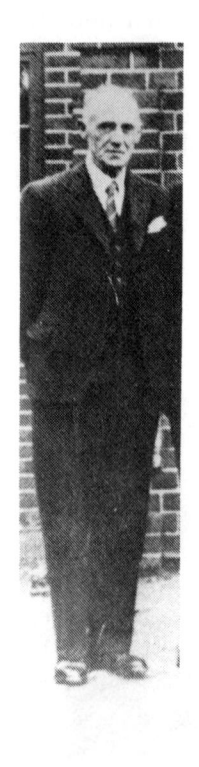

My Memories of Crowthorne Yesteryear and other accounts

Mr A. C. Goodband, Headmaster at Crowthorne C. of E. School.

(L. to r.) Miss Maud Green, Mrs Daisy Luckock, and Miss Gladys Burton, teachers at Crowthorne C. of E. School, standing outside the front of the main school building.
(Photo courtesy of Joan Franklin.)

CHAPTER EIGHT
MORE CHILDHOOD MEMORIES

OUR SEASIDE TRIPS. My first sighting of the sea, when aged 2½, was I believe at Southsea. I felt wonder and almost disbelief when, while standing staring at it, I also considered, what a lot of water, far more than in my bath! Where did it all come from? Later in the day, at the resort, I was bought and had handed to me by Mum, to eat them all myself, a whole bag of Smith's crisps. When I looked inside the bag, I felt it was such a big bagful of them and took a long time to eat them all. And when I pulled out the mystery (to me) blue bag of salt, Mum quickly retrieved it, saying, "You can't have that!"

Other seaside places we visited on coach (perhaps sometimes charabanc) trips from Crowthorne – mostly I think organised by the Crowthorne Inn – were Littlehampton, Brighton, Worthing and Bognor Regis. Some locals may also have gone to Bournemouth, but we did not go there. "Too far," my parents said.

THE FUNFAIRS. These were popular, fun and exciting, especially in the evenings when lit up and it was getting dark. And I liked the music. We went to them in Wokingham and Camberley, having 'a go' on the rides and the stalls – throwing rings, rolling balls, throwing darts and aiming for the coconuts. I liked the ghost train, on which I merely feigned fright, but disliked some of the rides that made me nauseous, such as the swinging-boats. Our money never went very far at the fairs and I can't remember winning anything.

OTHER SHOWS AND OUTINGS. We occasionally attended circuses locally, I think at Blackwater, where I believe some of the fairs used to be. I was not very impressed by them. The hard, wooden, form-type seats meant I was ready to leave long before the end!

My mother took us to ice-shows at Wembley, by coach. These were spectacular, with flawless skating. And the ladies' beautiful, colourful outfits, that usually glistened, served to increase my enjoyment greatly.

Mum also took us to London sightseeing, by train, visiting Westminster Abbey, The Houses of Parliament, St. Paul's Cathedral, Buckingham Palace, and many more places of special interest, to help with our development. One of her favourite places to take us to in the city was Madame Tussaud's waxworks, where I found it most interesting of all in the Chamber of Horrors. Mum and our Aunty Blanche

My Memories of Crowthorne Yesteryear and other accounts

often told us creepy stories – true and fictional – which always enthralled us, so I was in my element in the Chamber of Horrors.

Then Mum said, "How would you like to spend a night alone in here, with the lights out, for five hundred pounds?" It was certainly a great temptation, but my answer was a shivery "N..n.no."

Mum also took us to London Zoo, and Chessington Zoo occasionally. I particularly enjoyed watching the monkeys and chimps.

There was an unpleasant incident for me at London Zoo, when I was eight. In the monkey house a man in a raincoat and trilby, standing behind me, indecently assaulted me with his hand through my clothes. I did not know exactly what was happening at first. When I turned round to see, he stopped his actions, and when I turned my head away to watch the monkeys again, he repeated them. This, a few times. Disturbed, I eventually moved to where Mum stood, nearby (my sisters were with us), and told her quietly of it.

The place was quite full of adults and children and the man, on seeing what I had done, slipped off in a hurry towards one of the exits, moving people aside as he went. Mum, shocked at events, went after him, but once out of the monkey house he was too fast for her and she could not keep up with him. Returning to us, flustered, she said, "Disgusting, doing that to a little girl! He shouldn't be about, I'd like to tell everybody." But she did not do so and we soon left the zoo, having otherwise enjoyed the visit.

OUR HOLIDAYS. The only holidays away from home we had, when we were older children and in our teens, were holiday camp ones at Brambles on the Isle of Wight and at Gorleston-on-Sea, Norfolk. These were small camps, each for some six hundred holidaymakers. We never went to king-size Butlins, or other, ones. In the camps, Mum (Dad only went once, I believe) avidly joined in the games and other events and pushed my sisters and me into doing them too. We had a lot of fun there, made friends, dressed up for the fancy-dress occasions, and were 'on the go' all day. We'd split our sides from laughing at some of the antics that went on and made new friends. Those short holidays enriched my childhood and early teens a great deal.

ROYAL ASCOT. Mum also took us to Royal Ascot, again when we were older. This was a thrill to me. I had sometimes seen "posh people", in their finery, in big, posh, gleaming cars being driven along Crowthorne High Street and over Lightfoot's Hill (the section of Bracknell Road by Lightfoot's garage), before further making their

My Memories of Crowthorne Yesteryear and other accounts

way to the racecourse. But *we* went there by bus.

From the heath I was always overjoyed to see the royal procession, with the horse-drawn carriages of principal royals: King George VI, Queen Elizabeth, Princesses Elizabeth and Margaret Rose, colourfully making its way along the course. I enjoyed the races too, also very colourful, besides being thrilling.

The occasions were most delightful. My experiences there led me to wanting to be a female jockey when I was older. But I grew too large for that!

Mum also took us to the Royal Military Academy at Sandhurst to see the Passing Out parades, and in particular to see members of the Royal Family who used to go there, only one each time in my experience, to take the salute. On one particular occasion it was Princess Margaret. As she was driven, in the gleaming royal car with its small insignia flag flapping at the front through part of the grounds for the ceremony, we saw her from a good vantage point free of other people Mum had taken us to.

Looking absolutely lovely and perfectly made up, she waved to us. Her features, to me, were like those of a beautiful doll. I was very excited and absolutely enthralled at seeing her.

THE CINEMAS. We had many outings to the local Plaza; then, after it was burned down early in my teens*, and with some reluctance because the Plaza had been so superb a place, to the Odeon and the Arcade in Camberley, as well as to the Ritz in Wokingham.

---

* Press cuttings, dated July 4th 1949, in relation to the Plaza cinema fire (as supplied by Crowthorne Fire Brigade), state as follows:
 'The Star', evening newspaper (London), quote: 'Flames were already leaping through the roof when Berkshire and Reading Fire brigade were called to the Plaza Cinema, Crowthorne, Berkshire, early today.
 'For some time the firemen had to concentrate on preventing the flames from spreading to other buildings.
 'The cinema, which had recently been renovated, was seriously damaged.
 'Firemen salvaged a sum of money in notes, silver and copper.
 'This was the 25th fire attended by the brigade in 15 hours.'

(And from an unidentified newspaper) quote: 'The Plaza Cinema, at Crowthorne (Berks.), was completely destroyed by fire during the early hours of today. A little while before the blaze a film called "The Fatal Night" had been shown.
 'Fire brigades from Reading, Wokingham, and Bracknell were called, but so fierce were the flames that they had enveloped the building from end to end before hoses could be brought to play.'

My Memories of Crowthorne Yesteryear and other accounts

Once (probably in my childhood) I also saw films in a small cinema in Broad Street, Wokingham, known as "the flea-pit". I don't recall its actual name and believe it closed down within a few years of my visit.

The costs of the seats in the Odeon, Arcade, and Ritz were, not surprisingly, higher than at the Plaza. We had to travel by bus to the cinemas, which created inconvenience and additional expense, and the Camberley ones seemed too posh to me compared with our oh-so-cosy Plaza. The Ritz, at Wokingham, however, was not so grand as the Camberley cinemas, where we felt comparatively more at home!

As in the Plaza, the film was given to breaking down sometimes, to soon bring about boos and foot-stamping, especially when the situation was prolonged. Once at the Ritz this was for nearly two hours, during which some patrons walked out. Others in the auditorium were walking about, talking to others, and generally preventing themselves from being cheesed off! I used to hear such expressions as, "Come on, get it fixed! We've paid you," called out on such occasions.

Seats in the Plaza had cost 2/3 (11p) and 1/9 (9p) for the best, and 9d (4p) for the cheapest 'down the front' ones. Patrons who sat there used to get a stiff neck from looking up to the screen. Courting couples always sought the back rows, especially *the* back one.

I was in the cinema once with Mum, when a man wearing a large hat came and sat in front of her. For a while she put up with not being able to see the screen very well, then gently lifted the man's hat off his head, tapped him on the shoulder (whereupon he turned round) and handed him his hat. He simply took it from her and put on his lap. Throughout, not one word was spoken between them, while I was feeling 'jellyish' about what could happen!

People took picnics to the Plaza, including flasks of tea and bags of food, and some did this regularly, when, especially in the interval, they could be heard munching apples and making a noise with crisp packets. I would try to sit as far from them as possible, but sometimes had no choice!

There were three different programmes weekly, each screened for two days (Mon/Tues, Wed/Thurs, Fri/Sat), and the cinema was closed on Sundays. The programmes consisted of a main film (1½ hours), a support film (1 hour), trailers for future films at the cinema, and the Pathé News. I am not sure if advertising was involved, but feel it likely – a little anyway. However, perhaps I am thinking of the other cinemas mentioned here.

On Saturdays, mornings or afternoons, there were special matinée programmes for children. I attended them sometimes, when we were obliged to sit in the lower (bottom or front) half of the auditorium.

However, I preferred to be out playing with my friends – especially in the summer-time, when we had many nice, warm days.

I liked the Tarzan films at the cinema, with Johnny Weissmuller in the role, his partner, "Jane" (possibly played by Maureen Sullivan), and Cheeta the chimp. Also, I liked the George Formby ones, when he played his ukulele (good foot-tapping stuff). And the detective Charlie Chan (Chinaman, I think) ones appealed to me too, with his regularly uttered phrase, "Let Charlie pass," when he wanted to pass people.

'Gone with the Wind' was too long for my young stamina. I lost concentration mid-stream (even though there was an interval) and to sit watching the film after that was like watching paint peel! Laurel and Hardy films – "Now look at the fine mess you have gotten me into," (regularly uttered by Oliver Hardy to Stan Laurel) – were a joy and a source of great laughter to me. Love story, musical, and western films were those I liked least. So, detective, other mystery, and comedy ones were my favourites.

OTHER POPULAR STARS. I was named after Shirley Temple, the child star 'rage' at the time (she being 6 years old when I was born). I still have a collection of black and white postcard pictures of many of the stars who entertained us all so much in the dear old Plaza and other cinemas. Heart-throb of many women and girls was Errol Flynn, also Cornel Wilde, Rock Hudson and Cary Grant, besides of course Clark Gable. I did not have a particular heart-throb among them. Of the admirable female stars I liked in the films were Myrna Loy, June Allison and Barbara Stanwyck. Jeanette Macdonald and Nelson Eddy appealed to me with their superb singing. Bette Davis and Margaret Lockwood I thought special actresses also.

OUTDOOR PURSUITS. In the summer we went swimming in Heath Pool, Heath Ride. Mum took us, all riding our bicycles. It was difficult to ride them through the deep white sand of Heath Ride. Big brown ants flourished in the woods that abounded Heath Pool, which were a real nuisance to us when wanting to sit there and when we got undressed and later dressed. We were once going to hang our clothes on trees (mostly pine), but saw that the ants were also scurrying up and down their trunks and along their branches!

We had lots of fun in the lake, the water of which always looked dirty and had pieces of tree branches, stones and assorted debris in it. I am sure we had many mouthfuls of the dirty water, but never seemed to suffer any ill-effects.

Near Heath Pool was The Heritage "Nudist Camp", as we called it.

My Memories of Crowthorne Yesteryear and other accounts

We used to speak of the place and wonder about it sometimes, while having the odd girlish giggle at some of our imaginations. The Heritage was surrounded by a tall wooden fence.

One day, when about 9, I was dressing in the woods near Heath Pool after our family swim, and heard a rustling sound in nearby bushes. Glancing that way, I saw a naked man standing looking at me from behind a low bush. Our eyes locked for a few seconds, before he turned and hurried away, showing me his tanned backside as he did so. I mentioned the business to Mum as soon as I was dressed and had joined her, and she said, "I expect he's an escapee from The Heritage!"

INDECENT EXPOSURE. The above incident was probably an innocent interlude, but I feel that cannot be said of the following. One afternoon I was riding my bike along New Wokingham Road (towards Bigshotte School), alone, also when about 9, when a man came from behind one of the Nissen huts that were positioned yards from each other along 'my' side of the road. As I rode nearer the hut, he came to the front of it, where, 20 yards or so from me, and I was getting nearer to him all the time, he stopped. Then, facing me, he dropped his nether garments to his ankles.

Nervous, I continued cycling, all the while keeping my gaze ahead though observing him out of the corner of my eye. He was statuesque. I fearfully accomplished an errand before cycling home the 'long way', via Nine Mile Ride and Old Wokingham Road, so as not to have to pass him again. I arrived home and told Mum of the incident. "Where?" she shrieked. "*Tell me where he is? I* want to see him." (To tell him off, of course!) I told her where and she charged off on her bike, with me calling behind her, "I don't expect he'll be there now." I was right, he wasn't! She returned home disgruntled.

SWIMMING POOLS. Mum took us to Martin's Swimming Pool, in Milton Road, Wokingham, where there were adult and children's pools. The latter had a very appealing chute, I excitedly went down time and time again. Mum had trouble getting me out of the water when it was time to get dressed and go for the bus, for I so loved being in there.

"*Please* let me stay in a bit longer, *please.*"
"*We have to catch the bus. Hurry up, or we'll leave you here.*"

By the pools there were flower-beds, and sloped lawns, on which families sat relaxing in the sunshine and having their refreshments.

We also went to the Blue Pool, at the town end of London Road, Camberley. I liked this pool too, but was not so impressed by it as

Martin's. There was not the right atmosphere somehow, and the water always seemed colder than at Martin's.

We would also go to King's Mere lake, off Nine Mile Ride, not to swim but sometimes to paddle. Queen's Mere lake, very deep and dangerous I was told, lay nearby, behind much screening of vegetation and fencing. I did not venture near it as, also, it was out of bounds I understood.

OUR BARGE TRIPS. During some summers Mum took us to Windsor to visit the castle and to have barge trips on the River Thames. The latter I found somewhat boring, especially after the first one! And in bad weather they were especially so, with more-or-less the same scenery throughout what seemed an endless period of time, but was only a couple of hours or so at the most. Our going through the locks was a novelty, though also only on the first occasion.

We also had boat trips on the Thames, or maybe the Loddon, from the Reading area. I cannot remember where we hopped aboard there, maybe at or near Loddon Bridge, or Pangbourne.

FOREST FIRES, CHIMNEY FIRES. Forest fires, and others needing the attention of the local Fire Brigade, were quite commonplace in my childhood. I remember them particularly on the forest ground (probably of the Forestry Commission) off Old Wokingham Road, near the mouth of Ellis Road. They started in a small way, of course, and it was soon after this that my friends would alert me to it, and add, "Come and have a look." Excitedly, I would go there with them! Soon the fires spread, usually as we watched them burn. The brigade, helped by other local men (who had often arrived there first), usually had the fires under control within a few hours, unless they were more serious, when much longer was involved.

During my childhood house chimney fires were a fairly regular occurrence. We always knew when there was one in our area. The acrid smoke, we saw and smelled, and also sometimes sparks coming from the top of the chimney and falling onto the roof of the house concerned, were the indicators.

Householders, whose homes were affected by the fires, were alarmed about them on occasions (and others living nearby were too), when they would sometimes seek help and advice. But mostly folk knew well how to cope with the fires – especially if a man was at home – and took this in their stride, without flapping. I don't recall ever seeing a fire-engine at a house with a chimney fire (or hearing of it), but probably there was on occasions.

My Memories of Crowthorne Yesteryear and other accounts

FRANK ASHBY. The chimney-sweep of the time was the short and ever-cheerful, Mr Frank Ashby, who used to travel about the village in his little red van, with his brushes affixed (I can't be sure, but maybe on its outside, or he had some of them there). He also appeared, soot-black, wearing his work clothes, and carrying his brushes, at the local churches, following some weddings. This was, traditionally, to bring good luck to the newly-weds.

I think Mr Ashby came to us once or twice to clean our living-room chimney, but mostly Dad cleaned it himself. He did this by felling a suitable holly-tree, or sawing off a holly-tree top, measuring about 4 ft long. Then he attached the end of a rope to near the tree's lower end, fixed the end of the tree into the top of the chimney (having first dropped the main part of the rope through it) and, indoors, by the hearth, pulled on the rope, thus allowing the holly-tree to travel down the inside of the chimney, cleaning the soot from it simultaneously. We were assured a good job of it will have been done. Of course, everything in the room had been well prepared beforehand against the inevitable mess! Dad used the soot on his garden, as being "good for it."

When, on occasion, our open fire refused to burn on first being lit, we helped it to by sprinkling a small amount of sugar or the gratings of part of a candle onto the paper and sticks. Sometimes both were necessary. Whatever applied, it always worked well.

Once, my mother employed my sisters and me sieving the coal (with a garden sieve) in our coal shed, when it had become necessary for *someone* to do it. The job took hours and left us very warm and filthy, but we had carried out a successful task.

SNOW. Many of our winters seemed to bring snow and my mother used to persuade my sisters and me to go out playing in it. I used to protest that it was "too cold," but it made no difference.

"Go on, get your things on and out you all go!" So we would dress up in our coats, hats, gloves, scarves and wellingtons and, at least as far as I was concerned, with barely a modicum of enthusiasm, venture out in it.

We never had a proper sledge, but made do with planks of wood and suchlike to pull and push each other and our friends along on. And sometimes Dad 'knocked something up' for us for the purpose. We had snowball games and fights, the boys much preferring the latter, usually starting them. Within an hour of our activities beginning we were very warm!

CAROL SINGING. When snow fell before Christmas we went carol singing in it (we went every year anyway). This was to

My Memories of Crowthorne Yesteryear and other accounts

people's back doors in Pinewood Avenue and Ellis Road. Sometimes the snow reached halfway up the calves of our legs as my sisters, friends and I trudged through it, in the dark, from house to house. Well wrapped up and carrying our torches, I did not mind being out in the snow then. There was a magical element about it, cold or not, and the prospect of our carol singing boosting our pocket money emphasised the excitement.

There would be up to five of us at a time, rarely boys in the party who were not very interested. We sang parts of three popular carols, concluding with the jingle 'We wish you a merry Christmas, a merry Christmas', etc. Mostly, the householders then came out to us and put money in our cocoa tin we carried for the purpose. The very rare contribution of two shillings (10p) was the largest amount from a householder we ever received. Sixpence (2½p), or less, was the usual, and our collection would total six to seven shillings (30 - 35p) at the end of our 2½-hour stint. We were happy, but also tired and anxious to be home by then, and our share helped us to buy Christmas presents for our parents.

When any householders did not open their doors to us – and we were convinced they were at home – dismayed and downcast, we would purposely leave their gate open on leaving. On one occasion, by contrast, a lady, on opening her door to us and popping coins in our collection tin, kindly invited us inside her home for cups of hot cocoa and biscuits, adding, "You must be cold, poor dears." We were pleased to accept, though did not want to be held up!

JACK FROST. As there was no central heating in our home for many years, our bedrooms and hall were very cold in the winter and sometimes, we would wake up to the shivery conditions to find pretty, frozen 'lace curtain' designs on our windows. "Jack Frost has been again!" Sometimes the windows remained like this all day, and icicles hung from trees and other objects outside as well. When the frost on the windows thawed, they 'ran' with condensation (we regularly had this trouble) and Mum wiped them down with big cloths. If she delayed doing it, pools of water formed on the window-sills.

We widely used winter clothing of all kinds, especially for outdoors, and regularly took hot-water bottles to bed with us.

DOGS AND CATS. Dogs ran loose in my childhood and roamed amongst us as we played, sometimes in groups. People who had dogs always had a kennel in their garden for their pets, and dogs did not go into homes as much as now. I would see a dog mounted on

My Memories of Crowthorne Yesteryear and other accounts

another at times and in all innocence once asked my mother, "Why do dogs get on top of each other?"

"You know why."

"I don't."

"Well don't look at them. Do something else!"

Once on a warm day, in Pinewood Avenue I saw a neighbour's dog foaming at the mouth and dashing about wildly, almost in circles. I left the scene like a startled rabbit!

Much later, in 1963-'64, when I was living in Cromwell Road, Camberley with Gordon, my first husband, our son Michael and *maybe* our daughter, Susan, or I was pregnant with her (I can't be sure, who was born early in 1964), a rabid dog was reported to be loose there. All householders were advised to stay indoors as much as possible, and report to the authorities if they saw the dog. Armed troops of the local units were sent out, to go on foot across commons and so on, searching for the affected animal. Eventually, after several days, it was found and destroyed. The very serious and alarming incident, in the summer of 1963 or '64, created national, maybe international, news and put Camberley firmly on the map.

When I was young, puppies – other than pedigree ones, which were mostly sold – were always *given away* to people who wanted them.

Many people had cats, probably more of them than had dogs, while some had both, and kittens, soft and fluffy, particularly appealed to young children. Kittens too were given away, never sold, to always keenly awaiting recipients.

A BEARABLE PUNISHMENT. On an occasion that I was naughty, but I don't recall the facts, Mum, I knew, would be 'after my blood'. I would either receive the lashing of her tongue – she was very practised at – or hear her threat of, "You wait till your Dad comes in, he'll give you a clout." If he was there at the time of the wrong-doing, he probably would have carried it out anyway!

I decided to protect myself by placing two thin colouring books in the back of my knickers, in readiness for any slap through my clothes, if it was coming. It was! In fact *three* fierce slaps, and I didn't feel a thing. "Let that teach you!" Mum thundered. It did. It taught me, what a good idea it was to put the colouring books in my clothes for protection, an action a friend had told me about, or I had read the advice in a comic. I kept the truth from Mum, or she may have made sure I was then given the real thing!

My Memories of Crowthorne Yesteryear and other accounts

Above, Shirley, Virginia (Virgy), Christopher F. (evacuee), and Glennis Woodason, on the edge of Martin's swimming pool, Wokingham (circa 1941).

Left, 'Syd' Woodason, bricklayer, with daughter Shirley (aged 9), during a break from building his garden shed.

Right, Virgy (left) and Shirley Woodason (aged about 5 and 9) enjoy knitting in the garden of their home, 'Sydellen'.

My Memories of Crowthorne Yesteryear and other accounts

The one time Plaza cinema, High Street, Crowthorne (previously St. George's Hall), decorated for VE Day or VJ Day, 1945. (*Also appeared in Our Memories of Crowthorne Yesteryear.*) (Photo courtesy of Joyce Earney.)

CHAPTER NINE
MY WELLINGTON COLLEGE GROUNDS EXPERIENCES

THE LAKE. Of the great joys of my childhood, my walks in the Wellington College grounds rank high. These were with my mother and sisters and later with my friends. I liked everything about the college grounds. Most appealing was the large divided lake with its bridge we would walk slowly across, taking in all to our left and right as we observed the still water, the reeds growing in parts of it (mostly near its edges), and water birds, including swans sometimes, afloat.

Occasionally we stood for a while by one of the white painted, wooden fences, situated at both sides of the bridge, known as The White Bridge, attracted by the beauty and appeal of the lake and all concerned with it. At other times we walked straight over the bridge and made our way around the lake by way of the pathway that meandered by its shores.

Here, as we trod the springy, peat-surfaced path, through the beautiful woodland of assorted trees (silver birch and I think beech and copper beech among them), we could often still observe the lake through the foliage. The whole experience was one of joy on every occasion.

Mostly we entered the grounds from Waterloo Road, through the college gateway and down the winding, sloped, gravelly roadway between tall trees and wild shrubbery, to the lake and bridge. Or we entered the grounds by a footpath beside the Iron Duke Hotel, alternatively by the main (roadway) entrance from Sandhurst Road known as The Mordaunt Gate (or gateway in this case). These, especially the latter, were the long routes for us, from the bottom of Pinewood Avenue, but were good for a change.

THE PRETTY, 'GENTLE' WALK, AND ROCKERY.
The entrance beside the Iron Duke afforded us a very pretty and 'gentle' walk too, that we always thoroughly enjoyed equally, especially in the spring and early summer.

The other great appeal to us in the grounds was the marvellous and popular "Wellington College rockery-garden", as it was known for miles. The largest of all those I had seen, the rockery seemed to have everything a sunken garden of its kind could possibly have. Little concrete paths and steps led one through it, which was full of a variety of plants interspersed with pools of water and little waterfalls. It had me entranced and eventually Mum, when with me, would almost have to pull me away from it. *"Come on, you can't stay here for ever, we have to go home,"* she'd say impatiently. But I would still linger by it, the colours and scent from the flowers also being of great appeal, and have to catch her up, as well as any other members of the family, or friends, that might have accompanied us.

Nearby was a large playing field, where often, in the summer, a cricket match was in progress. These always attracted a number of spectators. The Grubbies tuck-shop was in the vicinity.

THE SWIMMING POOL. The college outdoor swimming pool, nearby, was usually out of bounds to the villagers and other visitors to the grounds. It lay behind high wooden fencing, surrounding it, which had in it a tall, also wooden, locked gate. My friends and I felt compelled to see what we could of the pool and would look through the knot-holes in the fencing to get a satisfying peep. There were never any bathers in the pool at these times. Everything in the college grounds was a delightful change to us as children, from our everyday surroundings in Pinewood Avenue, much as we liked *them*.

SKATING. Referring again to the lake, we would go to the college on occasions in the very cold winter time, when sharp frosty conditions hung about all day. This was when we would see the lake ice-covered, with people 'skating', walking and standing on it. There were the obvious dangers. Even so, I dared myself to go a little way on to the ice where other 'dare devils' were sometimes. But on the final of these occasions I heard the alarmed cry of, "It's cracking, get off!" I then 'flew' off it with a bunch of others, to eventually look around, when I saw the person had been right. But everyone made it to the bank without mishap. I did not go on the ice any more after that!

A few times I saw a boat or two on the water, in the summer, but mainly there were none on the lake. I never saw fishing taking place there as a child, but have done since.

The college grounds absorbed all four of the seasons in quiet, majestic style, which the villagers and others never failed to appreciate and thoroughly enjoy. I strongly feel a situation of this kind still exists there today, although a number of changes have come about there, including some housing development, as visitors are regularly observing.

THE SPEECH DAYS. When the Speech Days took place every summer at Wellington College (this being in June, immediately before or, more likely, after Royal Ascot Week) a number of the parents gave custom to the Waterloo Hotel nearby, and other establishments of the kind in the village. Each time, I observed dozens of them in their finery by the hotel (in Waterloo Road and the nearby college grounds) and in the hotel grounds. It made a good picture, similar to seeing the high society Royal Ascot racegoers in their fashions and smart outfits.

My mother worked at the Waterloo Hotel before I was born, or in my very young childhood, although I have no personal details of this. But I recall her helping there as a waitress, in the hotel and marquee, on the college Speech Days. She told me of the lovely food that was served, including strawberries and cream, which particularly stayed in hers and my mind.

I *RESIDED* AT THE COLLEGE IN MODERN TIMES.
Although my mother was in service at The Lodge, Wellington College, I personally did not enter any of the college *buildings* until 1991, when on a week's course for writers. This involved my sleeping in one of the dormitories, studying by day in the library (where also my group met), and enjoying many variations of music in several other buildings (including the fine Chapel), since an excellent music festival in its many forms was taking place there too. My attendance in the chapel was of particular appeal to me and dining in the dining hall (where, hanging along one wall, I saw framed portraits of the respective headmasters of the college) helped to complete the pleasing and uplifting experience for me.

My Memories of Crowthorne Yesteryear and other accounts

Wellington College, summer 1991. (Photo - Shirley E. Peckham.)

My Memories of Crowthorne Yesteryear and other accounts

Shirley Peckham by part of the Wellington College lakes in summer 1991, standing precariously on mud!   (Photo - Peggy Mullings.)

My Memories of Crowthorne Yesteryear and other accounts

A section of one of the Wellington College lakes, summer 1993.
(Photo - Shirley E. Peckham.)

The Chapel, Wellington College, that also suffered bomb damage during the war (later restored), with Shirley Peckham in the foreground, 1991. (Photo - Peggy Mullings.)

My Memories of Crowthorne Yesteryear and other accounts

The Master's Lodge, Wellington College, summer 1991, that replaced the original Master's Lodge destroyed by a bomb during the Second World War, which also killed the Headmaster, Mr R. P. Longden M. A. *(See also picture on Page 239.)*
(Photo - Shirley E. Peckham.)

My Memories of Crowthorne Yesteryear and other accounts

CHAPTER TEN
RELIGIOUS ASPECTS

CANON COLERIDGE AND REV. A. C. NUGEE. As ours was a church school, religious matters featured widely there and we were closely connected with St John the Baptist Church. Canon G. F. Coleridge was the vicar of the church for most of my childhood years, being replaced in October 1946 by the Rev. A. C. Nugee, who was partially blind from wartime service injuries and always wore an eye-patch over one eye. He was a quite different character from the Canon, but pleasant enough and everyone seemed to like him. Often he was seen about the village with his brown dachshund dog, on a lead.

Canon Coleridge was a towering figure of a man, over six and a half feet tall probably. I cannot imagine what his weight would have been. He always wore long, loose black clothing and a white 'dog collar' appropriate to his clerical role. He had been a cyclist, but increasingly came to need two sticks to help him get about.

THE CANON'S APPEAL. The Canon always had a warm, ready smile and time to talk to anyone who wanted to converse with him. He never seemed hurried (his physical condition as time progressed, apart), and apparently took life at a leisurely pace. He lived in the Vicarage, adjacent to the school, and in retirement in St. John's Lodge, a dwelling near the church, in Church Street.

Canon Coleridge would come to the school often, and was a big part (his size aside) of what went on there. He was decidedly interested in the place, the staff, the children and everything connected with the running of the establishment. A cauliflower ear, from apparently having been a boxer in his time, was another of his features. We children were always happy about seeing him at the school, where he would talk with some of us in the classrooms and the playground, as well as with the headmaster, Mr Goodband, and the teachers. When very young I had to look up very high to see his face properly, such was his loftiness.

ST. JOHN THE BAPTIST CHURCH. Where the Canon really made us very welcome was, naturally, in St. John the Baptist Church, where I was baptised on July 29th 1934. We would all go there – head, teachers and pupils – on saints' days and others with particular religious influence, including, I believe, Empire Days, when we had celebrations in the school playground attended by our parents,

My Memories of Crowthorne Yesteryear and other accounts

and on Armistice Days. We would walk to the church from school, along the rough, unmade roads of Church Road and part of Church Street – lines of us in pairs, with our teachers keeping an eye on everyone.

After the service we filed back to school, if we had anything to collect, or went straight home for the rest of the day. I enjoyed the church services and the holiday as well, but was always keen to resume work at school the following day, or the following Monday.

SUNDAY SCHOOL. I also attended Sunday School, I believe in the C. of E. school and when I was older in St. John's church, during which time I changed for a while to attending the Methodist Church Sunday School, to see what I thought of it. Mrs Joan Asselbrough taught me there. Mrs Mildred Vaughan and Mr William Wheeler were there too, though not personally involved with me. Finding the Methodist Church Sunday School basically the same as the C. of E. church one, I returned to attending that.

I attended the Sunday morning family services at St. John's church as well and feel the Sunday School meetings there usually 'ran into' these, with the choice being for us either to go home after Sunday School, or stay for the family service. I did both, at various times.

MY CONFIRMATION. The Rev. Nugee prepared us for weeks preceding the event, on our understanding of the scriptures, during small gatherings in a room at The Vicarage. In December 1948, when aged $14_{1/2}$ (with others of my age group) I received confirmation into the Church of England in St. John the Baptist Church, carried out by the Bishop of Oxford, assisted by the Rev. A. C. Nugee. It was an early Sunday afternoon ceremony, for which the girls were attired in special white dresses and head pieces (small veils I think, held by a matching band), and the comparatively few boys wore smart suits. Our parents, and a few other people, also attended the very special occasion.

MY WHITE PRAYER BOOK. I still have the white prayer book given to me in commemoration of my confirmation by my Godmother, Mrs Bertha White, who, together with her husband Tom, were friends of my parents. They lived in Upper Broadmoor Road and had a daughter, Enid. I was given my second name, Enid, by my parents, as being "After your Godmother's daughter." As mentioned, my first name Shirley was after Shirley Temple.

Mrs White surprised me by coming unannounced into the school

My Memories of Crowthorne Yesteryear and other accounts

playground to see me one playtime, days before my confirmation, to hand me the prayer book. She wished me happiness for the special event and inside the book had inscribed, 'To Shirley, on the day of her confirmation, December 8th 1948, from B. White'. It was a lovely and pleasing gesture, I had not expected in any sense.

I attended and fully participated in my first communion service one week after my confirmation, when all of us who had been concerned did the same. Afterwards I attended them regularly.

Canon G. F. Coleridge.
(Photo courtesy of George Daniel.)
Pictures of Rev. A. C. Nugee appear on pages 302 and 303.

My Memories of Crowthorne Yesteryear and other accounts

School girls at Crowthorne C. of E. School in 1949. Standing, left, Shirley Woodason, right, Clare Price (now Mrs Mundy). Sitting (l. to r.) Rosemary White, Theresa Partridge, Jeanne Gange (later Mrs Roberts, now deceased), Janet Dorrell, (now Mrs Douglas), Pamela Davidson. (Photo courtesy of Clare Mundy.)

CHAPTER ELEVEN
CHRISTMAS, DOMESTIC, AND MORE CHILDHOOD MEMORIES

CHRISTMAS. The magical Christmases of my childhood still glisteningly stand out in my memory, such wonderful times filled with happiness. After the superb Christmas Day we would go to a pantomime at a theatre in Reading every Boxing Day afternoon – Aladdin, Jack and the Beanstalk, Red Riding Hood, Cinderella, etc.

For two weeks beforehand the days increasingly dragged as Christmas got nearer yet seemed further away. Christmas Eve was particularly exciting, when we would hang up our stockings in our bedroom and not be able to sleep for ages. Perhaps we were hoping for a glimpse of Father Christmas!

On *The Morning* we sisters woke in pitch darkness ("if you do, keep quiet and don't put on any lights," our parents had warned the night before). We felt for our full stockings at the foot of our beds. As quietly as possible, and whispering to each other, we took sweets, crayons, small toys, apples and tangerines from the stockings and bit into the edible gifts. One year, though, I sank my teeth into a fat blue crayon in the dark! A selection of larger presents: colouring books, paint-boxes, jigsaw puzzles, reading books, handbags etc., awaited us in the living-room. One year Father Christmas brought me a big book about monkeys and chimps, with coloured pictures of them in, that delighted me for weeks.

OUR CHRISTMAS DINNER. We usually had roast chicken, one of our own fattened up for the occasion, and all the trimmings. Sixpenny and silver threepenny coins were in the pudding, necessitating second helpings! We did not want much Christmas cake at tea-time, despite the crackers that sometimes accompanied it. For we were too full from all our hours beforehand of snacking on a wide variety of rich food and fruit, as well as drink, and having our dinner meal.

One Christmas morning I was taken, by a friend who was a member of it, to visit a large family in Old Wokingham Road. The woman of the house (a Mrs H) said that so far that morning, being in a "tizz" (at sixes and sevens), she had put tea-leaves in the cabbage instead of salt and stuffed the turkey with the dishcloth! I was glad not to have my dinner or any more of Christmas there!

WASH-DAYS. Mondays at home were entirely taken up with my mother doing our washing. Before the advent of school dinners my sisters and I would arrive home at midday to cold meat and bubble-and-squeak, followed by warmed up rice pudding, maybe with stewed fruit, or some of Mum's cold home-made fruit tart. Our clothes and other items were piled in separate categories all over the kitchen floor and clouds of steam escaped through the open door and windows. We would usually hear, "Mind where you are putting your feet!"

We had a gas boiler in a corner of the kitchen, which would be filled with water and lit 'first thing'. Sheets, towels, tablecloths, Dad's working shirts, and so on, were boiled in this, as well as our liberty bodices, knickers, pants (of Dad's) and vests. Small items, such as handkerchiefs, were boiled in an old pan on the gas-stove. Face-cloths (flannels) sometimes had the same treatment. Our gas meter had to have plenty of shilling coins put into it before all this began!

Mum did not have a wringer. I think she was put off them by, when a child, catching her fingers in the rollers of her mother's big floor-standing one, from which her longest finger on one hand remained slightly disfigured. So she wrung all the washing out by hand.

I was always glad when Wash-day Monday was over and Mum and our kitchen were back to normality!

STEAMED PUDDINGS AND DUMPLINGS. Given more time, Mum made superb steamed puddings, with dried or fresh fruit or syrup. She also made dumplings for the many lamb and beef (sometimes rabbit) stews we had, which I found enjoyable apart from the root vegetables and onions they contained. I never liked them, though had a particular palate for meat. We had the enjoyable fish and chips, mostly bought ones, sometimes.

Once Mum left a cold treacle tart in the oven for the family but, alas, when I fetched it out of the oven it was black with ants! They had trooped over the kitchen doorstep and into the back of the oven via a vent-hole, for a good feed. We had bother from ants every year.

On Sunday mornings Mum would take the joint from the oven to baste it, then would 'dunk' slices of bread in the fat for us to have on a plate each for a mid-morning snack, with a drink. It was delicious.

For Sunday tea we would have a pot of dripping, from the set roast meat fat, on the table. This we had on bread, often with celery when in season.

OUR BATH NIGHTS. My sisters and I had our baths, as young and not so young children, up to the age of about nine, in a tin bath in front of our living-room fire. The bath was placed on a towel and another was ready, warming, to dry us. When in the bath, I would feel very warm one side of me and cool the other, away from the fire, and always felt concern that someone might knock at our back door. The living-room door to the kitchen, and the back door, from the kitchen, were almost in line with one another. Our living-room hearth was opposite the living-room door and so if the back door was opened, to a caller or another reason, a cold blast of air would 'hit' the naked body of whoever was in the bath! I would not only dread a caller coming, when it applied to me, but also had fear of the possibility of a *man* being the visitor. My parents, provided they knew the person, would always invite the caller in – even if just for a couple of minutes. I hated any man, other than Dad, seeing me in the bath. But Mum said it was nothing to be concerned about and, "What have you got to hide?" Sometimes, like then, she left me speechless!

SYMPATHY. A caller to our home on occasions was a Mr Brant, we knew as "Bullum". He lived with his wife and family of four or five children at 'our end' of Pinewood Avenue and when anyone died in the immediate area (of only the Avenue, I think) Bullum brought the news to all the nearby householders and collected money for a wreath from us. Everyone trusted him to handle this, which he did well, and he would order and collect the wreath, also attach a message to the floral tribute: 'From all your neighbours in Pinewood Avenue', which would have included any who hadn't contributed to the collection. But I'm sure most, if not all, had. I wonder who collected for Bullum when he died?

The practice of wearing black armbands, or a black diamond-shaped piece of material stitched to the top part of the sleeve of one's coat, for several weeks – after the death of a close relative – gradually fell into disuse. People also wore black clothes a lot at this time.

PETS. Mr and Mrs Greville Bent (she was previously Mrs G. V. B. Burgoyne, before his sad, untimely death in 1943), of Crowthorne Farm, had a honey-coloured mongrel dog, named D-Day. Mum was still working at the farm then and sometimes when she returned home, D-Day would follow her. This resulted in me gradually coming to consider him a pet of *mine* – but I kept reminding myself he wasn't really.

D-Day was a loveable dog. He seemed almost human and I became very fond of him and made a great fuss of him. At times he was at our home more than he was at his own, but Mr and Mrs Bent did not mind. When he wasn't there, they knew he was likely with, or concerned otherwise with, us. I taught D-Day to beg for biscuits and he became

My Memories of Crowthorne Yesteryear and other accounts

very good at it.

When we went to the Plaza cinema, or to the village to catch a bus to somewhere, D-Day would follow us. At the cinema he would wait outside till we came out 2½ hours later. And he would wait by the bus-stop till we returned *there*; also a wait of a couple of hours or so.

If D-Day could have talked, and I feel sometimes he nearly did, I would have seen him as human. He would wag his tail vigorously, which always occurred when I made an appearance before him. He was part of our lives when Dutch soldiers were billeted in Nissen huts in Easthampstead Park towards the end of the war. A photo of him, me, my sisters (Glennis and Virgy), and Hans de Vos, one of the soldiers, standing in our front garden, appears on Page 99.

MY SPANIEL PUP. The parents (Rose and Fred, nicknamed 'Pop') of my great childhood friend, Jeanette Hatt, and her younger brother, Keith, of 'Carshalton', Ellis Road, had a pedigree cocker spaniel and often had pups at their home. I spent much of my childhood and into my teens at the Hatts home, where I was always made very welcome. The pups were of great appeal to me, being silky-coated and white, with various black and brown markings.

On one occasion, all the pups came to go to new homes except one, and Mrs Hatt asked me if I would like it. This pleased and excited me, but of course I had to ask my parents first. Dad left it to Mum to decide. She agreed with some reluctance. My parents were not really 'pet people'.

So I took the pup home, with instructions from the Hatts as to the care of the animal. He was lovely. I may have named him Spot, but cannot be certain now.

But my pet made endless puddles in our home and Mum became vexed by it. When I was there I could deal with this. But when at school, or elsewhere, Mum alone was faced with the trouble. She was increasingly losing her patience.

While I was at school one day Mum returned my pet to Mrs Hatt, who gave her a new rag doll to give me in replacement. I had had no idea any of this was to happen and arrived home to be given the news by Mum, who then said, "Mrs Hatt left this for you instead," and handed me the rag doll.

My 'paddy' boiled over – especially as I had had no warning beforehand of events – and I took the doll in one hand, just had time to look at its seemingly grinning face, then, almost tearful, flung it across our kitchen where it landed under the cooker. "*I do not want a rag doll in place of my pup!*" I let out, fiercely.

Mum didn't answer, but had the good sense to retrieve the doll, take it from my sight and I never saw it again. Jeanette, with her parents' co-operation, later said, "We'll keep the pup at our house and you can come there and see him whenever you like." So, a happy ending!

OUR CATS. For a time in my childhood we had sister black and white, smooth-coated cats, Tiddles and Toddles, as pets. Mum coped with these all right, but Dad wasn't so keen, mainly because of what they did in his garden, particularly scratching up seedlings.

Came the time when Tiddles and Toddles had kittens a couple of days apart from each other. One produced five of them in our hat, scarf and glove cupboard, and the other gave birth to four of them in our shoe cupboard. The mess can be imagined! The cats partly cleaned it up, and Mum did the rest. The cupboards, both in our living-room, were four feet from each other. When older, the kittens walked out of the cupboards and would be all over the room floor, when we had to be careful where we put our feet!

We eventually found new homes for all the kittens except one fluffy tabby one. We kept him for ourselves and called him Fluffy. Unfortunately, Fluffy came to be a rascal. He would catch birds and leave them dead on our garden path, disappointing and exasperating us each time. One day I scolded him for it and he slouched off. We never saw Fluffy again and did not know what to think of it. However, we still had Tiddles and Toddles, so did not miss him particularly and were pleased not to have to tolerate his nasty habits any longer. In the end he slipped from our minds.

Eventually a day arrived when my mother, sisters and I came home from somewhere to see a lady with a bike, that had a big, square, lidded, wicker basket on the front of it, leaving our drive. Dad was indoors and we asked him who the lady was. He soon revealed that she was a vet and he had arranged with her to take the cats away, for good, because of the trouble from them he had had in his garden. We were dismayed, disillusioned and disappointed, but could not really feel cross with Dad in the circumstances.

However, would we really, or ever, get over it? Our dear pet cats had gone! Well, we had to and we did. It took days – maybe weeks – but we came to accept the situation, as graciously as possible.

EGGS IN ISINGLASS. Speaking earlier in this chapter of my friends, the Hatts (who, I cannot emphasise more, were always very kindly and hospitable to me in my childhood), reminded me of

My Memories of Crowthorne Yesteryear and other accounts

how they used to put some of their hens eggs 'down' – as it was termed – in isinglass, a substance to preserve them. Only posh people (or affluent ones) had fridges then. There was one at Crowthorne Farm, for instance. A bag of ice cubes from it were used to try and reduce the swelling when I broke my leg some time previously. Most people who wanted to keep eggs needed to preserve them in a container of isinglass.

We, in our home, did not do this, because we always ate our hens and ducks eggs, in one form or another, soon after they were laid. In the winter, for a spell, the birds – chickens at least – had a rest from laying eggs, which is when those who had them in isinglass would no doubt have put them to use.

Sometimes our chickens would lay soft-shelled eggs, when we had to give then a good supply of grit to help their insides form shells.

I, being the eldest daughter, used to often have to feed our poultry after school when Mum was at work. This involved boiling potato peelings, then mixing and mashing them with meal till 'dryish-sticky'. The cockerels sometimes chased me in their run, and try to peck my ankles. Mr George Daniel, of King's Road, used to deliver and sell us chicken feed, regularly.

George Daniel (who no longer delivers chicken feed) on his 98th birthday, July 1994.   (Photo - Shirley E. Peckham.)

CHAPTER TWELVE
MY PARENTS

DAD (BRICKLAYER). As I mentioned earlier, Dad worked as a bricklayer for Spear and King, the one-time building company of King's Road in the village, for almost all his working life. This, except for a short spell employed at Jim Blunden's building firm, of Old Wokingham Road.

Although he found bricklaying hard work, most of the time, he enjoyed it as well and would refer to his role as "on the building". His work took him all over the place, mostly in and about Crowthorne, building homes and other buildings (he was involved once with the building of a school at Frimley), putting extensions onto already constructed places, and so on.

He once told me, "What I don't like is, when my colleagues and I are building something for someone, and the person stands close by and forever watches us work and asks questions on what we are doing. It interrupts us and takes our minds off our work so! What's more, they don't understand the technical side of it anyway!"

Dad also used to say sometimes that a fellow, not necessarily but on occasions, working for Spear and King, had got the "D.C.M.". I did not want to plead ignorance, but one day could hold back no longer, so asked what this meant. "Don't come Monday", he replied. In other words the man had been given the sack, instant dismissal, for it always applied that the command was given on a Friday afternoon.

As you may have already realised, Dad was an introvert and I think my shyness came from him (though periodically I am extrovert as my mother was; being I am a Gemini this fits the situation, two persons in one shell, as it were). Dad also had a dry sense of humour and in some cases his own brand of jokes developed crusty exteriors with age! He would tell the same ones over and over again. "Dad, we have heard that one," we'd say, wearily, before he got far into it. But he would carry on telling us it as though we had not interrupted him. At the end he would smile gently, as we roared with laughter, and I particularly used to see the funny side of the constant repeats. Often more so than the joke itself!

LOCAL FOOTBALLER. Dad played football locally as a member of Crowthorne Football Club. I cannot be certain, but was informed authoritatively by Mr Doug Clark (residing in King's Road today and who knew Dad well) that Dad played for the club's Saturday Reserve side for a time. (See picture on Page 86.) Later he regularly

My Memories of Crowthorne Yesteryear and other accounts

attended home matches at Elm Park, Reading, which he travelled to by bus "to watch Reading play." He was always so enthusiastic about it and one day I decided to go along with him, though had no interest in football really, to see a game. All this did was make me think what a good-looking goalie the opposing side had!

SENSE OF HUMOUR. Undoubtedly his sense of humour amused us all in the family greatly, which would even pull Mum out of a bad mood at times, or she would quip, good-naturedly, "Don't be daft.". One of his specials was: "Is it right to say the yolk of an egg *is* white, or the yolk of an egg *are* white?"

Keen to show off my grasp of grammar I replied, "*Is* white!"

"No, the yolk of an egg is *yellow!*"

Another (that he swore was true) was: "Two men went into a cafe, sat at a table, and one asked the other, "What'll you have, tongue?"

"Gosh, no!" was the reply, "I would never eat anything out of an animal's mouth. I'll have a couple of eggs."

Some days after our evening meal, Dad would amuse us children (possibly in part to keep us at the table for a while to digest our food), by involving us in a little game. He would take all the copper coins from his pocket: penny, halfpenny and farthing ones, and ask us in turn to guess the year dates on them. We really enjoyed this for, as well as the fun, we were keen to be successful, since Dad *gave* us whatever coins we guessed the right date of. Sometimes two or three of them would have the same date on – which was a really good win for one of us. On occasions one or two of us did not win any of the money, but were not despondent because of the success of the other or others against ourselves.

THE PRINCE ALFRED, HIS LOCAL. Dad was a regular in the Prince Alfred on Saturday nights, where he would drink two or three pints of beer. He used to play shove-ha'penny there too and maybe darts as well.

MUM (OF MANY ROLES). Caring, but often fractious in the home (probably at least in part because of all the demands on her as a housewife and working mum, coupled with often suffering from her asthmatic condition), Mum had boundless energy. She never stopped, and some days would complain, "I've worked my fingers to the bone!" Also would refer to housewifery and the demands of her young family as "slavery". She was vivacious, attractive (slim with black hair, gently turning grey eventually) and had a young outlook.

Her nerves were of steel. She got away with a lot when 'speaking her mind', but sometimes was up against the wrong person! One of her regular phrases was (and she didn't mind who she said it to, if she considered they deserved it), "I'll not have any of your nonsense, you're wrong and you know you are!" When I was nearby I sometimes found it very embarrassing.

HER 'OUTSIDE' DOMESTIC ROLES. Mum had a succession of outside domestic roles during my childhood and never had trouble getting a job. Once, when she had been working for Miss Churchill, next door, and it reached near lunch-time and she was not home (being nearly an hour overdue), I went to look for her. I opened the old lady's garden gate, before seeing Mum lying across her path, a yard from it. I was aghast! Was she dead or what?

I had to step over her, to race for Miss Churchill, who came with me to find Mum just starting to come round. Slowly, Miss Churchill and I helped her get up, and I gently led Mum home to our settee. Afterwards I asked her about the incident. She replied, "I must have fainted, have been doing too much work I expect." (It was warm weather at the time.) I watched and treated Mum for the rest of the day as though she were an item of rare bone china in my keeping.

Mum's domestic role at Crowthorne Farm (for Mr and Mrs Bent, after Mrs Burgoyne, widowed, remarried), meant that she could be there in two minutes from our home, as when working for Miss Churchill. This was very handy for her.

When I neared and then was in my teens, Mum's style of job changed as her demands in the home lessened in line with us children being more independent. Successively, I am not sure in which order, but roughly as I relate, she was employed in the following places.

HER OTHER WORKING POSITIONS. Mum worked for a short period, in wartime, at **Home Dainties**, serving the lunches to the customers of the very busy cafe every weekday. She went there mainly, I think, because she liked people and had been a parlourmaid in service, so was used to attending them in that role. She also had a favourable rapport, beforehand and while there, with the partners in the cafe, Miss Crane and 'Son' Reason. I had some lunches in Home Dainties, when Mum was there, and found them very enjoyable, especially Miss Crane's home-made raised meat pies, chips and peas, followed by her fruit tart and custard!

Betty Brown's olde-worlde cafe in London Road, Camberley, was where Mum worked as a lunch-time waitress, a position decidedly

My Memories of Crowthorne Yesteryear and other accounts

up-market for her, to which she travelled by bus. In this role she wore a neat uniform, including a crisp, white apron and matching cap. Mum loved the work and liked all the people she met while doing it. Sometimes she brought leftovers of bread and cake home, with her employer's blessing, for our chickens and ducks. One day, when doing this, she was in the middle seat of the back ones in the bus, with the scraps wrapped in newspaper on her lap, when the bus suddenly pulled up sharply. The parcel shot off her lap and all the scraps fell out on the floor. Stern-looking faces of the other passengers nearby directed towards her let Mum know what they thought of it. She crouched down and picked all the pieces up, etc., while saying sheepishly, "They're for my chickens and ducks," which did not melt the stern looks!

Mum's job as barmaid at the **Bush Hotel** in Wokingham, when I was in my early teens, was 'right up her street', more so than her waitress role. Here she met, and had wonderful conversations with, business people and many others, that held her interest. Sometimes she worked there at lunch-times, otherwise evenings, and during this time bought herself an old-style Mercedes car, following her having driving tuition and passing her test. Dad never drove and was a regular cyclist.

I was riding in Mum's leather-seated, comfy car one day, as a front seat passenger, and when she drove round the bend in Duke's Ride (by Albert Road) the car door 'my side' suddenly opened and I nearly fell out onto the road. There were no seat belts then. It frightened and alarmed Mum, who was also very relieved to find me still with her! Oddly, it barely troubled *my* nerves!

Mum's role as an auxiliary in the female wing of **Broadmoor Asylum** (now Hospital) did not suit her and she left after, I think, several months. Possibly friends of hers who worked there encouraged her to seek the role, and all the time she was in it I found her personality different from usual, reflecting how she was affected. I was glad when she had left the job and was back to her normal self. Some of the staff, in contrast, worked there contentedly – it appeared – for many years.

For a year or so Mum worked as an assistant in **Gale's bakery** shop in Crowthorne High Street (that is still there today, 1995), and was happy enough there.

Finally, her last job of all began from her helping Mr Michael Mason, of the **Mason's coal** firm in the village, by, during a prolonged postal strike in the early 1970s, delivering his coal bills to customers locally and in areas about Crowthorne. (My eldest sister

My Memories of Crowthorne Yesteryear and other accounts

Glennis, and John Priest, who became her second husband, worked for Mr Mason at the time.)

In her role, Mum drove her blue Mini, the car she "loved".

When the postal strike was over and Mum became well used to working for Mr Mason, she continued with the job. By then she did not only deliver the accounts – in Bracknell mostly – but collected the payments from some of the customers as well. On her rounds she encountered some uneasy situations, caused by householders opposed to paying for their coal, or needing more time to do so.

One threatened, "Clear off, or I'll put the dog on you!" Mum, not bothered for long by this sort of thing, was back at the offending people's homes next day with the enthusiasm she always carried out the work.

One day, in her role, she had to call at The Heritage nudist camp, Heath Ride, for purely the purpose of delivering their account. When her ring at the doorbell was answered (the door formed part of the very high surrounding fence), she handed over the coal bill and asked, "What is it like in there?" She was then invited inside for a conducted look around.

On her arrival home, I was very interested to hear all about it, and asked, "Weren't you embarrassed?"

"No," Mum replied, "I found myself only looking at their faces!"

Well, my parents brought me up not to tell lies, but was this one of Mum's white ones?

Left, Sarah Ellen (Helene) and Dudley (Syd) Woodason. (Circa 1950). Right, Helene with her beloved Mini, in 1976.

My Memories of Crowthorne Yesteryear and other accounts

Dudley (Syd) Woodason as a member of Crowthorne Football Club - 1930. Back row (l. to r.) Charles Collis, Louis Scuffle, Nelson Smith, Dudley Woodason, William Gear, Bert Fullbrook. Front row (l. to r.) Charlie Milam, Sam Mason, Bert Parker, Frank Clacey, Arthur Milam, Doug Spear, Maurice Woodason (youngest brother of Dudley, who lived in Ellis Road in married life). Further information concerning the picture: v. Ascot. Lovell Road. Lost 2 - 0.

(Photo - T. H. Greville, Maidenhead.)

CHAPTER THIRTEEN
THE SECOND WORLD WAR

BLACK-OUT. I was 5 1/2 when I heard the first siren on the 3rd September, 1939. The adults whispered in groups about the Germans and gradually the idea of war sank in for us children too. We learned about the government's stipulation of Black-out Precautions. Our curtains had to be changed for thick dark-coloured ones, drawn in good time before dusk, and none of our gaslight had to leak out! We still took candles to bed with us – the dangers, of possible fire, of this were not so apparent then. And hot-water bottles eased the iciness of our beds. Regularly hearing the 'Jerry' planes overhead, we were relieved when, during those long, often frightening nights, the 'All Clear' eventually sounded.

BOMBS ON CROWTHORNE. Some bombs fell in the village and the one I particularly remember hearing fell in a field off Old Wokingham Road (in the St. Michael's Cottages area, I believe), causing a big crater. Storms at night sounded like enemy air activity. These were frightening times indeed! Our air-raid warden was a Mr Timms, of Pinewood Avenue, who asked us children to look out for any silver-foil strips that had fallen, or been dropped, from enemy planes. Keen to help him and excited at the prospect, I went alone to look for them and was overjoyed when I found several of the strips in bushes along Lover's Lane, opposite our home. This is now known as Old Sawmill Lane, that leads to Old Wokingham Road, where (in the lane) there was the sawmills of Mr Jim Blunden, builder, whose premises were nearby, in Old Wokingham Road. Mr Timms made a 'big thing' of my find, when I went to him with the strips, "Very good, well done, very observant, thank you." I felt the proverbial 'million dollars'.

GAS MASKS, RATION BOOKS. Mum, Dad, Glennis and I, were allocated grey gas masks, while Virgy's was a 'baby' Mickey Mouse one, being quite a novelty. They were very claustrophobic to wear and smelled strongly of rubber, which they were made of. So after the initial try-on, we mostly kept them in their boxes!

Adults were issued with beige Ration Books, children had blue ones and expectant mothers, green. Shopkeepers sent the coupons weekly to a collection point in Bracknell. The Baptist Church, in the High Street, was also used for collecting our Ration Books, I believe, making it a widely used place in those times.

My Memories of Crowthorne Yesteryear and other accounts

Meat, fats, cheese, sugar, biscuits, clothes, shoes, sweets and other items were 'on ration', but not all of them at the same time. And sometimes food, such as potatoes and apples, was in very short supply so that the shopkeepers concerned had to more-or-less sell it on a sort of unofficial rationing system, to eke it out in the fairest way. I remember when apples were unavailable at all the fruiterers for weeks. (Grocery shops did not usually sell fruit and vegetables then.) Then I suddenly heard that Sworders, fruiterer's and greengroceries, in the High Street, had Australian ones in. Mum gave me money and I dashed there to have my choice, limited as to amount, of yellow and red ones. As an apple lover, still, my day was made! This of course would have been at a time of year there were no apples on folks' trees.

NEWS BULLETINS. "Here is the news and this is Alvar Liddell reading it." Those familiar words on the wireless introduced many news broadcasts during the war. My parents (Mum, when Dad was in the army) always made sure that we had one of our two accumulators charged up and I was usually selected from my sisters and me – "You are the eldest" – to carry these to and from Sid Townsend's garage in the High Street for the purpose. "And be careful with it, or you'll get acid on yourself, which *burns*," would ring in my ears, as I set off from home carrying the heavy, approximately 8 x 6 inches, accumulator by its carrying handle.

I would leave an accumulator there for 1 - 2 days, then exchange it for our other one, so that we always had a charged one working our wireless. The cost for this service was 6d (2½p), I believe.

While talking of Mr Townsend, I digress to say he also sold secondhand bikes and Dad once bought me one, of the number of them I had in my childhood, for 6/- (six shillings, now 30p), this when I was about 12-years-old. It was a small-ladies size, painted black all over and somewhat "aggy", a term we in our family used for any item, particularly of clothing, not of our taste. I think Dad had bought me the cheapest, right-size bike at Mr Townsend's. Mum exploded when he brought it home! "*What did you get her a thing like that for? It must have been the worst one he had!*" Before Dad could answer I sprang to his defence. "It's all right for me, I'm sure I'll like it." And in no time I was in the saddle and away up the road, leaving Mum subdued on the issue for all time. Fairly regularly she would chastise Dad, sometimes unfairly in my opinion. Mind you, he would give her the sharp edge of his tongue back sometimes too. We children wisely made ourselves scarce on these occasions, whether or not (often it *was* the case) we had caused the trouble!

My Memories of Crowthorne Yesteryear and other accounts

THE INFLUX OF EVACUEES. Officials, who came with them, decided who in the village had room in their homes for evacuees from London during the war. A double-decker bus-load of mainly the evacuees, parents and children, made its way down Pinewood Avenue. It pulled up before reaching the crossroads. The officials alighted from the bus and called on house-holders. Afterwards we found ourselves with a family of them: a man and his wife (Mr and Mrs F.) and their 2-year-old boy, Christopher, who were to occupy our third bedroom and share our kitchen and bathroom. It was a squeeze and we often did not have a good rapport with Mrs F., who often had a severe approach and would be harsh and unreasonable towards the youngster. Her husband, on the other hand, was a congenial, quiet man. He was away from our home a lot, maybe at work somewhere. Christopher was quiet, like his dad.

Came the time, after they had been with us for many months, that Dad tried to 'move them on' (I feel he may have enforced this, since we had had enough), and eventually they left our home with reluctance. We were very relieved and could spread ourselves out again in the bungalow. However, some time later we were all in our living-room, one dark evening, when I heard a noise from the front part of our bungalow. I told the others in the family of it, none of whom had heard it themselves. "You must have been hearing things," Mum said. But I knew I hadn't.

Then there was a louder noise from there, that startled all of us! Dad went to investigate and found the Fs had smashed a window of the third (that had been 'their') bedroom and climbed into the place! My parents were immediately cross of course, but got little more from the Fs than the forceful, insolent and defiant, "We're back and we're staying!"

For the sake of Christopher, mainly, they were allowed a few more days with us. Mr F. had to replace the broken window the next day. Then they were finally gone to our even greater relief! We missed the little boy though, who in my eyes had grown to be like a brother to us girls.

Later we had another family of evacuees, a man and wife (name unrecalled), who had twin unidentical daughters of ten years, Sylvia and Gay. All in the family were amiable and quiet-natured, which suited us well, compared with the Fs. Sylvia and Gay, who kept together regularly, played a lot with children 'up the road', whom they befriended, and not so much with us, whose games seemed not to match their interests.

It was very difficult for all concerned, though, having evacuees

My Memories of Crowthorne Yesteryear and other accounts

living with us, whose ideas were far different from our own. And their sharing our one toilet and kitchen with us was particularly inconvenient. Once, I was using the toilet and had shut, but not locked, the door (as was 'fine' when just my family were at home), when suddenly the door opened and the man evacuee started to enter. He saw me, sitting directly opposite him on the toilet, said, "Oh, sorry," and quickly reversed from the room, while I remained in position red-faced! On having mentioned it to Mum later, she said, "You must always lock the door while they're here, it's not like when we were on our own." Too true, in so many ways!

I believe all the evacuee children of school age in the village attended Crowthorne C. of E. School, which caused some overcrowding. Often three children had to sit and work at a desk for two, bringing cramped conditions that could not be helped or avoided. Our practice sessions at school (I remember them particularly when in Miss Burton's class) on what to do in the event of an air-raid were, on command, "Dive under your desks and stay there until you're told to come out." It remains in my mind as though yester*day* never mind about yester*year*. Despite the overcrowding and other inconveniences of wartime, generally we coped better than a lot of people imagine. There were the exceptions, sometimes emphasised, of course.

FOREIGN SOLDIERS IN CROWTHORNE. The first contingent were **Canadian** (mostly **French Canadians**, I think), who occupied their own building of Pinewood Hospital, previously Sanatorium. (This is detailed more in the account of Michael Ifould, later in this volume.) The men all bore injuries from service across the Channel. We saw them all over the village, in plaster-casts, bandages, and on crutches. They wore hospital-blue clothing and could be seen 'a mile off' in it, along with their white dressings. They always had a happy approach with the villagers.

One, who had lost his way, turned up at the back of our home one evening. He wore a bandage over his head and one eye, and black-out time could not have come in then, for suddenly – while sitting in our living-room with my family – I glanced up to see him (face and shoulders only) looking at me through the window opposite. It was like being confronted out of the blue by a figure out of a horror film! I squealed, pointing his way, "Whatever's *that?*" Dad shot outside, leading to the man being directed to Pinewood. He had seen our room light shining outside, which had led him to our window, and had looked in, hoping to get help.

There were social occasions in the village, including at Pinewood

My Memories of Crowthorne Yesteryear and other accounts

itself, for these troops. We had some in our home too, for happy evenings enjoyed by all. My sisters and I went to at least one Christmas party at Pinewood, which was laid on by the Canadians and was a lovely affair, when all the generosity that could be lavished on us by way of food and drink, was. Mum worked there for a while, helping mainly at social events, I believe. The soldiers, or some of them, were still there in 1943.

DUTCH. Later in the war, a contingent of young Dutch soldiers (there may have been other foreign ones too at some time, but not in my memory) came to the village, where they were happily welcomed. They were billeted in Nissen huts in Easthampstead Park. Social events were put on for them too, in the village halls and in people's homes, and very happy times they were. The Dutch soldiers and the Canadians before them, regularly visited the Plaza cinema, when it was 'full house' more often than not, with patrons standing at the back of the auditorium, who took seats as they became vacant, if lucky. Some stood throughout the entire performance.

Of the Dutch soldiers who came to our home – sometimes with musical instruments (or, my recollections can't be clear on it, this might have applied to the Canadian ones), for fun evenings of group singing, etc. – Hans de Vos held particular appeal. He was aged eighteen, and was special to us, while a number of the other men were not far behind him in popularity with us, one of whom we knew as Johnny. My mother kept in touch with Hans by letter after the soldiers had left Crowthorne for service in Java. Also, she corresponded for a time with his parents and his sister Lois, in Holland.

Hans survived action in Java, gladly, and returned to his homeland. Gradually Mum lost touch with him, and later also his family. However, when I was living with my first husband Gordon in Germany, in the '60s, I visited Rotterdam and by pre-arrangement also called on the then very elderly, widowed mother of Hans, living in a flat alone. We were thrilled by our first, and only, meeting and in an hour, long enough in her frail state, we came right up-to-date on our family topics. She was very happy and remained grateful that we had made Hans so welcome in our home during his time in Crowthorne and told me he was happily settled elsewhere in Holland.

When any of the foreign soldiers left Crowthorne, by the hundreds, an amalgam of villagers were at the station to see them off on the train. This brought many tears and verbal expressions of sorrow and regret. Many of the young women and soldiers had fallen in love with one another, so hearts were broken. I was there and saw some of the

My Memories of Crowthorne Yesteryear and other accounts

soldiers hand their Crowthorne girls tokens of affection, single red roses, and there were passionate hugs and kisses. Duke's Ride was thronged with people at these times. After seeing the soldiers off, the villagers left the station, dolefully, in groups, talking quietly about it.

CROWTHORNIANS WENT TO WAR. Many of the villagers, men and women, were called up and regrettably some did not return, while others returned with injuries. The father of a friend of my sisters and me, Pam Eckett, of Pinewood Avenue, was one I recall seeing and speaking with, as he went about on crutches. He came to our home, and on the ground by our back door lay a farthing coin. Having put the end of one of his crutches down hard on it, he said, "Got it," followed by, "at least my eyes are all right still."

CONSCIENTIOUS OBJECTORS. Some local men, and certain of them lived near us, did not go for military service for they were "conscientious objectors", Mum told me. This was almost like my being talked to in double Dutch! She tried to explain, but it wasn't until years later that I fully learned its meaning.

LOCAL HOME GUARD CONTINGENT. I was aware of this, and some of their activities in the village, and used to see the men about. I also knew some of those concerned. But my knowledge of them extends no further than this. I feel their headquarters in the area was in the Drill Hall at Wokingham, though have not been able to have this confirmed.

DAD WAS CALLED UP. My father was called up for the army in or about 1943. He had escaped call-up till then because of his work as a bricklayer. The telegram arrived one morning while Dad was gardening, and he read it in our front garden. "Well, that's it!" he said, resignedly, "I've got to go."

He joined the RAOC and was sent to a unit in Newport Pagnall, Buckinghamshire. It seemed unreal that he had left home. Mum and the three of us had to adjust to the new situation, as so many other local families had, who had been forced into it.

It was not easy for some time. Then we became attuned to his absence and were always pleased to see Dad home on leaves.

From Newport Pagnall he was posted to Osnabrück in Germany, when we welcomed his leaves more than ever. By then he had settled down well enough in his new role and I believe was never involved with any active service. To my (child's) brain it seemed dangerous for

Dad, and other British troops, to have been sent to Germany, the very country which was at war with us! I expressed this to Mum who explained the situation, putting my mind at rest. I have wondered since then how Mum received her housekeeping money in those times, for she always had "hungry mouths to feed and backs to keep clothed."

One day when Dad came home from leave and we all met him off a train at Crowthorne Station, he stood, cheerfully, with his kit-bag aloft and said he had some sweets and chewing-gum in the bag for us. We had, of course, greeted him warmly, then urged him to produce the 'goodies' there and then to quell our excitement.

Except for a smile having spread across his face, he did not respond at first, but by the nearby bookshop he stood the kit-bag down on the footpath, dived down to near its bottom and produced the packets of sweets and gum for us. We were overjoyed and thanked him 'a million times' before getting our teeth into them, and we walked home together.

"CUSHY". Dad said his army work over in Germany was "cushy", compared with that of his bricklaying role "on the building." I think to a large extent he was having a sort of holiday! And as he had rarely ventured out of Crowthorne previously – "Crowthorne suits me enough," he would reply when challenged on why most of the time he didn't want to go out of it – this really was a change for him, and except for missing his family, no doubt, apparently a happy one too.

DEMOBBED. Dad, I believe, then remained in Osnabrück and was demobbed towards the end of the war, in 1945, or perhaps early '46. He was given a navy-blue, his favourite colour, demob-suit and awarded some medals, that my sister Glennis retains. While serving he often recited his army number by heart.

SHORTAGES. Rationing continued involving some commodities till long after the war. Fruit and vegetables, still often in short supply, caused hardship at times. Schoolgirls, older than me, went potato-picking by lorry to fields in the Ambarrow area. Maybe other areas were involved too. In the warm, sunny weather, they would arrive home, at the end of weekday afternoons, tired and filthy. My friend and near neighbour, Pat Butcher, a year my senior, was one involved.

'POM' AND DRIED EGG POWDER. Both these were used as substitutes, to help the rationing, during and after the war. Pom was the popular dried potato that would be made up for use on

My Memories of Crowthorne Yesteryear and other accounts

such dishes as shepherd and cottage pies.

The dried egg powder was made into false scrambled egg. It was also used in cooking and baking a lot, by manufacturers as well as householders. However, the 'scrambled egg' it produced was bright yellow (instead of pale, of the real kind) and the taste was decidedly different from the genuine and could not have fooled anyone! *I* developed a palate for it anyway, and quite enjoyed it in the end.

I return to the subject (mentioned on Page 87) of Mr Blunden's sawmills. On passing this one day in my childhood, when the place was closed with no staff there, I saw small amounts of smoke rising from the middle of a collection of part tree trunks. Quizzing myself about this and wondering if there was a danger of fire, I stood in the lane observing it for a while, when I began hearing quiet voices coming from where the smoke was emanating. I was even more puzzled when I saw three boys I knew, of ten or eleven years, emerge from there. Apparently they were as surprised to see me there looking at them as applied vice versa. I asked them, "What caused that smoke?"

"We were *having* a smoke," said one. "We've got to get somewhere out of the way to do it. You don't have to let on." And I saw another of them stub out a cigarette.

Shirley Woodason, in wartime, when aged about ten years (school photo).

My Memories of Crowthorne Yesteryear and other accounts

Christopher F., evacuee at 'Sydellen' with his parents during the war, who was two years old when they arrived from London. Picture taken in the front garden before the bird-bath was built in the centre. Note the crazy-paving and the plants of pinks that 'Syd' grew a lot there.

My Memories of Crowthorne Yesteryear and other accounts

Marcel Messier when at Pinewood Hospital, Crowthorne, circa 1943, wearing his hospital Canadian army uniform with a cross on the sleeve. Identity of the children unknown. (Picture also appeared in *Our Memories of Crowthorne Yesteryear.*)
(Photo courtesy of Marcel Messier.)

My Memories of Crowthorne Yesteryear and other accounts

A Dutch soldier in Crowthorne (stationed at Easthampstead Park) during the Second World War. His note on the reverse gives the name of E. J. v. d. Wurd.

My Memories of Crowthorne Yesteryear and other accounts

Left, Dutch soldier, Hans de Vos, when aged 18, stationed at Easthampstead Park, during World War II.

Right, Dutch soldier, "Johnny" stationed at Easthampstead Park during World War II.

Above, Hans de Vos, Dutch soldier, with (l. to r.) Shirley, Virgy and Glennis Woodason, and D-Day, the mongrel dog (mentioned on pages 77 and 78), standing up in front of Shirley. The group are in the front garden of the Woodason family home 'Sydellen'. Behind them is the side of Miss A. F. Churchill's bungalow, 'Sherbornia', and part of a Crowthorne Farm building is on the right. Below, Hans de Vos and friend, Dutch soldiers, in the front garden of the Woodason family home, 'Sydellen'.

My Memories of Crowthorne Yesteryear and other accounts

Above, a group of young Dutch soldiers (of the Royal Netherlands Army), at Easthampstead Park, in 1946.

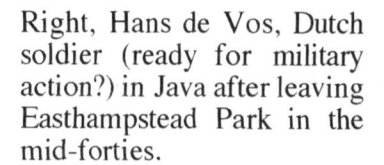

Right, Hans de Vos, Dutch soldier (ready for military action?) in Java after leaving Easthampstead Park in the mid-forties.

My Memories of Crowthorne Yesteryear and other accounts

Above, a group of Dutch soldiers (Hans de Vos on the left) in Java, after leaving Easthampstead Park. Below, the parents and sister, Lois, of Hans de Vos, pictured in the garden of their home in Holland (exact location unrecalled).

My Memories of Crowthorne Yesteryear and other accounts

Dudley (Syd) Woodason, in the RAOC, when stationed in Osnabrück, Germany during the latter part of World War II.

Dudley (Syd) Woodason (left) with a fellow member of the RAOC, when stationed in Osnabrück during the final years of World War II. A note on the reverse of the photo says: 'We had just left the dining-room' (well satisfied with their meal, hopefully).

My Memories of Crowthorne Yesteryear and other accounts

Above, a Crowthorne pin-up of the forties, Sarah Ellen ('Helene') Woodason, in her early thirties, bringing alive a Crowthorne wood, for fun! Below, Helene, left, having more fun, in the stocks (place unknown), with Kath Russell, of Broadmoor Estate. (Helene's note on the back of picture states "the devil's hat is made of steel and the ball is iron.")

103

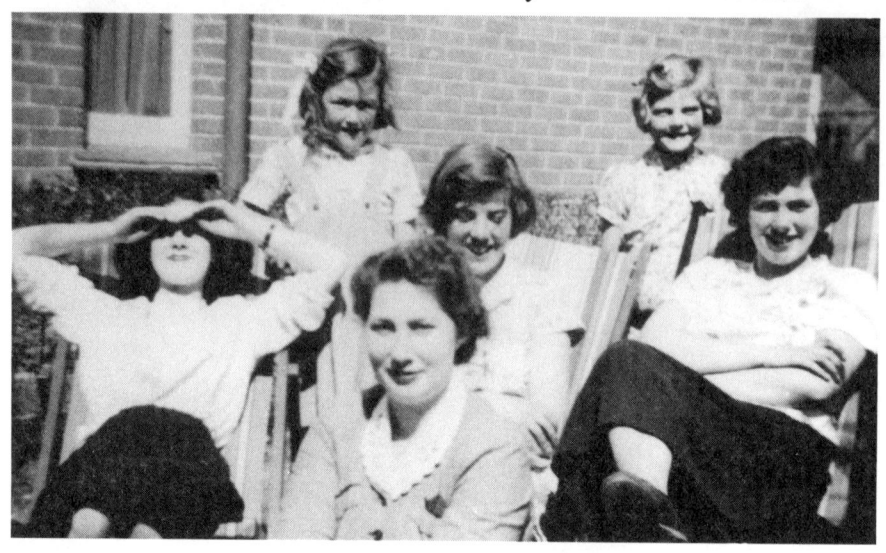

My Memories of Crowthorne Yesteryear and other accounts

Above, Pinewood Avenue friends and neighbours, left, Joan Watt (now Mrs Sayers); Daphne Robertson (now Mrs Johnson); Shirley Woodason; Virginia (Virgy) Woodason; Diane Wheeler; and Glennis Woodason at 'Sydellen', the Woodason family home, circa 1947. Below, Sarah Ellen (Helene), in sun-glasses, and Dudley (Syd) Woodason, sitting together, right, at Brambles Holiday Camp, Isle of Wight, sometime in the 1950s.

CHAPTER FOURTEEN
MY GROWING UP

ADOLESCENCE. I had learned piecemeal about 'the birds and the bees' in the school playground, from the age of 9, where sex was sometimes crudely discussed and giggled about. This also occurred away from the school and 'dirty jokes' being told, followed by rapturous laughter, among us became quite a regular feature.

When boys entered our ring at these times I felt the flush of embarrassment and their laughter following the jokes (many of which *they* told) was full-blooded and raucous. They would often humiliate us without hesitation and to see one of us embarrassed undoubtedly oiled their passion for this! I still remember some of the jokes, but wasn't tempted to tell you them!

The 'birds and the bees' subject was not part of the curriculum in those days, nor for many years afterwards. When aged thirteen and Mum *needed* to explain to me about menstruation, I asked her why she had not told me of "where babies came from and all those things."

She replied, "Well, it would not have been easy. If you get married and have a daughter you will know what I mean." So I learned most of the facts of life from my friends. I had hoped to gain a new insight into the subject on hearing (not from her) that Mum had a copy of "a really dirty book" in the house, *Lady Chatterley's Lover* by D. H. Lawrence. One day, when I was at home alone, I stole into my parents' bedroom and quickly searched through clothing laying neatly on a shelf in the top of their wardrobe – where I had earlier found they sometimes hid Christmas presents weeks before the event!

It was some minutes before, suddenly, my hands were on the book. Excited, I quickly turned pages for 'spice', but, alas, I wasn't able to find any, except for the odd dirty word here and there, when I heard someone coming. Wow! I just got out of the bedroom, from putting the book back in its place, in time! I believe it was one of my sisters having arrived home, and I didn't go to the book again. However one day, much later, I asked Mum about the contents of *Lady Chatterley's Lover*, though not particularly *her* copy. She replied, "It's not for children to know about," and is "very dirty." I finally read it and saw the film, in my fifties!

MY INTEREST IN THE OPPOSITE SEX. By the age of eleven I had become plump. Dad made no comment (the trait was in his own family, particularly applying to his mother and sisters, so he was used to seeing this), but Mum, who was average-sized, like all *her* family, seemed to have a feeling of pride about it. It was as though this trait in me mirrored in her mind her satisfaction of regularly serving me and the family plenty of "very good for you" substantial meals.

It did not bother me, particularly. I felt all right. But the former was definitely going to change as my life progressed. Mum talked to her friends, in my company, about 'the new me' and then told me, "It's puppy fat" (a regularly used phrase then, applying to plump girls approaching adolescence), which made me feel cuddly!

Except for Michael, I have mentioned, and the boy I fancied and was bullied over (as you have also read), the local boys of my childhood *and* teens did not appeal to me. And I did not seem to attract them very much. At school, I felt that the fact I did well in my lessons (and some of them, the boys, did too), in a sense encouraged them to stand away from me. However as related in my book *Our Memories of Crowthorne Yesteryear*, I only became aware in recent times (from his now late brother Jim) that Gordon Rowe fancied me in my young life. If only I had been told *then* ....!!

SEARCHING FOR "TALENT", THEY FOUND *US!*

In my early to mid teens, my sister Glennis and I, our friends Doris Denton (of Ellis Road), Ann Buckner and others, were discovered one evening by three lads from the Kiln Ride area of Nine Mile Ride (Wokingham) who had cycled to our part of Crowthorne to "look for talent" (girls they fancied). Near my home, in Pinewood Avenue, they pulled up their bikes beside us. We were interested in them straightaway! And the interest, that was from both sides, continued for some months. New faces of boys on the scene and them cycling all that way (4 miles or so) to see just *us*, which they then did most evenings, was really a highlight and appealing.

The lads, Pete, Morrie and Les, were devilish and fun-filled, which appealed to our sense of adventure, daring and being out-for-a-laugh. With us in tow, as it were, they got up to all sorts of antics about the village. Theirs were 'track bikes', with no brakes, and we mostly enjoyed ourselves with the bikes up in the Walter Recreation Ground. There, sometimes with us on the crossbars, and we would have goes on our own, they would charge up and down the hills exhilarated to the marrow. Oh, yes, there were the tumbles when the bikes sometimes carried on down the hill without us, which, physically hurt or not, we soon turned from dismay into laughs.

Once we were trespassing with the lads in the Wellington College grounds after dark. We were lost there half the time, as we rambled, sometimes through people's gardens. Suddenly, while in one, a house

My Memories of Crowthorne Yesteryear and other accounts

door opened and the figure of a man stood before it shouting, *"Clear off, the lot of you! Go on, clear yourselves out of it."*

"Move fast!" shrieked one of the lads, "Quick, let's get out of here. He's got a gun!" I could sense what felt like the juices draining from my system as, on looking the way of the man again, I saw by the light in his doorway that his arms were raised in such a position as for firing a rifle and felt I *saw* a rifle in his hands.

We charged through shrubbery, plants and over a fence to safety! Near breathless, one of our party said, "Cor, I think he meant business, that was close."

Another evening the lads (and, besotted, we helped) turned some of the local road signs around, to confuse the village motorists.

But when they were up to their tricks to spoil our olde-time dancing fun, in Pinefields hall, Waterloo Road, we could not turn the other cheek, as it were. We had invited them to the event, but they refused to accompany us. Incensed by their throwing small stones up to the outside of the hall windows in their efforts to get us outside, we also felt powerless. They didn't break the glass, but the man running the event stormed out to them and told them to *"Scarper!"* They obeyed, but as soon as he came back in the hall, they were back there and doing the same thing again.

We did not want them to 'win', by us leaving the event early to please them, so waited till almost the end. Then, all set to give them a good telling off, we joined them near the hall to see on their faces foot-wide grins and just had to fall about laughing with them.

We had some little 'romances' with the lads. I fancied Pete, though he fancied attractive Ann, who also fancied him. This caused me low spirits and I finally sent him a note, secretly, saying, "A thing of beauty is not always a joy forever." I had no response and their 'romance' continued. Before all this, however, the following occurred.

THE UNUSUAL SEASIDE TRIP. Mum, my sisters and I were booked to go on a day's outing to a south coast resort, with Brimblecombe's coach firm of Wokingham, and before the day we girls mentioned it to Pete, Morrie and Les, to avoid them coming to Crowthorne that day to see us on what we used to term 'a fool's errand' (expecting us to be, but finding us not there).

I don't know whether we were surprised or shocked to hear from them that they would also be going (it escapes me where the place was) *on their bikes! And would see us there!* Then, thinking they might be fooling us, we felt some relief. *But they weren't, they were deadly serious!* We told Mum of it who, concerned, said woefully, "Oh, we don't want them spoiling our day," and her concern remained.

The occasion arrived and we had covered two-thirds of our journey to the resort, when suddenly we saw through the coach windscreen the three lads in the middle of the road. To cut a long story shorter, the coach driver was obliged to stop and we heard that the trio (Morrie was injured about the face) had cycled the journey to there the day before and, after sleeping overnight in a nearby field, woke to find one of their bikes had been stolen.

In no time, after the driver had heard they had been cycling to the resort to see us, they were invited aboard, together with the two remaining bikes. They then travelled the rest of the journey with us. Morrie's severely grazed face had been caused by him taking a tumble from his machine onto the road.

Mum need not have been so concerned before the trip about what *might* happen, for at the resort the lads kept well away from us. We did not see them all day, but they joined us at the end of it for another lift, this time to Crowthorne. When they next paid us a visit, in the village, Morrie was still looking the worse for wear from his injuries, about which we were sorry and expressed our sympathy, and I asked them, "Would you ever do a thing like cycling to the seaside again?" I received a resounding chorus of "NO!"

DANCING. At the age of sixteen I went with friends to Broadmoor School one evening a week to learn modern ballroom dancing. These were run by local, Ted Brooker, an expert dancer, who was partnered by the aforementioned Ann Buckner. They also, while teaching us, danced individually with all of us in the class in turn. "Relax, relax," Ted would advise, while partnering me, "there's no need to be so tense." I gradually learned to dance as if floating on air. "You've got it right at last," he then gleefully said, "I knew you would."

And so began my wonderful social dancing times in and about the village. When a few years ago I was praised in a dance-hall at Highcliffe-on-Sea, near where I now live, by a man who I floated around the floor with, for being "far lighter on your feet than my wife who goes around the floor like an elephant, but don't tell her that" (she was sitting nearby), I was aware of the face and words of Ted Brooker again!

THE LOCAL HOPS. I attended these with keenness and confidence once I could dance properly. Mostly they were social evenings – games and dancing combined (completely the latter, in the second halves) – that took place in the British Legion and Pinefields halls. Then I went further afield, to attend dances in California-in-England, Nine Mile Ride, and at Arborfield Barracks (known as "Cali" and "The Camp"). We socialised with fellows, who weren't Crowthorne ones, at both. In many cases they were from all parts of the country. This was a novelty, and very interesting, in itself.

I also went, on Saturday nights a handful of times, to the Majestic and Pavilion ballrooms at Reading and far more frequently to the Agincourt hall in London Road, Camberley, this also on Saturday nights. I was not keen on the Reading venues, which lacked the right atmosphere for me, but at the Agincourt spent some happy occasions, in what was usually a very warm and overcrowded hall.

BRITISH RED CROSS SOCIETY. I remained a member of the local branch of the BRCS, otherwise known as the VAD (Voluntary Aid Detachment), throughout my teens and into my twenties, having progressed from cadet to adult member, leaving several years before I married and left the village. A Mrs Hands, under Mrs E. Moorcroft (who became Commandant in 1953), conducted our meetings in Pinefields hall once a week. I wore my uniform with pride and was successful in the First Aid and Home Nursing exams. Another senior member who was involved with us was a Mrs Worthington, of the 'White City', Broadmoor Estate.

My membership involved First Aid duties at fetes and other outdoor events in the village, helping to blanket bath an elderly blind lady in her home in Church Street, and looking after the children of visitors to the aforementioned TB sanatorium at Pinewood, in a hall that 'stood on its own' in the grounds. Children were not allowed in the wards, where patients had to be kept as quiet as possible.

By necessity, I wore my uniform to all these and other events. On Remembrance Sundays I marched with the branch and other local organisations, from the British Legion Hall in Wellington Road, down the High Street and along Church Street to the Lych Gate. There we attended a short service, followed by a long service in St. John the Baptist Church. On cold Sundays, I was very pleased afterwards to get home to Mum's hot roast dinner!

Sometimes we had to line up in uniform outside Pinefields to be inspected by senior members of the British Red Cross, who came from outside the village for this and other purposes. In navy-blue or black skirts, white blouses, navy or black blazers, if cold weather, matching ties and round berets with our Red Cross badges affixed, we looked smart.

My Memories of Crowthorne Yesteryear and other accounts

One day we were preparing for this and were lined up, when Mrs Hands said, "If any of you are chewing-gum, take it out of your mouth now."

I was one involved, so asked, "Where shall we put it?"

She replied, "Anywhere, out of the way, such as behind one of your ears."

I carried this out and when I went to retrieve the gum later, found it so badly entangled in some of my hair that I had to cut away a chunk of it to free the gum!

One day we had another girl join our group. As a new girl cadet (there were no boy members) she was keen to see how she fared in the role, as she "couldn't bear the sight of blood," she said! Well, she wasn't a member for long, for at the initial First Aid lecture from her joining, the lecturer had a figure of a skeleton hanging over a blackboard to point out to us what she was explaining, and the girl fainted soon after the lecture started!

Shirley Woodason, aged about eighteen, in her British Red Cross Society uniform, outside her home 'Sydellen', just before setting off one Sunday afternoon, on her 'racing' bicycle, to carry out child minding for patients' visitors at Pinewood Hospital. (Circa 1952.)

My Memories of Crowthorne Yesteryear and other accounts

Above, 'Pinefields', Waterloo Road (no longer used as a function hall, or any public use), in 1991. Below, the Lych Gate of St. John the Baptist Church, Crowthorne, in 1993, with part of the church in the background. Part of Waterloo Road, lies to the left, and part of Church Street lies to the right. (Photo - Shirley E. Peckham.)

My Memories of Crowthorne Yesteryear and other accounts

Victor Woodason, eldest brother of Dudley (Syd) and Maurice, and uncle of Shirley Peckham who was renowned for his manufacture of model aeroplanes (including those used for wartime identification purposes, see picture on Page 120) and other models: cars, etc..

CHAPTER FIFTEEN
THE IN-BETWEEN

IN REFLECTION. I now take a look back, before continuing my account that takes me through my working life, teenage years from my school days, and those of my twenties, including my first wedding and very early married life, before leaving Crowthorne for what lay ahead for me.

My memories, particularly those associated with Crowthorne, are so vast, *and* more and more of them come to me almost daily, that the previous chapters in this book, and those beyond, contain only a small example of them. This book would be a tome too heavy to handle if *all* my memories of my life in the village were included. Perhaps a third book from me on the subject is called for?

MAINLY HAPPY CHILDHOOD. I believe I came through my childhood well. Despite wartime occupying a large part of it, I was happy most of the time. The wartime 'hindrances' for me were: the frightening enemy air activity over Crowthorne and news of bombs having fallen on the village; our family having to cope with the overcrowding situation of evacuees in our home and other inflictions from them; sweet rationing, which seemed cruel (children could not see the implications behind the enforcement and nothing could take the place of sweets and chocolate for us); and the stark, blunt news arriving that my dad was to be called up to do his stint in the army and leave us temporarily. Once he had gone, I soon settled to the situation, accepted it well, and looked forward eagerly to his coming home on leaves.

Rather than inconvenient and a nuisance, I found the overcrowding and cramped conditions at school in wartime, because of the influx of evacuees having taken their place there, interesting, quite fun and a change. None of the 'foreign' children bothered me on a personal level, though I still kept company with only my regular friends in the playground.

At home, away (loosely, of course) from wartime, I mainly enjoyed life too. Sometimes my sisters and I clashed (three don't agree, being the apt phrase concerned), with often two of us being in disagreement with the other one. But not always the same two were against the same one sister. Our personalities are largely very different. Today we still sometimes have contrasting viewpoints, suggesting that how we were made is how we would stay! When we approached Mum, and asked her to sort things out for us, she would say, "Sort out your own squabbles, you're old enough. I have my own things to worry about!" The same applied to when we had fallen out with our friends. Oh dear, we often needed a mediator, maybe also a counsellor!

MY SCHOOL LIFE CHIEFLY HAPPY. During most of my school years I was happy too. Because I was academically successful, I had a fairly smooth ride, and my rapport with the teachers and fellow pupils was mainly good throughout. But no such phenomena is without its tarnish, I've found, and this concerned (a) some of the teachers, from time to time, who would 'get my goat' (using a phrase of my mother's), being unreasonable; and (b) apparently because of my success, some of my fellow, bright, boy class-mates (I did not notice it applying to any of the girls), in the various classrooms, adopted an attitude of resentment towards me on occasions. Often sensitive, I felt the sting of this, though I was soon able to 'throw it off', by thinking, *they* don't really appeal to *me* half the time anyway! According to what I have learned since on psychology, they likely saw themselves as threatened, which affects some people in all sorts of situations.

My failure to pass the very-important-for-my-future (though I did not see this at the time) eleven-plus examination, was a severe form of blight I encountered; and my being temporarily afflicted with school phobia (or whatever it was), was a further unpleasant incident in those formative years. I believe now that the situation probably came about from hormonal changes I was likely experiencing on having entered adolescence, as I had always been 'fine' and mostly relaxed in school beforehand and the teacher I had at the time, Miss Mohr, normally had an undemanding and unfrightening approach. But I cannot be sure, as Mum *didn't even mention* that I should see our doctor about it! I was very pleased to resume my education, as a mature student of Adult Education classes, in quite recent times, and, of course, was even more pleased at my success in the exams.

SUMMING UP MY CHILDHOOD GENERALLY. Fun-filled! And I loved to learn. I recall, at the age of six (when I grasped how to whistle, amongst other things), feeling absolutely wonderful whenever I learned something new, at school or otherwise, and then looked forward to my next item learned.

Of course, Mum and Dad were, to me, a fine pair of individuals! Sometimes they would be after my tail and ready to clout my hide or legs (on occasions carried out) for a misdemeanour, but they obviously meant well and had a lot of concerns and pressures with three children

My Memories of Crowthorne Yesteryear and other accounts

in an age-span of 4½ years, as well as many other anxieties Glennis, Virgy and I never heard about – though some we did were: "the mortgage", "the tax man", their ever-trying to "skimp and save". The former alone was easy enough and was natural in our lives, but for them to save, or try to, was almost a laughable idea they found to be near impossible!

And Dad's regular flutters on the horses (he backed them at Mack's, the 'bookie's', in the High Street) never seemed to produce the success he hoped for. He never told us, Mum either, though, what he may have won or lost. She would say, "He can't be winning, or we would know about it!" Well, I'm not so sure.

Below are just a few more of my memories for you (do you see what I mean?), relating to the first section of my book, before you read on:

SCOTTS' EMULSION. In our kitchen, on a high shelf, where my white mouse in his cage had been positioned till I raffled it, Mum kept a large bottle of horrid-tasting, thick, white medical emulsion (I think called Scotts' Emulsion). As children we were told by Mum that it "is good for you", in some way. I would fly out of the house and up the road when I saw Mum reach up for the bottle, as I knew she was going to spoon it to me. She would call out, "You're having it, so you might as well come back here now," and add, like she always did when we were to take what to us was nasty medicine, "hold your nose when you take it, and then you won't taste it." This always worked, but we could nevertheless taste it to an extent after releasing our grips on our noses. When we needed to take tablets – usually Aspro – Mum would crush them up and put the powder in a teaspoonful of jam for us. This was successful, too. I had many unexplained headaches as a child, and was given Aspros this way for them by Mum. For much of my adult life I've been prone to headaches too.

MILK OF MAGNESIA/COD LIVER OIL. We had to take these too, from time to time, and I found them quite palatable compared with Scotts' Emulsion.

SENNA PODS. Mum regularly took senna-pod liquid, herself, at breakfast time, after covering the dried pods in a cup of boiling water the night before. She carried this out about three times a week, and often instructed us to have the revolting stuff too. We hated drinking it and definitely had to hold our noses then! Mum swore by the good effect of senna pods and would get into 'quite a state' if any evening she went to prepare some and found she had run out of them.

ASPROS. Mum also swore by the good effect, or that she thought if not always experienced, of Aspros. For some years, when I was in my teens and early twenties, she took one or two of them every bedtime, with warm milk, "To ensure I get a good night's sleep."

SAYINGS BY MY PARENTS (MOSTLY MUM, THOUGH) AND OTHER ONES, IN MY CHILDHOOD.
"Look at your filthy chops," referring to a child with a dirty mouth.
"She's like a house end," a crude description of any very overweight woman, especially if also of slovenly appearance.
"Get that tidemark off your neck," to a child with an only partially washed neck, showing the clean and the dirty part.
"I've got the pip," declaration of overworked and fed up wives and mothers.
"I haven't two ha'pennies to rub together." "I can't make ends meet." "I've barely anything between me and starvation." Expressions of mothers who were just about broke, which were heard most weeks, especially when weekly pay days – usually Fridays were nearing.
"Hand-me-downs," children's clothes that were passed down from one child of the family to the next or others younger, to get every possible bit of wear out of them to help the situation of money shortage.
"An old skinflint," a person tight with money.
"I'll knock your block off!" a threat, usually to a child by a parent, or other person, to anyone, implying "I'll knock your head off!"
"I'll smack you to kingdom come," I'll smack you relentlessly.
"In the family way." "Has a bun in the oven." A pregnant woman.

G.P's ADVICE. Referring again to our GP, Dr Chapman, he had an aversion (as I believe other GPs of those times did) to any patient telling him in his surgery what *they* felt they were suffering from. At such times, he would respond, "*I'll* tell you what you've got. I don't want *you* coming here and telling me what you think you've got." And he was deadly serious! Of course one didn't want to fall out with one's GP, so obeyed.

CANDY-FLOSS, ROCK, AND 'KISS-ME-QUICK' HATS.
On our visits to the seaside, we enjoyed ourselves on the beach with our buckets and spades, building sand-castles, collecting sea-shells, and so on. But on the pebbly beaches, such as at Brighton, a lot of this

fun was denied us, of course. Whenever there was a fun-fair at a seaside place we visited, too, we spent some time at it, having rides and trying to win something. At one of them there was a glass maze, I went into, and I couldn't find my way out of it for ages, though my sisters were successful quickly. The family was fed up, having to wait for me. None of these trips was without us being bought candy-floss, seaside rock, ice-cream in cones and kiss-me-quick slogan hats, the latter of which we wore all the way home in the coach as well, while we sang happy popular songs.

MY AVERSION TO GREENS. I hated greens, as a child, but Mum insisted I eat them every time she had put cabbage or the like on my dinner plate. "You must eat it, it is good for your blood, has a lot of iron in it."

"But I don't like it, and how can it have iron in (I was thinking of such as cast iron, knowing nothing of the other sort)?"

"Eat it up, or you'll get no pudding."

Oh dear, oh dear! Sometimes I would leave the greens and not get any pudding. At other times I would mix it with other food on my plate and eat it all quickly, whereupon I tasted the food as little as possible. Oddly, I loved bubble-and-squeak (of course, mashed potato and cabbage dry-fried together)! Perhaps one reason I didn't like greens is because of my continual dislike of caterpillars. However, when I used to visit Miss Churchill, next door, sometimes, if she had been cooking cabbage she would give me some elbow-hot cabbage water, in a cup, to drink, while saying, "It's very good for you, more so than cabbage leaves, for all the goodness has boiled out of them into the water."

I quite enjoyed the liquid. On telling Mum about what I had been given, and what Miss Churchill had said, she replied, "Well, I suppose she is right, but as I always make gravy with my cabbage water, you have it in *that* form here." I have eaten greens contentedly enough for many years since childhood.

PNEUMATIC TUBES. I recall a shop in Reading (possibly Jackson's department store, in Broad Street, that still has them) having pneumatic tubes, worked by vacuum, a suction method, in use, for when customers paid for their goods. The assistant placed the customer's money, paid for goods, into the end of one of them, which then disappeared through the tube (usually going upwards in the shop) to the cashier's office, somewhere in the premises, out of sight of anyone in the shop. The receipt and any change would be sent back

My Memories of Crowthorne Yesteryear and other accounts

through the tube, for the customer, after a couple of minutes.

CO-OP. My family's chief shopping store in Reading was the Co-op departmental one, where – because of them being Co-op members – my parents would collect "divi" (dividend) stamps, the value of them being according to the amounts they spent. This also applied when we shopped regularly in the Co-op grocery shop in Crowthorne. Between the time of my leaving school and starting work, Mum took me to the Co-op at Reading, to "rig you out for starting work." She was to spend twenty pounds there, on me alone! I felt really honoured and excited, and hoped my sisters wouldn't feel left out. They didn't show that they minded. With the twenty pounds, we obtained: a dress, a skirt, a blouse, some pretty underwear, and a handbag. It can be understood, I think, that having all these items bought for me in one day also felt an unreal situation to me. Many of my, and my sisters, clothes through childhood had been second-hand, passed from other families and some from jumble sales.

OUR PIANO LESSONS. My sisters and I were encouraged to be pianists by Mum, though were never in any way musical. However, against our pleas, she booked lessons for us, in my case, at least, with a Miss Yaxley (Kathleen, I believe), and later with a Miss Bartlett. Both ladies lived in the High Street, Crowthorne, the former in an end house of Cambridge Terrace, next to Townsend's shop where the lessons took place in the front room – and the other in the family flat above Bartlett's, the ironmonger's, near what was Rogers the baker's. Miss Bartlett had a metronome in use (standing on top of the piano) while I played.

For some of the time I attended at Miss Yaxley's home, Glennis did also, simultaneously, when we were taught the playing of piano duets.

Our practising at home on our piano, we had in our fairly small living-room, was forced on us by Mum. This had to be, agonisingly, for half an hour a day, usually after tea. We longed to be out playing with our friends instead. Sometimes we could hear them playing above our music, which piled on the agony!

ON STAGE PARTICIPANTS. When there came to be, during wartime, a talent concert for locals, in the village Plaza cinema, Mum insisted that Glennis and I took part, playing duets at the piano. I was very shy in those days and would have done anything to get out of it. But again my pleas (probably Glennis's too) did nothing to sway Mum's decision, and nervously I found myself on the stage, sitting by

Glennis (about the sixth act of the show), playing short passages of each of several tunes to the packed auditorium. Our nerves, mine the worst, I think, ensured that we made mistakes. But this was possibly not to the notice of the audience, unless some experts, like our music teacher, were in it!

We were only engaged in our act for about eight minutes, which seemed like half-an-hour, and I feel I speak for both of us in saying we were so very relieved to leave the stage and take our places in the auditorium by the rest of our family again.

COMEDIAN. A particular act I enjoyed that evening, and the only one I really remember other than our own, was that of Mr Edward Butler (known as Ted or Dusty), of Pinewood Avenue, as a comedian. I found him to be really funny, giving everyone many laughs. He was the first, or almost the first, act of the evening, which helped to set the scene happily for the rest of the concert.

PIANOLA. We had in our home for a while, in the room that had been occupied by our evacuees (later my sole bedroom) a pianola. It fascinated me, and seemed so unusual an object. I don't know where my parents got it from, or why. It was very unlike a piano to me and seemed secondhand. I feel we never had it in use, and I don't know where it went to. We didn't seem to have it for long. I would like to have heard it playing, but maybe it was past this.

A group of bricklayers in Crowthorne yesteryear times. Photo undated, but probably in the 1930s or '40s. L. to r. - F. Cripps; Maurice Woodason, youngest brother of Dudley (Syd); Bert Butcher. (Building in background unidentified, which looks like a public hall.)

My Memories of Crowthorne Yesteryear and other accounts

Victor Woodason, with some of his model aeroplanes, used for wartime (Second World War) identification purposes.

Copyright - Holton Deutsche Collection.

My Memories of Crowthorne Yesteryear and other accounts

CHAPTER SIXTEEN
MY FIRST AND ONLY JOB IN CROWTHORNE

WORKING FOR BUTCHER FRANK TALMAGE. I left school towards the end of July 1949 and two weeks later began work as a trainee cashier-bookkeeper for Frank James Talmage, Purveyor of Meat, Fish, Poultry and Game, of the High Street, Crowthorne. Previously I had not really known what I wanted to do on leaving school, but earlier that year Frank Talmage had approached the Head, Mr Goodband, to ask who, of the girls to leave that year, he considered most suitable for this role. He was given three names, mine included, and chose me from them because he had known my father in their school days, and knew the Woodason family well as a whole. This did not apply with the others, one of whom (Esther Bernard) was quite new to living in the village with her family. Oddly enough, Frank and his wife, Nora, were to become very friendly with Esther's parents. The family lived at the very top end of Pinewood Avenue. Esther, a tall, pleasant, quiet girl, had a younger brother, I think, Tony.

From making his decision, Frank Talmage approached my mother, who in turn told me that he was interested in employing me in the position of trainee cashier-bookkeeper, under and in the hands of Miss Dorothy Harfield, affectionately known by many as Dolly, but I preferred to call her Dorothy since I had not known her before. Convivial, bubbly and happy-natured, she lived with her large family in Upper Broadmoor Road and had recently become engaged to very tall and powerfully built, Des Reay, who was not of the area, but had moved there. Dorothy had worked for Mr Talmage for many years – from leaving school – and was to leave her position on or soon after marrying. Hence the need for her replacement.

When my mother told me that Mr Talmage had approached, her asking if I would be interested in taking the role, I was surprised at being asked and my first response was, "Oh, I don't know." I had also recalled that he always appeared hasty and severe when I went into his shop for my neighbour Miss Churchill's meat on Saturdays and the shop was renowned as being very busy. Even if Mr Talmage himself suited me, would such a busy place do so also?

Mum, keen I think for me to get into *a* (suitable, of course) job and earning a wage, encouraged me to take it and to tell him so soon, as "It may really suit you." So I went to see him and it was arranged when I should start.

I began there on a Tuesday (Mondays, like Wednesdays, were halfday closing at the shop when little actual business went on).

My Memories of Crowthorne Yesteryear and other accounts

Feeling some awe in my situation, I wondered, also, if I would ever come anywhere near Dorothy's popularity whom, I was soon to discover, was well-liked by the Talmages and a host of others, seemingly everyone. Needless to say, she and I came to have a good rapport too, and she soon had me initiated into the arrangements. I expected to work with her for months, rather than weeks, which turned out to be the case.

I wore a brand new, fashionable, 'new look' cotton dress in blue-check, which came to my calves, on my initial day and felt really grown-up for the first time. The day in total though seemed strange and very long for me, in comparison with my school ones. And thoughts of most of my working days being long like this was not a good prospect.

However, I soon found my work to my liking, the days seeming not so long as time progressed, and Dorothy was a good-humoured and patient tutor who guided me well. The office was large (room-size, unlike the 'box' ones often in butchers' shops) and customers came to either of two sides of the front of the office. Windows slid up and down for this, one to allow them to pay for their meat, the other their fish, poultry and game.

THE BOSS. Frank Talmage had a sharp approach that I felt uncomfortable with, but he more-or-less left me under Dorothy's wing to settle in and I did not have very much direct association with him for some time. My weekly wage when I went to the shop was £1-5s-0d (£1.25), while Dorothy's then was £3-10s-0d (£3.50). I, like her, was to be the firm's wages clerk as well as cashier-bookkeeper and to an extent act as secretary to Frank, who dictated letters to first Dorothy (till she left) and then to me. These were then hand-written on his business-headed writing paper. There was no typewriter at the firm.

THE MEAT SECTION STAFF. The white-tiled shop was very busy, with workaholic Frank Talmage (who was never still and bullet-in-flight quick with his movements) at the helm. Quiet-voiced and quiet-natured, fun-loving Irishman, Jim Beggs of Little Sandhurst was Frank's right-hand man. His pleasing manner went a long way in making up for Frank's shortcomings. But sometimes his sense of humour overspilled and, directed at me, caused me embarrassment, especially when in the company of others. He was a regular teaser.

Short, Fred Brasher, coming towards retirement, mainly delivered customers' orders, driving the firm's van. He would cover miles at this – the places I recall being Broadmoor, the area of the railway

My Memories of Crowthorne Yesteryear and other accounts

station, including the Ravenswood and East Berks Golf Club areas, Finchampstead Ridges, Finchampstead itself, and Eversley (possibly, too, Yateley), often taking him most of a day. Fred, with a quiet personality, had a very good rapport with his rounds customers. At the shop he would make sausages, mince, and be generally supportive to the team. Fred lived in Cambridge Terrace (a row of homes near the shop owned by Frank), with his wife Vivien and their only child, daughter Peggy.

Brian Ilott (of Hatch Ride) joined the staff straight from school, some long time after I went to the shop. He was to learn the trade, and was a bright, keen and willing employee. When he left his post (after I too had left there, I believe), he set up his own butcher's shop near Crowthorne station. This is no longer in being.

Very near, if not over, retirement age, Henry (Harry) Watts, of Manhattan Place, opposite the shop (where he lived with his wife, name unrecalled, but possibly Dorothy), became a staff member sometime after I did. Harry, short like Fred, was *very* quiet, and almost spoke in whispers. With what I considered a nervous tendency, he also though stood up for himself when necessary. For a time, while employed by Frank Talmage, he was released, as relief manager, to the then butcher's shop opposite the New Inn, near Sandhurst Halt, owned by Emily Louise Talmage (Frank's mother, widow of the late Edwin, who had also been a butcher in Crowthorne, ahead of Frank; maybe they worked together for a time too). Emily Louise lived in a detached house next to Hatfield's cycle shop in Crowthorne High Street. I had some associations with her and found in her a likeable character who suffered a little from senile dementia in her final years.

THE SANDHURST SHOP. For a short period while Harry Watts was there (and Dorothy was still in her role at the Crowthorne shop, so I could be spared), I also was sent to the Sandhurst shop, as cashier-bookkeeper, where staff shortages had created problems. In comparison with being at the Crowthorne shop, I found things almost 'dead' – with customers far fewer – and having kindly Harry in place of Frank working with me was sheer bliss. Applying to the two men, 'chalk and cheese' surely never fitted a pair more!

Frank asked me to print on a board, and put in the window at the Sandhurst shop, a notice for a bookkeeper being required there. I did this, with the message bold. Then the local policeman came in, in uniform, and said, "I'm applying for the job of *boo*keeper." Harry and I looked up with expressions as though we thought him mad. "*Boo*keeper?" we quizzed. "Yes," he replied, "who can't spell in here?"

Red-faced, though grinning, I admitted my error, put matters on the board right and have never spelt the word bookkeeper wrongly since!

THE HOURS. Back to the Crowthorne shop. All the staff had half days off work on Mondays and Wednesdays, when the shop closed, but the butchers and myself (Dorothy too till she left), had to work until 9 p.m. on Fridays dealing with weekend orders – mainly for delivery – for the following day. Frank rose every day at 4.30 a.m. and, after a quick breakfast, prepared the meat for the day's trade, boning and cutting it and dressing two windows. He was never noticeably tired and maybe this is why he expected perfection from his staff.

WORKING DIFFICULTIES CONCERNING THE BOSS.
Frank Talmage was very difficult to work for! His verve as applied to *his* work reached extremes and his tongue matched his sharp way. A character always clean-cut, he bore no frilly edges! Bespectacled, with thinning black hair combed back, he was short and as slim as a reed. Frank was very like Arthur Askey in appearance and as one ex-employee recently told me, he was "like a whirlwind!"

Always wearing black, ankle-hugging boots and over his clothes a beige smock and white apron, he would dart about the shop, sometimes sliding on the tiled, sawdust-covered floor a foot or two as he did so. Occasionally he laughed, mostly from what some of his favourite customers had light-heartedly said to him. Whenever it occurred, it was such a pleasant change that I felt like singing. One summer afternoon, I returned to the shop from lunch wearing a large, decorative straw hat and left it on my head while working, to test his reaction. Perhaps he would laugh? However, he appeared not to even notice it over the three plus hours concerned while, amused, the rest of the staff and customers were commenting on it throughout!

THE FISH SECTION STAFF. Various fishmongers came and went during my spell at the shop. Jack Sewell was there at first, then in their turn, a Mr M., then a comparatively young, bespectacled, chap whose name I cannot recall, and finally Tom Pepper, who, like Fred Brasher, lived in Cambridge Terrace (Frank Talmage's row of adjoining houses near the shop), with his wife Dorothy. Tom, whose account forms part of this book, still resides in Crowthorne, now in King's Road.

When the successive fishmongers were busy in the tiny, often flea-ridden (one told me), ramshackle shed at the back of the shop, plucking the birds, I would help out by serving their customers. This was between doing my own work. It was far from easy since I had to keep washing and drying my hands. Although I learned a lot about fish: skinning, filleting, cutting, etc., it was a very cold job indeed, particularly to the fingers, and of course even worse in wintertime, when my fingers went blue, then dead (my attacks in more recent times of Renaud's Disease may have had some bearing on this). The fish often had to be taken from boxes full of ice-cubes, there to keep it fresh.

SEXUAL HARASSMENT. The youngest of the fishmongers, the young bespectacled one whose name escapes me, once grabbed hold of me unexpectedly. We were 'out the back' of the shop, at the time. From walking towards him, I was going by him when, from grabbing me, he held me in a passionate embrace before plonking a humdinger of a kiss on my lips! I used to call these "smackeroos" and was stunned at what the man did. My total lack of response brought him swiftly to break away from me, when he looked shocked by his own action and totally embarrassed, before shooting off to return to his work in the shop. We continued normally as colleagues from then onwards, but I confided the incident to butcher Jim Beggs, feeling the need for someone there to know. He explained that the married man had problems in his private life, briefly detailed them, and said, "Didn't you know?" Well, I certainly had not known, but was relieved to have an explanation.

THE WAGES. Earlier in this chapter I gave details of the wages of Dorothy and myself when I first went to work at the shop in 1949. These were for a 42-hour week. One week, from preparing the staff wages, I mixed up those of two of the men, by putting one man's wages in the envelope of another, and vice versa – this on the Friday. Next morning Frank was waiting for me as I reached the office, the men having returned their wrong wages to him beforehand. I was severely up-braided and told never to make this mistake again, which can "cause no end of trouble." Oh dear, to be in Frank's bad books was to be reduced to midge-size. He soon threw it off though, as I did!

There was an occasion when, on arrival home with my wages one winter's evening, I accidentally flung them, in sealed packet, on our blazing hearth fire in mistake for something else. The flames soon gobbled them up. I realised what I had done immediately on seeing the charred remains in the flames, and shrieked, "Oh, Mum, I've thrown my wages (£6) on the fire!"

"Oh dear, can't you retrieve *any* of it?" she asked, but before her words were barely out, like me, she could see the impossibility of this. I think she *gave* me my keep that week, to help me.

FIRST AID. I was in charge of the shop's first aid box, that was often in demand, as the men were using sharp knives and choppers so much. With blood dripping from an injury they would first call out "Miss, a cut," or whatever, and hurry into the office, by which time I had the first-aid box out and open. This was when my Red Cross experience helped greatly as, with their blood still dripping – eventually on to the office floor – I had to set about briefly cleaning the wound and then 'slapping' dressing on it. Of course, plasters would not stick properly on the men's skin (it was too damp) and they did not want the inconvenience of bandages. They were often forced to wear finger and thumb stalls over dressings though, which I've since felt, being leather, were not very hygienic.

I was always especially ill at ease when Frank was the victim. He barely had the patience to wait for treatment, while shuffling his feet about on the office floor as though badly needing the gents! Talk about worse than a child ...! Before my time at the shop he had suffered a nasty accident in the shop, from slipping on a piece of animal fat on the floor and finishing up with a large steel meat hook (that hung from a steel bar fixed horizontally near the top of a wall) in his back. It had just missed a kidney! He was rushed to hospital and made a good recovery. I don't know how I would have coped in applying first aid to that injury.

One day I dealt with a bad cut on his finger, in the usual way. But within a couple of days he had collapsed with blood-poisoning (septicaemia), after looking ill and saying he felt it, though had continued working in the shop. He then, though feeling and looking 'rotten', conducted some of the administrative side of the business from his bed. I had to go to his bedside as part of this, when his face was as white as the sheets. Feeling compassion, I later mentioned how he seemed and looked to his wife Nora, who replied, "It's his own fault and he knows it. He should have stopped work and got the problem seen to earlier."

Frank's motto of "Work 'em off!" may have been all right as applying to colds (which he definitely did, never having time off to help the situation with any of them he developed), but as for the other side of the fence ... He was laid up for a week from his illness and still looked 'dicky' on his return to the shop.

On saying, above, that Frank and his staff would call out "Miss, a cut," reminded me to explain that it was the practice at the shop – as probably in most business places in those days – for the staff, including me of course, to address the boss as "Sir." or "Mr Talmage". and our colleagues – when in the boss's presence especially – as "Mr", etc., whatever surname. But increasingly, during my time there, the staff came to be on Christian name terms with one another. And the boss and all the staff – except Dorothy, when she was at the shop – addressed me as "Miss Woodason". Again, later, the formality was dropped and my Christian name only was used by them. Teenage members of staff who came there after I did, were addressed by their Christian name by the boss and other staff from the outset.

NORA TALMAGE. Frank's heavily-built wife, Nora, had attractive features, was pleasant-natured and always good to the staff. In some ways she was more like a friend to us, than the boss's wife. I think she saw herself, in her position, as something of 'the lady' though, for which (if right) I had no recriminations. She was always kindly and agreeable with everyone, that is what mattered.

Nora would bring her husband and the staff cups of tea and biscuits (from their home behind and forming part of the shop building) every mid-morning, and tea and her home-made cakes every mid-afternoon. She never failed us over this and whenever she could not do it herself she engaged someone else to. In my first few years at the shop she would sometimes leave their then pre-school-age daughter, Margaret Jane, with me in the office, while she (Nora) went out. The pleasant little girl would colour pictures in colouring books. The Talmages also had two sons. The eldest of the three children was Peter, and the other (second eldest child) Robert. All three children were likeable, well-mannered and polite.

Sometimes, during evenings, I baby-sat for Nora and Frank, when the children were problem-free, in line with their natures. Once, when I was baby-sitting for them, Frank and Nora arrived back at their home much earlier than expected, with blood-stains down the front of their evening clothes. I asked, "Oh dear, what has happened?" They replied that they had been involved in a road accident on the way to London and the crash had caused them minor injuries and damaged their car. This being still driveable, they were able to come straight back home, of course missing the event.

Nora once asked me to 'break in' a pair of shoes she had just bought for herself, by wearing them instead of my own in the office. As she took size 6 1/2, like me, she thought this idea a good one. I agreed to do it, for I liked her, and wore the high-heeled ones for two hours. If my bunions of today could talk would they make any comment of this, I wonder?

Still on the subject of shoes. I was on my way to work one dark winter's morning, when, while cycling, I noticed that I had a navy-blue shoe on one foot and a brown one on the other. This had happened while I prepared for work in a hurry in my poorly-lit bedroom. I couldn't be bothered to return home, didn't have time to either, so during that morning at work wore the unmatching shoes. No one commented on it, if they noticed.

When Nora had her hair permed, she would sometimes say to me the next morning, "Comb out my hair gently please, I hate doing it myself for the first time from having a perm." Well, so did I hate the activity, with my own, but I would oblige her by dealing with the task very carefully and she was always very grateful.

Nora's birthday was on December 29th and the date always caught Frank out, for, what with the busy spell in the shop from well before Christmas, all that he was concerned with regarding Christmas itself, and so on, often the birthday had arrived before he was barely aware his Christmas dinner had settled! One year he received a 'caning' from Nora for *forgetting* her very special day. On hearing of this, I suggested to him that I help him out in future, by reminding him in good time of her birthday. He was pleased to hear this and agreed with the idea, but added, "It would help me further if I also give you money to go and get the card."

I replied, "They should really be chosen, especially concerning the wording, by you."

"Oh, blow that!" he returned. "Use your discretion, you won't go wrong and you don't have to tell her."

From then on, Frank never forgot his wife's birthday. And, of course, neither did I!

DINNER DANCES. Both Dorothy and I (she went to far more of them than I did) were invited by the Talmages to butcher's special dinner dances, mainly in Reading. I cannot remember the organisation concerned, in which he held an important position (I think in the title was 'Master Butchers' and possibly 'Federation'). These were no-expenses-spared grand affairs and Nora would be in her element for weeks ahead preparing for her participation. She had some lovely evening dresses she wore for these and other similar events, and really looked attractive when wearing them. Her skin was flawless and she wore make-up well, also carried, on her arm or by hand, one of her selection of beautiful evening bags.

I felt somewhat out of my depth at the butchers' events and after attending a couple of them, politely declined invitations for future ones, by which time Dorothy had left the firm after marrying.

The Talmage family at home, 'Preston House', High Street, Crowthorne (that formed part of the building shared by their butcher's/fishmonger's shop), on the occasion of their eldest child, Peter's, twenty-first birthday, August 1959. Rear, l. to r., Robert, Peter, their father Frank (the butcher). Front, Nora (Frank's wife) and their daughter Margaret Jane.   (Photo - Shirley E. Woodason.)

Again, the occasion in August 1959 of Peter Talmage's twenty-first birthday, in the Talmage's home 'Preston House'. Rear (l. to r.) Mrs Bernard, Pinewood Avenue; Mrs E. Moorcroft, Forest Road; ? ; and Mr Rabbitts, friends of the Talmage family. Front (l. to r.) Robert Talmage; Shirley Woodason, staff member of their shop; George Pinchin and his wife, Rene, landlords of the Prince Alfred, friends of the Talmages.

CHAPTER SEVENTEEN
DOROTHY AND DES REAY

"THAT'S THE MAN I'LL MARRY." Dorothy's engagement to Des Reay led from her chance initial sighting of him in Crowthorne High Street, when she said to the woman she was with, "That's the man I'll marry." He was wearing a kilt at the time. As mentioned, he was not a Crowthornian, and I don't know when and why he came there. However, I am aware that the surname Reay has Scottish connections.

Des may have been as much as 6 feet 3 tall and, powerfully built, looked as strong as an ox. Dorothy was about 5 feet 4 tall, always wore smart, high-heeled shoes, and was quite slim. She had naturally-curly hair, she would lightly complain about: "I can't change the style. It wants to do its own thing all the time." I could see what she meant, but still admired her hair.

QUIET WEDDING. In February 1950, seven months after I had commenced work for Frank Talmage and Dorothy had taught me my job thoroughly, she married Des quietly at either Bracknell or Windsor Register Office (I cannot be certain which). For the event to have happened this way and at this time was most unexpected as far as the Talmages and the rest of the staff were concerned.

I heard the news from Nora and Frank on my return to work at the start of the following week. Having only recently received the news themselves, they were upset by the fact that the couple had not had a white wedding and not given them notice of the Register Office one. This was because in some ways Dorothy was like a daughter to them and accordingly they wanted to have a big part in her wedding, whenever it came about. They were therefore sorry about the secrecy from us of the affair. Dorothy was not going to return to work till the following week, having earlier booked a week's holiday from work – no doubt with their wedding and honeymoon in mind.

A CARAVAN THEIR FIRST HOME. The happy couple, Dorothy radiantly so, started married life in a caravan, somewhere in the village, and later moved to a house in Branksome Hill Road, College Town, Sandhurst, where I believe they lived for their entire married life. They had three sons. Sadly, the family suffered a series of tragedies. Their fate could not have been more undeserving. I am left with very happy memories of Dorothy, as are many other people, a number of whom knew her from their childhood days. She is still

My Memories of Crowthorne Yesteryear and other accounts missed, since sadly losing her life a number of years ago.

Dorothy (Dolly, née Harfield) and Des Reay (right and centre), and Dorothy's sister, June Harfield, in the garden of Dorothy and June's parents' home in Upper Broadmoor Road, following Dorothy and Des's wedding – February 1950.

CHAPTER EIGHTEEN
CONTINUING MY TALMAGE YEARS

THE SLAUGHTER HOUSE. A humane-killer was kept in a locked safe in the office and I was in charge of the key. The weapon was only used for slaughtering animals in the slaughterhouse, at the rear of the shop – once or twice a week usually. This involved pigs, steers and possibly heifers. I am not sure whether sheep were concerned and consider lambs were not. Silence fell on the animals' squealing once the humane-killer, that had been placed between their eyes, was fired. I was told they only felt momentary pain at the time, if that. One day, by request, I was taken to have a look in the slaughterhouse, a completely concreted, closed in and roofed-over area. There were cattle in a pen at one end. This was on a day there was to be no slaughtering, otherwise I would not have been allowed anywhere near it.

After a day's slaughtering, the slaughterhouse was thoroughly cleaned, using plenty of water and disinfectant, with hoses, buckets and stiff-bristle brooms involved. The men always wore rubberised, protective bibbed-aprons when working there, whether carrying out slaughtering or simply cleaning up afterwards.

An inspector from the Public Health Department of Easthampstead Rural District Council came to examine the dead animals, that would usually subsequently 'pass'. I do not recall any failing this, but do remember him failing organs of animals sometimes, the liver in particular that was diseased. Whatever was concerned, he took away, for maybe further examination and/or to be destroyed. Diseased organs did not necessarily, or usually, affect the flesh of the carcass itself, I was informed authoritatively.

A STEER ON THE RUN. One winter morning a steer escaped from the area of the slaughterhouse and was soon making its way ungainly, though rapidly, along the High Street, towards the Prince Alfred. Frank Talmage, Jim Beggs and another male staff member, quick to realise the problem, made after it and caught up with the beast opposite I. V. Scott's hardware shop (now Bob's DIY). There, according to my memory of how I was told the story, Frank and the other man held the steer while Jim went to throw a looped length of rope over its head to retain it. But in the process the animal made off again, causing Jim to slip on the icy road, slightly injuring and slightly concussing himself. He was taken by ambulance to hospital, but was soon released (maybe the same day) and quickly recovered. The steer continued towards the Prince Alfred and was eventually caught a little way into Upper Broadmoor Road, and brought back to the shop. It probably did not live long after that!

BASINGSTOKE CATTLE MARKET. Frank Talmage attended this every Wednesday, leaving the shop at noon to drive his large, powerful car there. This was when the shop staff, me included, had an eagerly anticipated relaxed hour in his absence, free from the constant necessity when he was in the shop to be 'on our toes'! (Nowadays, of course, he would not have got away with much that he did!)

At the market Frank would buy livestock to replenish his stock. He also visited other cattle markets at times, especially in the weeks leading to Christmas, when he always purchased prize-winning stock which he subsequently hung with pride in his shop. These being quarters, rump and fore ends, which he adorned with their bright-coloured rosettes. Having them there undoubtedly gave him self-exaltation and he would discuss the specimens with gusto with the customers, many of whom subsequently bought from this meat.

MEAT WHOLESALERS. Frank also bought 'dead meat' from the meat wholesalers, Borthwick's, of Reading. It would arrive at the shop in their huge covered-in lorries. This was meat of all kinds, including veal, which was an expensive meat delicacy, very much sought after by certain customers. I tried it once. It was, of course, very tender "as a woman's heart" (to quote Frank's phrase when asked by anyone if certain of his meat was tender), but did not have sufficient taste for my palate. Calves sweetbreads were considered the 'tops', delicate and rich in goodness, for feeding invalids on light meat food, as well as their brains – steamed in milk. Veal for schnitzels was also popular with some, likewise the often sought after escalope.

FISH FROM BILLINGSGATE. Frank bought his fish from Billingsgate Fish Market, in London. One of their representatives would phone the shop every morning at 8.30, when the fishmonger of the time was informed what was available, before giving his order, on behalf of Frank. Later in the morning the boxed fish would arrive by train at Crowthorne Station. If Fred Brasher, with the van, did not call there for it (though he mostly did, having been told when it would arrive), the station phoned the shop to say it was there, and very soon after it was collected. As with the meat, the fish was always of good quality, and 'daisy-fresh'.

PHEASANTS, HARES ETC.. Game at the shop was most often requested 'high'. When I first saw some of them in this state, alive with maggots, I cringed and considered, how can people eat that? But I was assured it was "lovely" and jugged hare, made from a hare that was high, was "rich, wonderfully tasty and produced superb gravy." I have not gone on to prove or disprove it ! One customer who liked buying hares high for jugging was a Mrs Bishop of Broadmoor, whose husband, Dr Bishop, was at the time Superintendent of Broadmoor Hospital. She was a superb woman, and a highly accredited customer of the shop, being one of the best, who treated us all with tenderness and unfailing respect. Also, every year she gave me a five pounds Christmas box (a white five pound note, these being in circulation then).

CHRISTMAS. We all had to work extra hours in the lead-up to Christmas, Sundays included some years (depending when Christmas itself fell), earning ourselves extra wages, but felt the tiring effects increasingly till this climaxed on Christmas Eve. This was when, particularly the men, were 'whacked' and almost ready to sleep through the holiday! Poultry, game and meat for Christmas orders had to be prepared. Sometimes the men were dealing with these up until midnight and would be back to work at 5 o'clock in the morning, having been in bed for so short a time.

Frank gave us a chicken, sausages and sometimes meat each for our Christmas-boxes. Grateful, kind customers also gave *me* Christmas-boxes of various kinds, such as boxes of chocolates, boxes of handkerchiefs, boxes of soap, etc., and money ones. I always did very well from the customers' tips at Christmas when, very grateful indeed, twice a day for several days – ending on Christmas Eve – I would go home with shopping bags full of gaily-wrapped presents and with the money making my purse bulge.

A CUSTOMER'S CONCERN. One winter's morning (not at Christmas) I was particularly cold at work while working in the office. We had an electric fire there, but the heat from it went out of the office windows, and the shop itself was cold, with its doors always open. My being cold in the winter was usually the case, and on occasions I would wear half-mittens on my hands, which also covered my wrists, to help out. It was about 10 o'clock when an elderly lady customer phoned to ask if I was cold. I told her "Yes." Then, half an hour later, a staff member of Armitage's departmental drapery shop, next-door, came to me and handed me a paper bag which contained a

My Memories of Crowthorne Yesteryear and other accounts

large, woollen, turquoise-coloured stole. She named the Talmage elderly customer, who had phoned me, and said that she had asked them (Armitage's) to deliver the stole to me, "To keep you warm," and put the cost on her bill. What a kind and thoughtful gesture. I rang and thanked the lady, of course, and was soon cosily wearing the stole, which helped my situation considerably. I came to wear it a lot, at the shop and away from it, over years.

THE TIPSY MISS! I was eighteen when the whole Talmage staff, as well as the Talmages themselves, was suddenly invited, on the actual afternoon, to a Christmas Eve drinks party at Armitage's, next door. This was partly because Frank and Nora Talmage were very friendly with George Armitage, who owned the shop.

Once there, at the end of the afternoon, with my colleagues and boss and his wife, we joined George and his staff in a small area of his shop, and sat on boxes and chairs. The drinks started to flow, but there wasn't a morsel of anything to eat. Out of my sight, the men merrily kept topping up my glass. What with, half the time I never learned! I think ever-fun-loving Jim Beggs was the main instigator, whose face bore a grin from ear to ear, bigger than anyone else's, throughout.

At the end of the less-than-an-hour session I went to stand up, along with everyone else, and found this difficult. I was decidedly wobbly. Outside the shop I was worse, felt I had rubber legs. Jim and one of the other men saw the problem and took one of my arms each to help me along. We were heading towards the Talmage's lounge, with some of the Armitage staff, George and of course the Talmages, to resume the party.

Once in the lounge I more-or-less fell onto the settee, and from then on was the comical star turn to make everyone laugh – even Frank! My observation of *him* doing it, through what seemed liquid eyes, giving a sort of triple-vision effect, was a joy. After more drinks (no food still), people began drifting away, when my inebriate state brought concern to Nora Talmage, who suggested I be given black coffee to make me sick. She soon provided this, which two of the party-goers, having a go each, more-or-less poured down my throat in their kitchen. This didn't work! Then someone suggested fresh air was the answer, and Jim and another male practically dragged me full circle round the large concreted area at the back of the Talmage house, which also did not bring the desired effect!

There came the final suggestion that I should be driven home and, this agreed, Jim piled me into the passenger seat, and my bike into the rear of the delivery van. Soon he was pulling the vehicle in at my home. There Dad was on his own, Mum having gone to a Christmas Eve social event. Jim told him that I had had "a little too much to drink" at the works party and Dad rounded with, "*I don't want anything to do with her like that, she'll have to sort herself out.*" Jim shot off and was very relieved to be going too, I expect!

In a fragile, subconscious way, I prepared myself for bed and went there without hearing barely another word from Dad, who remained disgruntled.

In the middle of the night I woke feeling very ill, causing vomiting. Mum, half asleep, called from her bed, "Are you all right?" Knowing it would suit her best, and Dad if he were awake, I replied with a weak, "Yes, thanks." A lie if ever there was one!

Next (Christmas) day, in great discomfort, I experienced my first ever hangover and decided it must be the last! Mum tried to tempt me with breakfast. I refused it. Then she spoke of our dinner to come. I said I would not want that either. "But you *must* have your Christmas dinner!" Never before had the word *must* had such worthless meaning for me and there would always be other Christmases. I insisted further that I would not want it. She was astounded! Dad kept himself scarce. I emphasised to Mum that I felt so ill. She suggested I have more alcohol, "Like you had at the party, 'hair of the dog' is the quickest cure." It was the first time I had heard the phrase. She soon explained, but I refused the idea adding that I "*do not want any more drink for the rest of my life!*" She told me that over the years thousands of people with hangovers have said that and not stuck to it.

I went for a walk and in the cold, crisp air 'took in' a number of village roads until, in mid-afternoon, I found myself by the Cambridge Terrace home of my work colleague Tom Pepper and his wife, Dorothy. Deciding to call on them, I rang their doorbell. Tom answered it, looked at me in surprise and said, "Hello! Gosh you were canned last night weren't you?"

I replied, "Yes," and briefly told him what had happened since. He invited me in, where they had a lady visitor. I was asked to stay and had a nice tea with them, by which time I had recovered. We also played cards and I won a few games. At last I was enjoying some of my Christmas Day, coupled with their very welcome hospitality.

MY GOOD LUCK. I had a bout of good fortune while working at Talmage's. I think when in my early twenties, there were some charity football tickets being sold week-by-week locally and probably nationwide. A person involved with them used to come into the shop and sell them to the staff, maybe the boss too, and each week – according to the league football results – a number of winners, for good money prizes, varying in size each time, came about.

I bought one a week, but without having any interest in football itself and not much interest in what I had bought, did not check it each Saturday night. However, one Tuesday a customer came to pay me for her meat and said, "*Someone's* lucky, isn't she?"

I asked, "And who would that be?"

"*Well you, of course!*" she went on, "winning on your football ticket." I truthfully replied that I did not know what she was talking about and wrongly guessed that she was having me on.

She continued, "*I can't believe you don't know. You've won a hundred pounds. Didn't you check your ticket?*"

"No," I replied, "I had no idea I'd won!"

On the following Wednesday I received the money, in great jubilation, which was hand-delivered to me in the shop, and thought, I'll buy my parents, my sisters and myself presents out of my winnings, followed by, now men will want to marry me for my money! Well, one of my, not serious, boyfriends of the time did come to say, "I hear you've had a good money win."

THEFTS AT THE SHOP! Money disappeared from the office, in two separate incidents, while I was working at the shop. The inside case concerned the fishmonger employed there at the time, Mr M, who carried this out systematically over some weeks, little by little. Some of the stolen money (notes, which, with Frank Talmage's co-operation and my determination to try and catch the thief, I had marked), turned up in the till of a bar in the Crowthorne Inn. They had been spent there by Mr M, a regular customer who, while always dapperly dressed, readily and regularly bought rounds of drinks for others and himself. The proprietor of 'The Crow' co-operated with us over this. The police were not involved and the man lost his job over the thefts, and for other reasons, also lost the house in Cambridge Terrace that went with it. He and his wife, who had moved to Crowthorne from elsewhere so that he could take the job, then left the area.

The other theft, years later, involved £66 disappearing one lunchtime from a cash tin in the office, left as usual unlocked in those more trusting times. This time Frank Talmage involved the police, and CID officers came to the shop to take the staff's fingerprints. Understandably my prints were found to be 'everywhere' in the office, including on its door and on the cash tin. We were told by Frank not to divulge to any customers what was happening if they showed their inquisitiveness as to what the men were doing there, while the shop was open. So we told some of them white lies.

Weeks later, during which the staff regularly wondered of each other whether any of them was responsible, the thief was arrested. Frank Talmage was quick to tell me of it on my arrival at work one morning. "*Who?*" I eagerly wanted to know. He explained it was the laundry roundsman, from a firm in Reading, who used to come to the shop each Thursday around lunch-time (it was a Thursday that the theft occurred) to deliver and collect the men's overalls and aprons. When I was there I would pay him from money in the cash tin, so he saw where this was. (I was at home for lunch, as usual, on the day the money disappeared.) We all at the shop had not suspected him, nevertheless, and were very relieved the matter was almost over.

The thief was subsequently found guilty at Reading Crown Court, for that and other similar offences, all carried out at firms' premises he called on in his job. He was sentenced to nine months in gaol. Frank was in court and later, after giving me the news, told me, "When they led him from the court his wife called out, 'Don't take my husband away. He is the father of our children.' But her plea was to no avail." Following this I could wear my new black coat I had bought just before the theft. If I had worn it earlier it might have appeared to Frank and others at the shop that I had stolen his money to buy it! Jim Beggs, who had bought a new suit just before the theft, apparently thought the same! We laughed together about our fears concerning our purchases and the theft, later.

THE JOVIAL FRANK. Once in the shop I caused Frank to roar with laughter – a record! I have a sense of humour, as did my Dad, but, the following was spontaneous and unintended as such. In the office there was a large wall clock that could be easily seen by me there, and by others from certain areas of the shop. The men did not normally wear watches because of the nature of their work and, particularly Frank, were forever calling out to me, "What's the time, Miss?" Because of the frequency of it, this became exasperating at times.

On the day in question, a Friday, we were as usual working late into the evening and it was about 8.30 when Frank called out for the umpteenth time that day, "What's the time, Miss?" Without hesitation I responded with the phrase of a well-known commercial advertisement for drinking chocolate of the time, the answer being, "It's chocolate time."

Directly I had said it I felt, what *have* I done? One does not do this

My Memories of Crowthorne Yesteryear and other accounts

to *Frank?* I need not have been concerned, for he stopped what he was doing, looked at me, for a couple of seconds was expressionless, then and burst into hearty laughter. The other butchers, ever ready for a laugh, joined in. I was stunned! This turned to a feeling of personal pride.

HIS RESPECT FOR THE DEAD. Just before any funeral processions were to pass the shop, Frank would show his respect by dropping the window blinds, and while the cortège was passing the premises he stood silently to attention (with sometimes a meat chopper or knife in his hand at his side), whether customers were there or not. When the cortège had passed he would put up the blinds and resume work as before.

THE KING'S DEATH. On the morning (Wednesday, February 6th 1952) of King George VI's death, Frank gave the news to the staff, that had come through on his wireless as he was in his home preparing to go to Basingstoke Cattle Market. It was quite a shock to us all. We had not expected it even though the king had been ailing for sometime.

The king's funeral was nine days later, and widely televised. We had had a television set at home for some years (to our great excitement at first), starting off with a 12" screen one, and I do not recall what size applied at this particular time. The main coverage was to be at mid-day and early afternoon. In the morning, Frank told all of us on the staff not to return to work at the usual time 2.15 (when the shop opened in the afternoon), but to see all the funeral coverage and then return, concluding that he would be late opening the shop.

We were grateful to him and I took him at his word – saw all the coverage, though the latter part was a discussion by parties afterwards of the event, and returned to the shop at 2.55, to find it open, customers being served, with Frank and the other staff present, which had apparently been the case for some time. Frank, on seeing me back, gave me a black look for my innocent 'sin', but didn't dock my pay!

BROADMOOR PATIENTS' ORDERS. We received small batches of single orders for sundry meat items (such as sausages, occasionally steak or chops) and fish ones, from Broadmoor patients. These, which had been sent to us from the hospital en bloc, had to be prepared and billed separately, and all delivered there together. Days later they were paid for in one payment. Never did the patients' full names accompany the orders, but instead we were only given Christian

My Memories of Crowthorne Yesteryear and other accounts

names accompany the orders, but instead we were only given Christian names with them (which may not have been their real ones) – such as Jim, one herring; Bob, four sausages; and so on. I cannot recall there being any female names amongst them, so maybe those patients did not order from us. It was my understanding that either the patients were able to cook the items for themselves, or had it cooked for them specially, in the hospital.

Other shops in the village also received orders this way from the Broadmoor patients, including clothing ones. The patients had their own money to spend on the items and some were quite wealthy I was told.

The one-time Talmage butcher's/fishmonger's shop pictured in 1993, forming part of 'Preston House' where the family also lived. The shop is now (1995) Larby's, butcher's; Butties (a cafe) and Alan's, hairdresser's. Butties was where the Talmage fresh fish shop was, and the butcher's one was to the left (as now), while Alan's formed part of the Talmage's living accommodation.   (Photo - Shirley E. Peckham.)

Bob's DIY (fairly close to Larby's), the handyman's shop and garden centre, of Robert (Bob) Barber (corner of High Street and Napier Road, in Crowthorne), pictured in 1993, which previously was I. V. Scott's, Ironmongers, and as some people recall it, the premises of Morrison's, the dairy people.

(Photo - Shirley E. Peckham.)

CHAPTER NINETEEN
FINAL ON TALMAGE'S

HOWLERS. I have found, in the main, butchers are often jovial and fun-loving and despite Frank Talmage's shortcomings, which meant that the staff should never even contemplate larking about, we had some fun at the shop together. This was both when he was there, sort of behind his back, and on the rare occasions that he wasn't. He did not go away on holidays. The staff had two weeks a year for theirs.

So, by necessity, we ensured he did not know what fun and games we were up to a lot of the time! Don't be under any misapprehension, reader, that we did not work hard at the shop, we did, very hard.

It was Frank who brought us the news one morning that his friend, George Armitage (of Armitage's shop next door), had just been taken to hospital (we had seen the ambulance call and leave there). "Why?" we asked. "What's wrong?"

"He's swallowed his false teeth," Frank returned.

This sounded like a joke, but as Frank wasn't normally given to wit, I quizzed, "Swallowed his false teeth? How come?"

"He did it while laughing, his plate got stuck in his throat, the men were working on him in the ambulance as it left his shop."

Well, we believed it then and didn't know whether to laugh or cry over poor George's predicament, while hoping he would be all right, of course. George was a great laugher, and I hope the incident (which he recovered well from, though did not want it discussed) did not quell this trait of his. I expect he probably laughed with Frank sometimes. As Frank and Nora had many friends, I feel it likely that socially Frank was a far different personality from the one we experienced at work. "He was like his father (Edwin)," I've been told. I have no personal knowledge of him. *He* (Edwin, also a butcher, as mentioned) died long before I came on the scene. A very elderly one-time Crowthornian speaking to me recently of *Frank* Talmage, he knew well for many years, said, "He was a hard nut."

Further on the light side (no pun intended), Frank once asked a young assistant, fairly new to the shop, to "put the lights out," meaning lights (sheeps' lungs) for cat food, and the chap switched off all the shop lights. Another time an apprentice asked if he should wipe the "constipation" off the tiled walls, which were running with condensation.

Jim Beggs once came to the office and gave me a neat little *newspaper*-wrapped parcel (as all meat and fish was wrapped, with

My Memories of Crowthorne Yesteryear and other accounts

white paper under it, like with fish and chips in those times) and said, seriously, "That will see you through the week." I wasn't suspicious, for he had sometimes given me such as a few sausages wrapped up before. On opening the parcel straightaway, I saw to my horror two bullock's eyes looking at me! By which time Jim was back behind the counter grinning like the proverbial Cheshire cat!

When a gent customer asked Jim for "A nice piece of skirt," he replied, "You'll find that in the office." However, I never heard such a response when any man asked him for "a nice leg" of anything.

Frank always showed great concern whenever he was aware that any customer's spouse (male or female) was ill. He would ask the 'fit' party, each time he or she came into the shop, "How is (naming the patient) now?" etc. He would sometimes have the response from a man (which mostly applied), "Well, she's now complaining about everything." Frank would respond, "Oh, she's better then, that's always a sure sign of it."

BIRTHDAY BUMPS. When I reached my 18th birthday, a work day, several members of the staff (the fishmonger of the time included) suddenly burst into the office, took hold of my hands and ankles and bumped me up and down on the floor eighteen times. My back, and the rest of me, seemed to withstand its repeated contact with the lino-covered floor, but I still called out "No! No!" protests – to no avail. Their task completed, they set me back on my feet, quipped, "Happy birthday Shirley," and happily trooped in line out of the office.

THE PONY. Margaret Jane Talmage, Frank and Nora's young daughter, had a pony she kept in a field in Wellington Road, and sometimes brought it to the back of the shop where the family had a garden and lawned area. One day Margaret Jane and her mum suggested I mount her pet and, after some hesitation, I did so. But only for a long enough period to be photographed on it!

STAFF UPSET. Periodically at Talmage's staff, individually, walked out, having had enough of Frank and his ways which had reached a peak. They would take off their apron and smock and determinedly leave the shop. Frank, concerned, would go after whoever was involved each time, catch up with him in the High Street and plead with him to return to the shop. I presume he also apologised and said he would mend his ways. The staff always returned to the shop with him and resumed their work. Frank would be noticeably pleasant to the man after this, for a couple of weeks.

My Memories of Crowthorne Yesteryear and other accounts

Once Frank severely irritated me, as he did Dorothy sometimes when she was there. After days of trying my patience, I could stand no more. I needed some information from him (only he could give me) before I could carry out certain bookkeeping work, and after asking him several times for this, over a couple of days, he appeared to be totally ignoring my enquiry. Then one morning he came into the office for his own purpose, when I asked for the information again. This caused him to turn and look at me, though he said nothing, before ignorantly turning his head away from me again. With that I slapped closed the ledger I had been working in and winged it his way with force! It just missed his head, crashed against a cupboard door behind him and then onto the floor. Frank, speechless, looked at me again, this time with surprise and horror! I burst into tears and fled from the office, towards his living accommodation at the back of the shop, dragging my coat I'd grabbed behind me. Nora saw me pass their kitchen window and came outside to ask, "What's the matter, Shirley?"

I soon told her and she replied, "I thought it would be him," and invited me into the house. There she said, "I'll put the kettle on for some tea and get the biscuits out. Stay as long as you like or go home if you want to."

I replied, "Thank you, but who will take the customers' money in the office?"

She responded, "*He'll* have to, it'll serve him right, he's always upsetting somebody, *me* included," something of which I was aware! She used to confide in me over various incidents.

I gratefully stayed with her for forty minutes, having the refreshments, then went back to the office and carried on with my work as before. Frank was doing his work, normally. At the end of the day I apologised to him for my out-of-character action from his causing my patience to snap. He replied, "Thank you, that's all right, I deserved it."

A CUSTOMER UPSET. Frank would upset customers from time to time, who would afterwards say to me, "But I keep coming because he and his place are always so clean and his meat always very good." So he got away with it usually.

But one day his actions ensured one lady customer was badly affected. Legs of lamb were regularly in short supply, because too many people wanted them, and Frank would accordingly say to me that, when taking orders, I must try to "push" the shoulders, or part shoulders, instead of legs, onto customers who phoned the shop for them.

The particular lady, who was a pleasant, quiet-natured customer of

My Memories of Crowthorne Yesteryear and other accounts

some years standing, came into the shop and asked Frank for half-a-leg of lamb, which was an unusual request for her. He sold it to her, though with some hesitation, *I* noticed, but don't think she did, for he was short of legs again that day. After wrapping it, he put it in her shopping bag and she came over to the office to pay. But before she did so another lady customer came into the shop – one of Frank's favourites who would never buy anything other than what she requested. She too asked for half-a-leg of lamb. With that, Frank unhesitatingly dashed over to the first customer, then, by the office and without a word, took her shopping bag from her, removed the parcel of meat from it, unwrapped it as he returned to the second customer (who wasn't really aware of what he was doing), quickly picked up half-a-shoulder of lamb, weighed and wrapped it, then darted over to the first customer again (who *was* aware of events) and put it in her bag, saying to me at the same time, "Same price." He then went and sold the half-leg to the second customer.

The first one retained her dignity and paid for the half-shoulder, after which she said to me, "Shirley, I will never come into this shop again, no matter what. His meat may be good, his shop clean, but ..." (his principles of course didn't match these, according to her recent experience). I did not blame her for her decision and was sorry I would not see her in the shop again.

RUDE RESPONSE. On an occasion when Frank, as usual, was busy in the shop but with no customers there, a business associate of his, I knew well also, phoned and asked me if he could speak to him. I put my hand over the mouthpiece (my regular practice when I had to call out anything to any of the men from a phoned enquiry, in case the necessary *shouted* back answer was not – or not in its fullest form – for the ears of the caller) and called out to Frank that the fellow wanted him on the phone. He replied with irritation, "What does the b----- want?" I replied that I didn't know, but would ask him, whereupon I said to the chap on the phone, "He wants to know what the b----- wants!" He responded, "That doesn't surprise me with him. Tell him I'll try again another time, when I hope for better luck!"

FRANK AND THE PRESS. One year, while I was at the shop, a patient escaped from Broadmoor Hospital. There had been a handful of such incidents in my life before, causing some unease in the village. I cannot recall who was concerned this time (or when, exactly, the incident occurred), but maybe it was John Straffen, who slipped to his freedom for several days in 1952, when I was eighteen. Frank

My Memories of Crowthorne Yesteryear and other accounts

Talmage was somehow involved in incidents following the escape – *not* in any way with it – and before the capture. I have forgotten the details, but they and he grabbed the attention of the local press, of course, and, from them, rapidly, the national press. Frank was in great demand by newsmen and had difficulty carrying out his work as well as attending to the pressures of the media.

However, he did both well, for a while. In the meantime, I was having to take constant phone calls day by day from the Press Association in London and national newspapers, all wanting to speak to him. He could not have known whether he was on foot or horseback half the time, as he was continually dashing from shop to office and phone, back to shop, back to office, etc. And in the shop, customers, the press and others, were forever wanting to talk to him about it.

He gave a series of interviews on his story to local and national newspaper reporters, who were among those who descended on Crowthorne like flies and headed into the shop.

Frank, I felt, coped with it all magnificently and may have enjoyed a lot of it to an extent. He appeared to like being the centre of attention over this and may have seen it as being good for business also.

However, when he came to read the various reports in the national press of what he was *supposed* to have said, none was accurate! He was furious, and said, "I would never have given them the interviews if I had had any idea of what would happen! I'll never help newspaper reporters again! *Or* believe everything I read in the papers!" He remained downcast over simply that for a couple of days, when I was aware of feeling sorry for him, considering the contrasting part he had played so unrelentlessly in the affair.

RATIONING. During the days of rationing, fish was not involved, but meat was. I had to cut, with scissors, small 'fiddly' meat coupons from customers' Ration Books and send them weekly to the Food Office at Bracknell. This was every Monday morning concerning those from the previous week. I cannot recall the amount of meat per person per week on the system, but it definitely was not enough for some. Possibly, I can't be sure, offal was exempt from rationing.

Besides the time of rationing – years, I think – there were times when certain items of meat were in short supply at Talmage's. Customers who wanted to buy them didn't of course 'want to know' about this, and were really dismayed, almost disbelieving, if their desired choice was unavailable. This led to us devising a system, from my idea, of referring to various meats in a kind of code when necessary between us, to, as far as possible, prevent customers from being upset.

My Memories of Crowthorne Yesteryear and other accounts

It was particularly necessary when any of them phoned the shop and, from my taking their calls in the office, I had to call out to the butchers to ask if certain meats were available, some of which were but in very short supply. Otherwise in calling out their response to me the butchers could 'give the game away'.

Rabbit became 'tibbar', veal 'leav', pork 'korp', liver 'rivel' and so on. The system worked well and no customers ever asked if we were in part speaking a foreign language in the shop! Sometimes, then, I could sell certain types of meat in short supply to a customer, who had phoned for it, without one already in the shop, who also likely wanted it and who would have to be disappointed, being otherwise aware. That customer in the shop would then be less perturbed.

After the war and while rationing was still in progress, Frank introduced whalemeat to the shop, the first butcher's shop in the village – and always the busiest, with most customers – to do so). This was to help out the situation of meat shortage generally and Frank hoped it would 'go down well' with customers, while being aware that its low price, 2/- (10p) a pound, would be appealing. As was often the case at the shop, particularly the fish shop, advising customers on products available and their prices, a notice chalked on a board was put 'out the front' giving news of the whalemeat in stock.

The whalemeat resembled liver in appearance and had a slightly fishy taste – otherwise one of its own. Not surprisingly, it was viewed by customers with suspicion at first. However the adventurous, daring ones soon bought it and in no time sales picked up. It became quite popular and we always sold out. Word got round that it was 'cheap and cheerful', which alone made it a winner with some, and of course it was the appealing, fat and bone free.

JOINED BY MARY. For a short time during my long employment at Talmage's, my cousin Mary Woodason (my Maurice and Aunty Chris's daughter, younger sister of Maurice, junior, now of Owlsmoor, and the late David), of Ellis Road, came to work in the office with me. It may have been only on the busy Saturday mornings, at least at first, then the other days too. However, the work did not suit her and she left by mutual agreement with Mr Talmage.

HOWLERS CONTINUED. The butchers, in Frank's absence, once locked me in the walk-in meat fridge, after I fell for their "just take a look at (something they mentioned) in there for a minute." Animal carcases and pieces of meat hung about on steel bars and offal lay on a block. From locking the inches-thick, wooden door – with a handle only on the outside – they switched off the light by the only switch, also outside. I dare not move lest any of my bare, or indeed clothed, flesh touched some of the meat. My shouts of *"Let me out, you fools,"* went unheeded and I was left there, distinctly uncomfortable for several minutes, before they put the light on and opened the door. Of course, they all wore mouth-organ-size grins and as I went by them, trying to preserve some dignity, I quizzed, "So that was funny, was it?" They were then laughing so much, and bent double with it, that they could not respond. Can my claustrophobia of today be blamed on the incident, I wonder?

Another time one of them put spoonfuls of salt instead of sugar in a colleague's mug of tea, who unsuspectingly took a huge mouthful before spitting it yards, not the way of any stock I must add!

A fishmonger, of the successive ones there, put sprats and, at other times, ice-cubes, down my cleavage, when my dress or blouse allowed. But none of the men could be blamed when a wasp once walked into the back of my sleeveless dress, via an armhole, and stung me near my spine, causing Nora Talmage to render first aid to me in the bathroom of her home.

ATTEMPTS AT CHANGING MY JOB. On more than one occasion I came close to relinquishing my post. I liked my work, the staff, *and* the customers, mainly, some of whom tried the patience of us *all*. Also the place was 'handy-home' for me. Frank though was regularly difficult and unreasonable as my boss.

I applied one year for a clerical post at the electronics firm Racal at Bracknell, where my cousin Denis Evans was working. The interview went well, after which the interviewer said, "This is not a place where you are interviewed for a job and then go away and never hear another thing. We'll be in touch." I never heard another thing!! Why are some prospective employers like this, I wonder? As my experience relates, it's not just today it happens.

Anyway, I probably would have had some travelling problems to and from there at times, had I acquired the post.

Frank riled me one Saturday, by insisting I work overtime one evening when I had a pre-arranged social commitment for then. It led to me carrying out the work and, as he was out, leaving him a note to say I was leaving his employ and therefore would not be at work on Monday. I went to the event late.

On the Sunday he came unannounced to my home, to my annoyance. Mum said to me, privately, "You'll have to speak to him, take him to my (and Dad's) bedroom and see what he has to say." This was the only available room suitable at the time.

We sat on chairs by the double-bed a yard apart, facing each other, and Frank poured out his regrets of events associated with my decision, apologised and finally said, "Will you please come back? I will mend my ways." I was determined, after making my decision, that I'd not be coaxed to change my mind, but three things altered this. He had apologised, etc., he was of mellifluous manner as he sat there, though I shouldn't have fallen for that, and I wanted him out of the bedroom and away from our home so that I could resume enjoying my Sunday. After briefly issuing ultimatums, therefore, which he agreed with, I told him, "All right, I'll return." He went away, chuffed, and was pleasant towards me for the following two weeks at the shop. Unfortunately he could never keep this up for longer in any such situation, regarding anyone!

LOSING THE INCHES! In 1955, aged nineteen, I embarked on my first serious diet, from the instructions on a leaflet given to me, as requested, by Dr Chapman. At first though, in his surgery, from my telling him of the problem, he said, "Oh dear, not another! I have fat people coming here wanting to be thin, and thin people coming here wanting to get fat. You are not overweight. But pop on the scales." He soon changed his tune when the reading revealed 13st 2lbs, "You *are* overweight!"

"Right!" he went on, "I'll put you on a diet, which you must follow to the letter. If you don't, I won't want to see you again for *anything*." Oh, his words reverberated through me like an avalanche! Finally, he advised, glaring at me (he always had one lens of his spectacles covered over white), "And remember, no sugar means no chewing-gum even. There is sugar in the coating that gets down one's inside." I left the surgery, keen to get it right to please him and, and not least so of course, myself.

I struggled hard with the diet, which I carried out strictly, and was successful in losing three stones in several months. Customers in the shop and other people outside it were remarking, "*Well done! Don't you look nice?*" all the time, and at the dances I was getting more partners than ever before. But I wondered whether a particularly nasty septic thumb (from cutting it slightly when opening a tin of meat) I suffered during that time was made worse by the dieting – maybe caused it to develop? The doctor, from my asking him this, said that resistance to infection is indeed lower than usual at such times.

My Memories of Crowthorne Yesteryear and other accounts

I WAS ACCOSTED. I had been at Talmage's for less than a year when I was accosted in Pinewood Avenue, at the top of the hill by the Walter Recreation Ground, by a man aged thirty to forty in a white vet's van from Reading (the details were displayed on its side). I was going home for my lunch, soon after 1 p.m., and as I got to the place he pulled up, on the opposite side of the road to me, facing the way I had come, alighted and walked towards me beckoning me to stop. I thought he was going to ask me directions to somewhere. There was no other soul about.

I stopped and got off my bike and he put a leg each side of the front wheel and placed his hands firmly on the middle of the handlebars. Then he looked me directly in the face and said, "You're beautiful." I knew I wasn't and said so, at which he insisted. "You are, you're beautiful."

Unease mounting within me, I tried in vain to pull the bike from his clasp and told him I needed to get home for my lunch. Then, still grasping the bike, he said he wanted to meet me later on and if I didn't agree to it he would not let me go. "I'm going to the Allen's," he continued, "to attend to one of their pigs (the Allen family had a smallholding two-thirds down Pinewood Avenue, and kept pigs), and after that I want to see *you*."

"All right, what time and where? I'll meet you," I returned, calling his bluff, in an attempt to escape.

"At quarter to two, just past the Allen's," he said, releasing his grip on the bike. Then, threateningly, "*And don't you let me down, or I'll come looking for you!*" With that he returned to the van and called out of the window, before driving off, "*Don't forget, don't let me down!*"

It was my half-day from work. Continuing to feel uneasy, I continued my journey home. The van, and no sign of him, was parked outside Allen's and I shot by it. Glennis, my eldest sister, was the only one at home. I told her of the incident and, amused, she asked, "Will you be meeting him?" I nearly responded, "Of course!"

I told her I was going to grab a bite to eat, then go and get a view of the road from behind our garden fence by our front gate, through knotholes in it, to see what the man did from leaving the Allen's. Glennis, still amused, came with me and we crouched behind the fence together. This caused us to giggle. Ten minutes later the man appeared, climbed into the van and drove very slowly down Pinewood Avenue towards us. He stopped the vehicle on reaching Pinewood Avenue/Ellis Road crossroads, 150 - 200 yards from where we were, and looked about him while remaining in the van.

This he carried out for some time. I was concerned that he might at any moment leave the van and come looking for me on foot. If he showed any sign to, I knew we would have to run very quickly into the house and lock the door. Glennis, who didn't seem to want to see the serious side of the business for a second, said in fun, "In a minute I'll stand up and shout, *'Here she is, come and get her'!*" I gave her an unsisterly nudge!

At 1.50 the man slowly turned his van and equally slowly moved off into Ellis Road, heading towards Old Wokingham Road, and I guessed and hoped that was the last I would see of him and the vehicle.

However, one Sunday evening some months later, while being driven by friends in a country area on the outskirts of Reading, I saw what may have been the same van (I hadn't taken note of the number of the one in *the* incident as I would today) in the driveway of a smart-looking house. And thought, is this the offender's home?

INVITATION DECLINED! A short and chubby, bespectacled, elderly, henpecked husband (noteworthy and respected locally), a Mr D., used to come into Talmage's shop regularly with his smartly-dressed wife, and while she was buying their meat he would toddle over to the office with his walking stick and engage me in general conversation.

He then began bringing me gifts, first the odd sweet, then boxes of sweets, or chocolates. I enjoyed them all, which he always passed to me discreetly behind his wife's back, literally, as she stood yards away at the counter choosing their meat.

My next present from him was a beautiful butterfly-shaped brooch with white and amber stones, I still have today. Then, on one of our quiet Monday mornings I was helping the butchers by cleaning the outside of the shop windows, when I saw the old man with his stick toddling along the footpath towards me. He stopped when he reached me and began chatting. I was responding, though by my also carrying on working it should have made it obvious that I did not want to be held up. Then, suddenly, he said, "She's gone away for a week, to London, do you want to come up?"

Gathering what he meant, though surprised and not wanting him to know I understood him, I made eye contact with him and quizzed, naively, "She?"

"My wife. She's gone to London for a week. Are you coming up?"

"Up where?" I turned away from him and carried on with the windows.

"To our house, while she's away?"

"*Good gracious, no!*" I returned. "*I am far too busy for that.*"
"So you're not coming then?"
"No, my time is always full. Now I must get on with my work, I have to soon finish these. And I've a full social life."

Looking totally dismayed and in almost disbelief he shuffled off, disconsolately, and didn't speak to me, alone, at the office again, nor anywhere else I encountered him. And, of course, I had had the last of his gifts!

The next morning I confided in Nora Talmage of the incident. She was astounded. "*No, Shirley, you surprise me!* Whatever was he thinking about? Don't tell anyone else, *please*. It would kill his wife."

THE WANDERING HAND! Broadmoor nurses, formerly attendants, were always held in esteem in Crowthorne, which I expect still applies. But indeed one, a Mr H., aged in his late thirties or early forties, who was always known as a respectable family man from the estate, with a wife and two children and a customer with his wife at Talmage's, seriously blotted his copy-book with me one day.

It was my half-day from work, one Monday, and I was going by bus to Reading. Waiting by the Prince Alfred for the bus, I saw the man there alone, who came over and started to chat in a general way, similar to how he did in the shop. When the bus arrived, I got on it ahead of him and he came and sat by me. He heard me ask the conductor for a return ticket to Reading and did the same.

We hadn't got far into the journey, when the man suddenly, without looking at me, put a hand on my knee. *Very* surprised at this, I said nothing and handed it back to him, whereupon he returned it straightaway to my knee. This continued several times and I was returning his hand to him more forcefully on each occasion!

This seemed to incite him to go further, for then he placed it higher up my leg, to part-way under the hem of my dress. Without wanting to alert other passengers, or the conductor (this I was sure I could deal with myself), I then pulled his hand away even more forcefully. That didn't deter him either, who remained speechless and expressionless throughout, for as we arrived on the outskirts of Wokingham he put his hand up my skirt to almost cover it.

Enraged I pulled it out and 'chucked' it at him furiously, saying, "*Please let me get out* (of the pair of seats), *I'm getting off here!*"

"*Here?*" he returned, "You're going to Reading, you bought a ticket for there."

"*I've changed my mind! It's Wokingham now!*"

"*Why?*" My scowl towards him while I moved down the bus aisle,

My Memories of Crowthorne Yesteryear and other accounts

leaving him sitting there, should have given him my answer.

As with the previous distasteful occurrence, I turned to Nora over the business the next day. *"Never?"* she responded, "He's a respected family man of this village, with two lovely children. *Please don't tell anyone else.* It would devastate his wife. What *was* he thinking about?"

Well, I didn't pass word of these matters on to anyone and don't have the answers to her questions. However, although I have always been a reliable secret-keeper, without using their names, I decided to tell you of these incidents, my reader.

Left, Shirley Woodason, aged twenty-five, in 1959, looking over the clothes-line while astride Margaret Jane Talmage's pony in the garden of 'Preston House', the family home and shop. Her navy-blue and white dress didn't seem to hide the fact that it was time she shed the spare inches again! But the pony didn't complain! (Photo - Nora Talmage.)

Right, Shirley Woodason, aged eighteen (left), with her eldest sister, Glennis, in the back garden of their home, 'Sydellen'. Shirley is wearing a black and pink skirt she sometimes wore to dancing evenings at the Agincourt hall, Camberley.

CHAPTER TWENTY
A DIRE EMERGENCY OVER MY MOTHER

SWELLING OF THE NECK. Sometime (which *my* memory tells me was in my childhood, but which each of my sisters, independently, consider must have been in my early twenties, according to *their* memories, adding that the event was after they had married and left home) my mother developed a swelling on one side of the front of her neck.

She had for years, at least through my childhood and beyond, suffered from asthma and allergy problems, house dust and open fire ash dust being two of the causes. Dr Chapman diagnosed an over-active thyroid gland being responsible for the throat swelling which, he added, would need to be operated on months later when it was 'ripe'. In the mean time Mum was to drink an obnoxious mixture of iodine and milk several times every day. She would hold her nose to do so, so as to taste it as little as possible.

PANIC STATIONS! I was still in bed early one morning and Dad was up preparing for work – in fact had just left our bungalow to go to the shed to get his bike out, when the emergency arose. Suddenly I heard alarming choking noises, that had started by small coughing sounds, coming from where Mum was still in bed, in the bedroom across the hall from mine. I leapt from my bed and raced there, where Mum was propped up on an elbow and grasping at her throat with both hands, looking terrified while the choking noise continued.

Having quick presence of mind in the situation, I raced through the bungalow to the back door, hoping I could catch Dad before he left for work. I was in luck, for as I opened the door he was passing it with his bike. Another minute and he would have been right away from the premises. "Dad, quick, put your bike down, come to Mum, she's choking, possibly to *death!*" I yelled. Certainly this was how the situation looked to me.

We charged through into Mum, who was still making the choking noises and grasping at her throat with her eyes bulging. Dad advised me, frantically, "*Get the bottle of brandy!*" I raced and got it from our living-room. He used something to try and get the cork out, but it would not budge – instead it broke up and bits of cork fell into the liquid. Eventually he gave Mum some of the brandy and she began to improve a little.

We could not have had a phone at the time, and neither did our immediate neighbours, so Dad told me, *"Quick, go and get the doctor, tell him how bad your Mum is!"* I threw some clothes on and discovered, on getting it out, that my bike had a very flat tyre, maybe a puncture. But there was no time to pump it up!

DOCTOR IN NIGHT WEAR. I was soon charging on it along the gravelly Ellis Road, to the tarmacked New Wokingham Road and to Dr Chapman's house and surgery, Quatre Bras, on the corner of Duke's Ride and New Wokingham Road. He answered the door, wearing pyjamas, a dressing-gown, and bedroom slippers. I told him the story in rapid fashion. "Right, you go back home," he replied. "And I will follow you, probably passing you on the way."

When half-way along Ellis Road, on my return journey, the doctor in his small car overtook me. And when I arrived home the car was outside my home, together with an ambulance. A few neighbours had gathered by our gate and more were to arrive there.

HOSPITAL. As I reached our back door, Mum was being stretchered out by the ambulance men, now quiet and no longer choking, but looking very pale. She was duly loaded in the ambulance and taken to the Royal Berkshire Hospital, Reading.

It was about 8.50 a.m. when the ambulance pulled away from our home. I went indoors, to where my father had remained and Dr Chapman was with him, still in his pyjamas, dressing-gown and slippers. He left soon afterwards, and Dad went to work also.

CYST. A few hours from her initial attack Mum was operated on at the hospital. With Dad, I visited her the next day, when her neck was heavily bandaged and she was pallid-looking. "Thank you for helping to save my life," she whispered. "I nearly died didn't I?" I didn't reply and she went on, "I'm sorry if I frightened you."

I told her, "You couldn't help it," and added, "What caused it?"

"Well," she said, "It wasn't thyroid trouble after all, I had all that nasty iodine in milk for nothing." I was aghast, especially knowing what she had to go through in having to keep taking it while the swelling grew!

"What was it then – the lump?"

"A cyst on my windpipe, which was gradually closing it as the cyst grew. It had almost closed my windpipe completely when I began all that choking. If I had been on my own I probably would have died." I shuddered at the thought.

"So our doctor made a mistake?" I quizzed.

"It appears he did not recognise the real trouble," she replied. And we said no more on the particular matter other than she continued, "The doctor here said I will have a fine, silver-coloured, scar around the base of my neck when it heals for the rest of my life, but I'll be able to hide it with choker necklaces and high-neck blouses or jumpers."

HER HOMECOMING. After a week in hospital Mum came home, still wearing a bandage, but far less of it than before. She was weak at first, but improved day by day. And from a red, very fine scar, it gradually turned to a silver one. Mum made a good recovery and more than once said to me, "How would you like to have your throat cut open from ear to ear like I had done?" Well, I certainly didn't say I would do!

INQUISITIVE NEIGHBOURS. Not surprisingly, nobody I told believed my account of Dr Chapman coming to see Mum in his pyjamas – though the folk at the gate had seen this for themselves, of course. People in those times always showed much interest in neighbours' medical problems and when an ambulance (I cannot recall them having sirens or flashing lights then) came to anyone's home, this mounted, and up to twenty people would gather to watch the proceedings. Naturally, everyone was concerned and sad at the tragic events, but folk appeared to be put on a 'high' seeing the patient on a stretcher, especially if they also caught a glimpse of the stricken face. They would talk about it excitedly, "I saw his (or her) *face*!" Definitely it was a moment of one-upmanship!

My Memories of Crowthorne Yesteryear and other accounts

Sarah Ellen (Helene) Woodason in the 1950s, in healthier times.

CHAPTER TWENTY-ONE
IN YOUNG WOMANHOOD

GRAN'S DEATH. Having been ailing for some time, my Gran Woodason died fairly suddenly in the mid-1950s when I was in my early twenties. I was aware she had been suffering from dropsy, now referred to as water retention. Dad brought me the sad news of her death at Talmage's, while on his way home from work one afternoon. I felt very sad. Mum, on holiday on the Isle of Wight at the time, came home in time for the funeral at St. Sebastian's Church.

CROWTHORNE FARM ESTATE. In or about 1952, preparations were well ahead for the building of the Crowthorne Farm Estate. It was not going to affect us in our family much. I do not think builders' lorries and so on were to pass our home for it and, when built, residents would not be driving by either, for the farm building itself was to remain, and is still there. If I am right, the entrance to the estate is in Old Wokingham Road.

However, the effect on us was, the local council concerned contacted my parents, before the estate was built of course, to ask if they would agree to having sewage pipes to the estate taken through our garden. These were to be laid from the roadway outside our premises, along our driveway at an angle, and, again at an angle, through our back garden, to the farm field at the right of it, where a number of the homes were going to be built.

My parents had to think seriously about this, weigh up the upheaval situation concerned while the work was going on, consider if there could be any problems at any time after the work was done (if they agreed to it) and if not for them themselves, for any future owners of the property. They were offered compensation from the council, but also had to decide how this measured up 'longside the other considerations.

They came to agree to the idea and the work was carried out late one summer. We had a certain amount of bother and there was the inevitable mess to contend with because of trenches having to be dug for the pipes to be installed. But the workmen minimised the inconvenience and lifted shrubs in their 'path' with the greatest of care, afterwards replacing them just as carefully. Overall, we felt they could not have done a better job. Commendable! And we came to have no trouble from the pipes having been laid there – for a length of about 200 feet.

ACCIDENT WITH OUR GAS GEYSER. Dad had always been the one to light this, in our bathroom, to ensure it was done correctly, mainly because of the dangers. But one afternoon, while he was outside gardening and Mum wanted a bath, she said to me, "Can you put the geyser on for me, to save your dad having to be called in from the garden." I hesitated, not liking gadgets and being aware of the possible danger of this, too, then agreed to it because the operating instructions were on a card hanging on the geyser.

I took a box of matches into the bathroom and nervously followed the instructions before me, line by line. Lighting a match when appropriate, I held it the way of the geyser. Result, there was a terrific explosion and I shot from the room like a deer in flight, into the arms of my shocked mother who was alarmingly on her way there to see what had occurred. "What the heck happened?" she shrieked.

"It blew up!" I replied. "But I'm in one piece and not even dirty."

Dad dashed into the house looking shocked and disturbed, and thrust at us, "*Whatever's going on?*" We told him and *he* exploded! "You know *I* always put that on, why didn't you call me in?"

The bathroom was in a mess, with the geyser, particularly, blackened and the inside of the bath had debris in it. Dad summoned the gas company who said the geyser, old anyway, would have to be replaced. The replacement was a new, modern, water *heater* – the word 'geyser' had been dropped from apparatus of the kind. The water-heater could be operated easily by anyone. However, that did not prevent me from always being wary of its use!

DIRT TRACK RACING. With or without boyfriends, I went with my sisters and/or girl friends to watch dirt-track racing at California-in-England, near Arborfield Barracks, some Sunday afternoons. We found this thrilling and there were spills, some serious, that used to worry us a bit, especially when any rider was taken to hospital. On one of the early occasions we went there, we saw what looked like a superb place to stand and watch the racing (no one else stood there, like they did everywhere else around the track). But we soon knew why the place was unoccupied, for during the next race we had dirt 'thrown' all over us from the bikes shooting round a corner nearby. We never stood there again! We cycled to these events and always arrived home grubby and over-warm. However, we would have a bath, our tea, and soon be leaving home again freshly dressed to catch the coach at the Prince Alfred, to return to Cali. for the Sunday evening dances.

DANCES. The dances were *every* Sunday night (7.30 - 11.00) and I attended *every* week for a spell of three years, besides other weeks before and after that period, in all weathers and sometimes when feeling under the weather! I once went with a raging toothache, from which I had to have a tooth extracted the next morning. I just couldn't miss the events, that were always so good. Many of the men who went there were soldiers from Arborfield Barracks.

The dance-hall was on the first floor of the two-storey building, that later was burned down and the bar was in a separate building nearby. There was a cafe area to one side of the dance-hall itself.

On the stage there was always a live band, very often the popular Bob Potter one, who was a fantastic drummer. There would be a mix of modern and old-time dancing, but mostly the former. Guest vocalists included, on one occasion, the famous popular duo, Pearl Carr and Teddy Johnson, and another week I was told that a player in the band was a brother of Max Bygraves, but I never gained proof of this.

The ballroom had a superb floor – perfect for dancing on, and in the centre was a section of squares of opaque glass under which coloured lights flashed on and off. They were particularly in use when the main lights in the hall were dimmed. Also there was a revolving glass ball hanging from the centre of the ceiling above the opaque glass section, that in its turn gave a dancing-lights effect on the walls and floor. When slow 'smoochy' dances were in progress, towards the end of the evening, the dimmed lighting effects gave a very romantic situation, which caused us to dance very close to our partners.

Part of the Crowthorne Farm house, in 1993.
(Photo - Shirley E. Peckham.)

Hazel Wells, of Cambridge Road (now Mrs Sergison), left, and Shirley Woodason, on holiday in Jersey in 1953, after a 'rotten' sea crossing and the return one was worse! (Hazel was one of Shirley's dancing companions in their teenage years and beyond.)

CHAPTER TWENTY-TWO
MY SERIOUS BOYFRIEND RELATIONSHIPS

JIM AND I. At eighteen, my first real boyfriend was Jim Reilly, of Napier Close in the valley. He was twenty-five and his father (Christian name and that of his wife unrecalled) farmed at the time at Crowthorne Farm. Jim and his younger brother Pete helped their father there sometimes and that is where my sisters and I met them. Pete, though, sadly lost his life in a road accident. Following this, Jim and I began a relationship.

We had good times and I was taken by him and his parents in their car to visit relatives of theirs in Gloucestershire and Southampton. However, Jim did not want to learn to dance and go dancing. This being my great love, meant that the attraction was sufficiently strong for me to attend dances as often as possible.

Jim came to propose to me, but I had to refuse because I felt too young and unready to settle down. Also, the dancing situation was a considerable factor and my feelings for him were far less than his for me. It was very sad for us both when these elements meant we had to part. I had found him to be a very nice man.

JOCK AND I. At Cali. (the California-in-England dances) I met a tall, light-ginger-haired Scotsman, from Edinburgh, named John, known as "Jock", Ritchie, who immediately swept me off my feet! I was wearing a neat black dress with several cloth white daisies stitched randomly down the front, and as soon as we set eyes on each other there was mutual attraction. Jock was a corporal in the Queen's Life Guards and stationed at the Army Apprentices College at Arborfield Barracks as a drill instructor. We were soon dancing every dance together and I wasn't surprised when he asked to walk me home the six miles from the dance-hall, instead of my going by coach. Some of the other girls from Crowthorne agreed to do the same with men they had met that evening, and about four pairs of us walked the route together. It was a fairly mild, lovely moonlit night, very romantic.

Our walk took us along Old Wokingham Road, after we turned off Nine Mile Ride. We had stopped for many kisses on the way and eventually continued this, before parting, by the then sawmills in what we knew as Lovers' Lane (now Old Sawmill Lane).

Jock asked me to see him the next week at the dance-hall but with the greatest reluctance I had to refuse this for I was going on holiday to the Isle of Wight with my mother and sisters for a week. I felt torment about the situation, as I badly wanted to see him again soon.

However, we arranged to meet at Cali. the week after my holiday instead. I came to enjoy my break on the island, but kept thinking of him while away.

GOOD TIMES AND CONFLICT. Jock and I were soon courting seriously after we got together again. We attended dances together at Arborfield Barracks and Cali. and had eyes for no one else. He had a friend, Stan ("Nobby") Clark, who courted a friend of mine, Moira Griffiths (they later married, a week before I did), and often the four of us were together.

Jock came to my home, where my parents often did not know what he said because he was softly-spoken and had a very broad Scottish accent. I never had trouble with this though. We would also go to the pictures a lot, at Wokingham and Camberley, and had some trips to London for sight-seeing together.

On one occasion, after we had done this and were sitting in a railway carriage at Waterloo Station waiting for our journey home to start, a group of army apprentices from their college at Arborfield came to enter the carriage that, except for Jock and I, was empty. They spotted us quickly and immediately had twinkles in their eyes and banana-wide grins on their faces. Then one said to Jock, "Ai, Ai! Sir," and looked from Jock to me and back to him, before, "Would you rather we took another carriage?"

Jock replied, while running his eyes over the group, "*Gosh, yes and as far away from this one as possible!* Whatever are you lot doing here on the day I've come?" They didn't answer and shot along the platform out of sight.

We were very attracted to one another and after some time began heavy petting. This led to Jock wanting to 'go all the way' with me and I couldn't agree to it without us at least being engaged, and he had not even hinted at this let alone proposed. Nowadays the situation would be different, I expect I would not have hesitated, but then there was a stigma attached to such things. I thought of my parents too and did not want to let them down. They had always relied on my sisters and me to act sensibly, adding, "we know we can trust you."

When I refused and explained why, Jock said, "You can't really love me if you don't."

I replied, "And you can't really love me if you force me to against my will."

This happened time and time again and eventually we agreed to part because of it. I was broken-hearted.

Periodically we came together again, to part again soon after for the same reason. On one occasion we were together I said to him, "*Please*, if you ever come to be posted from Arborfield, say goodbye to me first, we have had such good times, been so close – don't just go."

"Of course," he said, "I'll promise you that."

One Tuesday morning, after not seeing Jock for some weeks in our apart-from-each-other situation, I arrived at work to hear Frank Talmage tell me, "There was a phone call for you yesterday afternoon (Monday, my half-day). It was someone called Jock."

"What did he want?" I asked anxiously.

"He said to tell you he was being posted from Arborfield, *this* morning," which was the one on which I was receiving the message, "and was ringing to say goodbye." I felt sick and only subconsciously carried out my work for the rest of the day. The days following weren't much better. Very gradually I got over it and him.

JOCK'S SECRET. Some weeks later Jock's friend Stan let me into a secret of Jock's, he had confided in Stan. This was, all the time Jock was courting me so strongly he was engaged to a girl in his native Scotland! I was staggered, though not by then sorry to hear of it. Stan continued that all the time Jock was courting me he did not know what to do, continue with his engagement or break it off and continue his relationship with me. In the end, maybe because of my refusal to his importuning, he chose to keep his fiancé.

JOCK'S SURPRISE LETTER TO ME. Many years later, when I was married and living in Germany with my first husband Gordon and our two children, I had a surprise letter from Jock who had somehow obtained my address (though did not say in his letter how). He also was living, temporarily, in Germany with his then wife and was there, now in civilian life, concerning his job as a representative of Budgen's the grocery chain.

In his letter he said he hoped I was happy, often remembered our good times together, and was happily married but without children. There was no address on his letter, so I could not reply to it. I felt very happy and honoured that he had written to me, which helped to make up for how our relationship had ended.

My Memories of Crowthorne Yesteryear and other accounts

Above, Glennis, left, and Shirley Woodason, teenagers, in the early 1950s, in a Broadmoor wood. (Photo - Joan Watt.) Below, Glennis with her mother, Sarah Ellen (Helene) Woodason, on holiday in the 1960s. (Dog unidentified.)

CHAPTER TWENTY-THREE
MY DANCING CONTINUES

SOME INCIDENTS CONCERNED. I had other short-lived amorous adventures, as well as 'light' associations, with partners at dance-halls in the area. And besides soldiers I was involved with at the Arborfield Barracks dances, on Thursday nights, I also had involvements with some soldiers at the Agincourt hall in Camberley. These were members of the RAOC and stationed at Blackdown and Ash. As with the Arborfield REME ones – as well as Jock, of course – they were from all parts of the country, an aspect I enjoyed and found very interesting. I was quite attracted to the Liverpool (Scouse) ones I met regularly and liked their accents.

Mostly the soldiers I had the company of in the Agincourt were pleasant and no trouble to me, but one became a nuisance. I wasn't keen on him and he continually pestered me even when, regularly, I was dancing with other partners. Eventually after a long time of causing me annoyance in the hall and spoiling my evening he went a little too far with his pestering, while we stood by a stack of chairs at one end of the hall. Extremely exasperated, I gave him a push and he fell backwards over some of the chairs, with his arms in the air. I then grabbed one of his hands and, without thinking, sunk my teeth into the back of it, leaving me shocked at what I had done as he screamed!

Men in charge of the event came over to us and asked me what the trouble was all about. I told them the whole story and they took the fellow outside and said he would have to stay there. I was concerned about leaving the hall myself at the end of the evening, in case he was waiting there to get his own back on me. But I saw no sign of him when I did.

The next week he was at the dance again, with his hand bandaged, and came up to me specially to say, "Your bite turned septic. I've had a bad hand all the week."

I replied, unsympathetically, "Good, I hope it's taught you a lesson." He did not reply and walked away.

Sometimes after the Agincourt dances and while my friends and I were awaiting our taxi for home, cars with men in would pull up and from the cars they would ask us, "Coming to a party?" We didn't risk it, and our declining brought, "*Icebergs!*"

One midnight I received a terrible shock. On arriving outside the Prince Alfred by taxi from the Agincourt, I collected my bike from the nearby flat behind Charles Mason, gent's hairdresser's (now Patricia Hurst, ladies hair stylist). My eldest sister, Glennis and her first husband, Roy Gibbons, lived in the flat at the time. On cycling alone down the hill of the unlit Pinewood Avenue, by the wooded Walter Recreation Ground, I saw in the shadowy area of bushes to my left (as I rode towards it) what looked like a cigarette glow. Someone was apparently there smoking. There wasn't a sound, except for what I was making.

Gathering courage, I continued riding, my path being three or four feet into the road from where the glow was. As I approached it, presumably the *man*, without a word, walked into the road towards my path. When, still cycling, I reached him, still apparently with the cigarette in his mouth, I was sufficiently close to the smoker to brush along the front of him with my left arm.

My heart was thumping from soon after I saw the cigarette glow till when I arrived, thankfully in one piece, indoors, where I started to feel easier. I never found out who the man was and why he acted like he did.

On a similar occasion, I had been to a dance, had returned home by taxi and had ridden my bike from Glennis and Roy's flat to my home. On arriving there, I cycled down our drive to be met by a man who had been dancing with me in the hall. He had cycled the six miles or so in the time I had waited for the taxi and travelled home in it, etc. Besides shock, on seeing him, I was greatly alarmed.

I pulled up before him and asked in a firm, raised whisper (as my parents' bedroom was nearby), "What *are* you doing here? What do you want?" They were silly questions, I suppose! He answered incoherently, and I continued, "If you try anything on, I will scream, very loudly, and my parents will come out, from their bedroom *there*," and I pointed to it.

He advised me to put my bike down as he wanted a few kisses. I obliged and that is all that happened, to my great relief. I then suggested he be sensible and get on his way back to Camberley, adding that I would see him at the dance-hall the following week. My heart was working overtime till I was indoors!

DANCING AT THE RMA, SANDHURST. On several well-spaced-out evenings over some years I attended special occasion dances at the Royal Military Academy, Sandhurst. I think they may have been at Christmas time. However, they were really wonderful affairs in a marvellous, large ballroom, with an equally marvellous band (or orchestra) playing each time.

Always the local Police Balls used to be held there, on which evenings people not attending, never me (it was by special invitation only), would joke, "This is the night to commit a crime!" One of the bands that played there sometimes was Ivy Benson's All Girls Band, with Ivy as leader and all female players. It was very popular.

Whenever I and some of my friends attended *any* dances at Christmas time, from my idea, we wore silver glitter in our hair that we had scraped from the front of Christmas cards. This would be 'picked up' by the lights in the often dimmed dance-halls and give the desired sparkle effect to our hair. By the end of the evening and the next morning, though, our scalps were very itchy! In my own case I wore clothes in particularly bright red, bright green, or black (sometimes a combination of them), with gold jewellery, to the Christmas season dances, and similar to the New Year's Eve ones.

MUM AND DAD'S VIEWS ON US. Mum and Dad said we were good daughters – having not really given them any trouble in our childhood and, particularly, as teenagers (also, as far as *I* alone was concerned, in to my twenties) before we left home on getting married.

Dad also said a few times, "If girls and fellers get themselves into trouble together and find themselves in the family way, the girl always has to take the can back." How right he was!

He and Mum were thoroughly relieved this didn't happen to us, and with them having three daughters they must have always been very anxious about it.

Once, I was being escorted home from a dance at midnight by four soldiers. We were on foot spread across Pinewood Avenue enjoying our conversation when, about 200 yards from our bungalow, a thunderous male voice boomed out from its direction, "Shirley, is that you?" It hit us like cannon-fire!

"*Blimey, who the 'ells's that?*" asked one of the soldiers.

"My Dad," I responded, disconsolately, "fancy him coming out like this looking for me."

"He sounds mad."

"Shirley, is that you, *will you answer me?*" Dad was more and more agitated, walking towards us, and I was somewhat fearful of what would happen if and when he reached us.

"Yes," I responded, "and I'm all right."

"Well, you're late and your mother and I can't go to sleep till you're in. Who's that with you?"

"Four men, who couldn't be nicer, escorting me home."

"Will you tell them to clear off now and come home with me."

The soldiers said, "We're going, we've got the message! Good Luck!" And they shot off down Ellis Road.

My Memories of Crowthorne Yesteryear and other accounts

I had hoped I might see them again, but my chances had been ruined.

When I married Gordon we were both virgins and I had been his first ever serious girlfriend, he said.

When news got round of my engagement to Gordon, we mostly received congratulatory messages, expressing their joy, from people, but a soldier friend of mine serving his national service at Arborfield Barracks said to me, solemnly, "Have you ever read the book *Married Quarters*?"

I replied that I had not done so and had not previously even heard of it. He advised I try and get it and read it. I quizzed him on the book's content, but he preferred to say no more on the subject – maybe did not want to concern me too much!

I then more-or-less ignored the comments, but obviously did not forget them, nor did I ever come by the book.

Many years after my conversation with the fellow I came to recall his words more and more, when my role as an army wife had times of distinctly showing me its downside and Gordon was so devoted to his career that I wondered sometimes if he was more married to it than to me. The marriage was a happy one however, but the army itself (as applying to him) on occasions got uncomfortably in the way for me.

And when, sixteen years after our wedding, Gordon betrayed me and our two children – aged fourteen and twelve – by taking on another woman during one of his enforced and prolonged service postings away from us, I thought of the message I had received from the national serviceman more than ever!

MY VIEWS ON MY PARENTS. As a relative on the paternal side of my family said recently, "They were like chalk and cheese." Yes, but nevertheless, and they would have their disagreements regularly without a doubt, their marriage held for over fifty years, which speaks for itself. They were devoted to us, their three daughters, and gave us every care and attention through the good and bad times, which never faltered. It was mainly Mum alone who took us on outings and holidays, while Dad's sense of humour brought laughs and many smiles at home. 'Helene' and 'Syd' died 3 1/2 years apart, in the 1980s, Mum following Dad, bringing the inevitable sense of loss and sadness.

CHAPTER TWENTY-FOUR
THE SANDHURST CADET

At the Agincourt hall one Saturday night I met a Sandhurst Cadet who came to partner me for successive dances. I believe the cadets were not really allowed to go there, by order of the academy, or sometimes this applied. At first – dressed in smart grey slacks and a dark-coloured smart blazer, with a badge on the lapel – I was unaware he was a cadet. When he told me, I was quite impressed at having him as a partner.

When the interval at the hall arrived, we were both very warm, having done so much dancing and with so many people there, and I told him I was going outside for a "breather", which I usually did in the interval when there. He said he would come with me and soon we were walking away from the hall, gently, towards the Duke of York. He then asked, "Where shall we go?" With walking along footpaths about the hall purely in mind, I replied, "I expect you know the best places." Only very much later, did I come to learn that this was apparently the wrong thing to have said!

He suggested we walk in the Royal Military Academy grounds. I felt this fine. There was still some daylight – which was fading fast though on the summer evening, and I knew it was pleasant there with large manicured lawns, trees, shrubs and a big lake. But I had no intention of going far. In fact my body had cooled down sufficiently long before we even entered the academy gates.

However, holding hands, we were both obviously enjoying the walk and as we were passing the lake, with it then practically dark, he took me in his arms and kissed me on my mouth gently, which I enjoyed. He did this on several spaced out occasions, between which we had moved near to the academy building itself.

Then he said, "Would you like to come to my billet?" At that, and why I don't know (though I had had little of *any* experience of either), I mistook the reference of billet to that of mess. And feeling he meant a place where other men (in this case), some with their female partners, would be gathered socially – as in messes – I agreed but, without making him aware of it, with some reluctance. I was still a somewhat shy individual and did not therefore 'feel' like being in the company of strangers in such an environment, instead wanted to continue my evening at the dance-hall. As I did not want to disappoint him by refusing, I decided I would go there with him, make the most of it and hopefully we wouldn't stay long.

Soon we were climbing the steps of the academy towards the door at the right of them, where the horse and rider go on the Passing-out

My Memories of Crowthorne Yesteryear and other accounts

Parade occasions. After he had opened the door we went through there and, inside the place, which was otherwise silent and deserted, he led me along a passageway to the left of the staircase. From there we came to turn right and walk along a corridor with closed doors on each side of it. After a while – and with still no one about and no sounds from anywhere – he stopped by one of the doors on our right and opened it, before saying to me "in there" and he beckoned me inside ahead of him.

I went in without hesitation, wondering all the time though of the quietness in the corridor and within the room for there should have been a cacophony of social chat filling my ears. When I saw inside the room my heart sank as I realised my unfortunate mistake of confusing the reference of billet and mess. Here I was in a modest-size room, sparsely-furnished (just adequate), with a single bed protruding into the centre of the room, its head against a wall – in the Cadet's *billet*. As I stood stock-still, speechless, by the foot of the bed, contemplating the situation, he, having slid into the room behind me, shut the door and turned the key in its lock. Then he immediately took it from the lock and put into one his trouser pockets, before drawing me towards him and kissing me again, this time more passionately.

This over, *"Take your jumper off,"* referring to my evening-top, *"and get into bed!"* he commanded. He'd already taken his blazer off and the alarm bells that had been ringing in my head reached crescendo point! But I knew I had to play the situation coolly.

"No!" I replied, "I didn't realise you meant here, I want to go back to the dance-hall and the dancing. My friends will wonder where I am. Will you unlock the door, please?"

"Get your jumper off and get into bed!" he repeated, more forcefully.

"No!" I advised again. *"Now open the door, let's go!"* I looked about the room, then at him. The expression on his face had changed. He was no longer the man I had met in the dance-hall. His eyes were lustful. My mother's teachings on my needing to beware of some men and situations with them flashed into my mind, as one of the Cadet's hands moved to the fly area of his trousers.

He again refused to open the door, adding, "and it's no use you screaming. There is no one here. They have all gone away for the weekend."

Feeling alarmed and petrified by this in my 'isolated', imprisoned situation, I forcefully reverted my mind to items in the room. Referring to a framed photo standing on a chest of drawers of a small group of people, I asked, pointing to the picture, "Who are these people? They look nice."

"My family," he replied, "they live near Oxford. Now get your jumper off and get into bed." And he again took me in an embrace, to which, like the other, I was barely responsive. "No, tell me about them, your family. Tell me who they all are in the picture."

"*Never mind about them!*" he returned, angrily. "*Get into the bed!*"

It should have been obvious to him then that I would never do this, as I said, "They're your parents in the picture, aren't they? And your brother and sister perhaps?"

"Yes, I am very proud of them."

"I should think you are. They look fine people, a lovely family. Now what would particularly your parents think if they were aware of what is in your mind in this room tonight." He looked thoughtful, but made no comment.

I then turned my attention to a chart hanging on the wall close to his bed, of square shapes, some with crosses filling them. "What does this represent?" I asked, referring to the chart itself.

"How long I still have to do," he replied. "Every day I mark off a square and it lets me see how long I still have to do to complete my time as a Cadet." He went on to tell me how long it was before his term was completed.

"Interesting," I concluded, "will you open the door now."

He did not respond at first, then slowly put a hand in his pocket and brought out the key. He offered it to me in the palm of his outstretched hand. I didn't take it, but said, "Thanks, will *you* open it or me?" He shrugged his shoulders slightly, then turned and unlocked the door. Grabbing his blazer, he beckoned me outside ahead of him.

I was very pleased to eventually be out of the academy building and down the steps, and we made our way back to London Road, lightly holding hands and periodically making small talk. When we neared the gates of the grounds, he suddenly said, "Thank you," as we walked.

Surprised, I asked, "For what?"

"For back there."

"But I didn't do anything, so .... "

"I am grateful. Most girls wouldn't have been like that. I appreciate how you were."

I was quite taken aback by his comments, but glad to have heard them in the situation. Then he went on, "I'll walk you back to the dance-hall, but when we get there I must leave you. You know why, don't you?" I didn't know, definitely, but guessed it was because he would need then to find a girl more willing than I had been with whom to spend the rest of his evening.

My Memories of Crowthorne Yesteryear and other accounts

Next morning Mum was flabbergasted at my story.

"You could have been *raped!*" she blurted. "You might be twenty-two, but you shouldn't trust men, whatever your age. I've told you before."

"But he was a *Sandhurst Cadet*, looked a real gentleman, and smart in blazer and slacks."

"It doesn't matter, they're all the same. This could have been a News of the World story. You could have been murdered."

"Well I wasn't raped, nor murdered, I'm here and believe I handled the situation well."

"You were lucky!" she conceded, scornfully, and if her look could have killed .... !

CHAPTER TWENTY-FIVE
GORDON, MY FUTURE HUSBAND

WE MET AT CALI. A year or so after the incident with the Sandhurst Cadet I met Gordon Robson, a REME corporal, at California-in-England dance-hall. He was with a bunch of other soldiers, all friends, and was tall, dark-haired and a good dancer. I was with friends too, as usual, and the fellows regularly danced with us all varying their partners. Then, increasingly, as our Sunday evenings at the dance progressed, Gordon was dancing with me more than with the other girls.

Except for his good way of dancing and my dancing well with him, I wasn't very impressed with him at first, considering him to be something of a show-off, which irritated me. I have never liked the trait in anyone. However, I came to accept it, or threw it behind me, and found myself liking him which eventually grew into my falling in love with him. But long before the latter he asked me for a date, for a weekday evening, at the Ritz cinema in Wokingham.

DATES. On the week concerned I had dates on two evenings with other fellows, for the Ritz. So I quickly had to decide on a third evening to meet Gordon there, who had invited me to choose one. I enjoyed all three of the occasions and on the final one wondered if the girl in the box office had noticed my three evenings at the cinema with different chaps that week. If so, she probably thought, good for her, or she doesn't seem the faithful kind.

Gordon confided in me after we had been courting some weeks that before we had started to go out together, and he wanted to discreetly find out more about me, he cycled to my home and rode by it to hopefully not only see it but to see if I was about. He was trying to get the feel of my home situation. However, I never saw him then and he didn't see me or my family. He always rode racing-type bikes and for a time a Claud Butler.

VISITS TO HIS PARENTS. Gordon took me to meet his family in Aldershot, where they had settled because his father Stan, a regular soldier, like Gordon's situation, was in the Royal Army Catering Corps. (I cannot recall if Stan Robson was still in the army when I went to visit them. But if not, he hadn't long come out of it.) Besides also his mother Sarah, known as "Sally", Gordon had a brother, Brian, in the RAF, about a year younger than him, and a much younger sister and brother, Sandra and Alan. Brian wasn't very often

My Memories of Crowthorne Yesteryear and other accounts

at home. The others were schoolchildren. I saw my being taken to visit the family, and the visits continued, as being a sure sign of our relationship cementing.

POSTING. Our love grew and I came to think of us hopefully marrying. But then Gordon received news of a posting to a unit in Germany. He was very devoted to his career so, although disappointed at leaving me, he went off enthusiastically, promising to write. I knew I would be writing and sending him many letters. He also advised, on my asking, "What will I now do with my social life, I'm so attached to dancing?"

"Still go dancing, have boyfriends if you want them, be happy, that's what is important to me."

I was quite amazed by his response, though pleased that I was to be allowed free rein in his absence, with his blessing. However, I was determined I would stay faithful to him. "Well, thank you," I concluded, "and this will be a very good testing time of our relationship." He agreed.

I MET BOB. So I continued with my dancing and at one of the Arborfield Camp dances soon met a fair-haired Scot, lance-corporal Bob (surname unrecalled) of the REME, who was short in comparison with the loftiness of both my previous boyfriends, Jock and Gordon, each being over six-feet tall. Bob was about my own height and quiet-natured. Also, he came to prove, a true Scot through to his marrow. He greatly loved his mother country.

Bob was not in the army long-term, as Gordon was, and, probably doing his national service, was only half interested in it. He suffered from athlete's foot and kept the trouble under control with creams, but once said to me he could probably get out of the army on medical grounds if he stopped treating the trouble and the condition stayed at its worst, while telling the powers-that-be he was regularly applying it! However he did not do this.

Bob had barely learned to dance, so wasn't very good at it. I coped with the situation all right, finding it worth my while when I realised I was warming to him. We had a good rapport from the outset. He was concerned at regularly treading on my toes on the dance floor, but I laughed it off each time and would playfully hug him and say, "Don't worry sweetheart, it's not bothering me."

OUR RIDES IN 'FLOSSIE'. Bob and I started to date. I cannot recall going to the 'flicks' with him, but may have done. Our dates were usually out in his old car, with weak-spring seats that nearly had one sitting on the car floor! He called the car 'Flossie' and she took us for lovely rides in the Berkshire countryside on summer evenings. We would stop at beauty spots for a while, also visit pubs on our routes. The extremely pleasant occasions always made us very happy.

Early in our relationship I mentioned Gordon to Bob, how involved with one another we were before he had to go away, and how we were writing to each other very regularly with the idea that when Gordon returned here for good (he would be home on leave on several occasions as well) we would resume our courtship.

I added, "But he said I should still go dancing and have boyfriends if I wanted them."

"Gosh, he's trusting, isn't he?" Bob replied, and I agreed. He continued, "Well, if you're happy to go out with me, we'll have to enjoy ourselves with the brake on. We mustn't let him down." I felt that was very nice of Bob, and that is what we did.

TO STIRLING 'OLD-BANGER-STYLE'. When I heard from Bob that he was going to drive to Scotland for five days leave, I jumped at the idea of maybe accompanying him there to visit my youngest sister Virgy and her REME husband, Bill, who lived in Stirling and were soon to have their first child, who came to be son Stephen. Bob agreed I travel with him in his old banger, Flossie (this being prior to 1960, MOTs hadn't come in). I was very excited at my romantic thoughts of sharing such a long journey, both ways, with Bob like this. When I booked my holiday at work there were twinkles in Mr Talmage's eyes over how I was going to travel to and from Scotland. My parents had no qualms about it. "We trust you, you'll be all right," said Mum resignedly.

TWO MORE PASSENGERS. A few days before we were going to leave on the trip, a Thursday, Bob told me, "Two of my friends from the camp are coming now as well. You don't mind, do you?" Because I was so keen to go, I could say no other really than, "No, of course not." But it dampened the situation for me for a little while as I considered, now I'll have to share Bob with them. However, I hoped that I would still have the front passenger seat. As mentioned, *all* were practically springless though.

STEERING FAILURE AND A CLOSE SHAVE! We left Crowthorne at mid-day on the journey that was to take seventeen hours, with Bob driving Flossie throughout. All was going reasonably well (we made a happy foursome and, yes, I did have my chosen seat), until we neared Carlisle, where one of the passengers was going to end his journey. Then the car's steering failed, sending Flossie snake-like across the road. "*Wow! The steering's gone,*" said always unflappable Bob in matter-of-fact style. He stopped the vehicle, before carefully driving to the home of the passenger who was to leave us.

Soon the father of the passenger came out and helped Bob and his son work on the car to get the trouble right. It took about an hour and a half, then we were on our way again.

But it was dark and about ten o'clock at night when, not far over the border into Scotland, we were coming towards a T junction, with a brick wall across the road immediately beyond it, when it looked to me as though the car was going to be driven straight into the wall! "*Watch out!*" I yelled to Bob, "*there's a wall!*" Flustered for a complete change, he pulled the car up sharp. "*Phew!*" he hissed, "thanks, sorry about that, I went to sleep. Keep talking to me, please, to keep me awake." I did so, non-stop from then on, even though I was tired myself. The other passenger remained fast asleep, curled up on the back seat, throughout!

Soon after we had crossed the border into Scotland, Bob said, "Flossie will be excited now, she always knows when we are nearing home." This tied in with his strong devotion to his beloved Scotland.

After a train ride from Glasgow, where Bob had dropped me off as he wasn't driving to anywhere near Stirling, I arrived safely at the home of Virgy and Bill and spent an enjoyable five days with them. The journey home, with Bob only, as the other two passengers we had had were on leave for longer, was uneventful compared with the Scotland-bound one. I enjoyed having Bob to myself this time.

My relationship with Bob gradually petered out over the next few months and he came to be posted from Arborfield. He had, however, meant a lot to me and has a distinct place in my memory.

GORDON'S RETURN. I was very happy and excited when Gordon came home on his first leave from Germany. He was to arrive at *my* home during the evening of a Monday. I had booked to have a perm in the morning, at Katrina's, the hairstylist in Duke's Ride. But on the previous Saturday I had contracted a serious dose of 'flu and had difficulty, because of it, completing my work at Talmage's that day. Nora Talmage, seeing the state I was in from the condition, gave me a ticking off for working till the end of the afternoon and not going home – with an obvious temperature and my throat on fire – much earlier.

I had to spend the rest of the weekend in bed, but decided to get up and go and have the perm on the Monday morning rather than cancel it, or Gordon would have seen me on his arrival at my home looking 'a mess'. I couldn't have that, the rest of my life might have depended on it! When my mother knew of my leaving my sick bed to have a perm she didn't hesitate in saying, "*You're a clot!*" unsympathetically. She never suffered fools gladly. I was concerned about possibly passing germs on in the salon. But I coped without my condition causing me any real problems and my action didn't appear to worsen it.

When Gordon arrived at my home, at about 7 p.m., I was back in bed sitting up and smiling at him as he entered my bedroom. My mother had already told him I had 'flu, but he didn't care, he said (meaning about possibly catching it himself), and made his way to my bedside.

Ignoring the germs, he was soon kissing me and kissing me, "You are still lovely, with your super hair-do, 'flu and all," he said. "I might even get in your bed in a minute!" Laughter made me cough and splutter. What a romantic reunion!

MY PROPOSAL IN GREEN LANE. So we resumed our courtship, often walking at night holding hands along the quiet roads and lanes of Crowthorne, stopping every now and again to embrace. Except for the little we made ourselves, there was barely a sound from anywhere.

One moonlit evening in Green Lane, Gordon held me in an extra lengthy embrace. Guessing his long-term intentions, matching mine I knew well, I asked suddenly as we drew apart, "Will you marry me?" It was not even Leap Year and I immediately thought, what *have* I done? *I* shouldn't have proposed to *him*, surely? However, he responded, "Yes," leaving me statuesque, then filled with excitement, and I thought, we are going to get married, how wonderful!

We continued our walk, while making plans in brief about our future together. Then Gordon said, "I will have to ask your Dad for your hand in marriage."

"*Surely not*," I replied, trying not to giggle, "I thought that sort of thing had died out."

"No, and I want to do it," he said, firmly. "Please arrange it for me."

I knew my dad would think this very funny and felt my sisters' husbands-to-be (they had married before me) had not carried this out.

Gordon also said that he would have to ask his C.O. if he could marry me. Even more surprised at this, I responded that he didn't even

My Memories of Crowthorne Yesteryear and other accounts

know me. "No," he said, "but it's routine, I have to ask him, *can* I marry, and give your name. But *who* I want to marry is far less relevant than I want to marry itself." He added that permission is unlikely to be refused, which he had never heard of happening.

Days later Dad had the expected chuckle and agreed to Gordon taking the last of his three daughters to marry, "*Off my hands!*" (Virgy had married two years after Glennis had done and I was going to marry two years after Virgy's wedding – in 1955, 1957 and 1959. We always said afterwards that we "worked this well to give our parents time to save up for the weddings each time.")

MY FUTURE MOTHER-IN-LAW. We had the blessing of our family and friends, but there was only one thing standing in our way, Gordon's mother, the now late Sarah (Sally) Robson. She felt our marriage-to-be (*any* marriage for him, I think) would have an adverse effect on Gordon's career! Then, abruptly leaving a family gathering at my home to celebrate our pending engagement, she and her husband Stan had been specially invited to, she refused Gordon's attempts to pacify her. Some weeks later she stirred things up again by reminding her son that I was three years older than he was. "I don't care if she's *thirty*-three years older than me!" retorted my loyal husband-to-be. He had very fond feelings for his mother, which cracked temporarily when she was like this.

THE RINGS. On what turned out to be a very wet pre-arranged day we went by bus to Windsor to choose an engagement ring for me. Excitedly, we went from jeweller's shop to shop and I saw the perfect ring to suit me in the window of one – gold with a zircon (turquoise-coloured) stone surrounded by diamonds. I hoped that the £30 asking price was not too much for Gordon, who hadn't given me any idea of what price range for my ring he had in mind, or would find suitable to his means.

The ring fitted exactly and Gordon happily bought it. I was then invited to choose my wedding ring at the same time. This came to be a plain gold one, just like my mother's, and cost £6. We left the shop jubilantly, with the boxed rings nestling in one of Gordon's suit pockets, and headed for a coffee shop.

There we enjoyed scones and coffee. But while still there we fell out! This was after I had asked Gordon if I could see the rings again, while we were in the shop. "No," he said seriously, "that is for later." I couldn't believe it and told him I was disappointed. We left the shop, not very happily. But this didn't last long.

My Memories of Crowthorne Yesteryear and other accounts

When we arrived back in Crowthorne I took Gordon straightaway to meet Nora and Frank Talmage in their home, it being the end of their half-day closing afternoon. I wasn't aware if they were in, or not, for there had been no pre-arrangement of our visit. They *were* there and were delighted I had thought of taking Gordon to meet them. We spent a happy twenty minutes with them, when they wished us a wonderful future together. Next day Nora made a particular point of saying to me that she and Frank were very grateful and impressed that I had specially taken Gordon to meet them, on our engagement day.

Later, on our special day (the morning had been very wet though while we were in Windsor, brightening afterwards), Gordon proudly slipped my engagement ring on my finger. It was a wonderful moment and we were very, very happy. The wedding ring was to stay in its box until the Big Day.

Left, Gordon Robson, REME corporal, the late 1950s, before he married Shirley Woodason, in St. John's Church, Crowthorne, in 1959.

Right, Cpl. Gordon Robson, REME, at the back door of Shirley Woodason's home, 'Sydellen', in 1959, before they married later that year. (Photo - Shirley E. Woodason.)

My Memories of Crowthorne Yesteryear and other accounts

Above, Shirley Woodason in her early twenties (early 1950s) with her "delightful" friends, Mary, Jeff, and little Sheila Ramsey, of Ellis Road. Below, Shirley Woodason, second from right, at Broadmoor, with other guests, following the wedding of their friends, Stan (Nobby) Clark of the REME, Arborfield Barracks, and Moira Griffiths, of White City, Broadmoor Estate, in August 1959. Diane Davidson is on Shirley's right and Stella Axford is on her left (man unidentified, possibly Diane's husband or who became so). *(Sorry about the feet loss!)*

CHAPTER TWENTY-SIX
MY SISTERS' AND MY WEDDINGS

GLENNIS. As mentioned, my sisters married ahead of me. Glennis's wedding was on June 25th 1955 (one week after my twenty-first birthday), her husband being Roy Gibbons of Frimley, who had been in the RAF. They met at Cali. dance-hall. Virgy and I were two of the bridesmaids. Glennis and Roy first lived in the flat in the High Street, Crowthorne, I mentioned in recent chapters, and then set up home in a new bungalow built on the plot of land, where we used to play as children in the little wood that stood on it next to our family home 'Sydellen'. My father and Roy (a carpenter) built the place together.

Glennis and Roy came to have a daughter, Caroline, but the marriage was dissolved after a few years. Glennis then came to marry John Priest, of Finchampstead, an employee of Mason's the coal merchants in Crowthorne. They have a son, David, and lived in Farnborough (Hampshire) for many years before retiring to New Milton, in the south of the county (where I live also), in 1989.

VIRGY. In 1957 Virgy married William (Bill) Fairless, of the REME, Arborfield Barracks and I was the single bridesmaid, in a pale turquoise dress. They too had met at Cali. dance-hall. Virgy and Bill went to live in Stirling, after he was posted there. They came to have three children, sons Stephen, Robert (Bobby or Bob) and Graham. After further stints with the army in Nairobi, Germany, and various UK units, Bill left the army after 12 years and the family settled in the New Forest town of Ringwood, where currently they are the proprietors of The Chocolate Box in the town centre.

SHIRLEY. So, even though the eldest sister, I was "left on the shelf", many told me. I heard it so often that I began believing it, but knew it unlikely that I would be 'an old maid'. My times of having fun, especially when dancing in wonderful company, continued, as did my job. Then along came Gordon and we planned to marry on the 29th of August 1959, my parents' twenty-eighth wedding anniversary, in St. John the Baptist Church, when I would follow in theirs and my sisters' footsteps.

To ensure Gordon and I were within our rights to marry in St. John the Baptist Church one of us had to stay for at least three nights, during the preceding fortnight, in the parish of Crowthorne. I lived in that of Wokingham Without, whose church is St. Sebastian's and Gordon

My Memories of Crowthorne Yesteryear and other accounts

was stationed at Arborfield Barracks. I therefore spent those nights at the home of Mrs Barbara (known as Louise) Burtwell in Cambridge Road, mother of my friend Barbara Burtwell, later Mrs Spong. Mrs Burtwell was an invalid at the time, suffering from arthritis. I was grateful indeed to her for allowing me this facility and after my wedding I surprised her by calling on her and presenting her with my wedding bouquet of pink rosebuds, lily of the valley and maidenhair fern. This was my special "thank you" gesture. She was most grateful to me and very touched.

I was in St. John's Church for the mid-morning services when I heard the banns called for our wedding. I can't be sure, but Gordon may have been with me on at least one of the three occasions.

At 8 o'clock on the morning of my wedding day (a glorious, sunny, late summer day), to the gratification of the Reverend Nugee, he laid on a special communion service at my request in St. John's church. The vicar made a particular point of saying to me, in the churchyard after the service, "I wish all brides-to-be would do that." Less than a dozen people attended, including Nora Talmage who accompanied me to the church.

During the morning, after the service, when I was back at home and fully relaxed leading to my 2.30 p.m. wedding, I decided to write a note of reassurance to Gordon in case he was feeling nervous about events ahead. He had been staying overnight in the flat we were to rent, at 'Bramlea', Wellington Road. After writing the note (below) I asked a friend of mine in Pinewood Avenue if she would hand-deliver it to Gordon for me and she agreed to do so. Gordon was pleased to receive my message, which he later passed to me and I still have it in its envelope:

"Sydellen", Crowthorne.
Saturday August 29th, 10 o'clock.

My Darling Gordon,

Good Morning, and what a lovely one it is. Let's hope it continues through the day. Well, I hope you are feeling OK, and not too nervous. As for me, I feel fine and very happy. It won't be long now before we are united together. Oh, darling, it's wonderful and thank you for being such a first-class husband-to-be. Now keep your chin up, darling. I love you for always. See you at 2.30.

All my love, Shirley XXXX

And when I joined him in the church, I whispered, "Hi, Mucker!" which was an army greeting, friend to friend, that we had adopted and

My Memories of Crowthorne Yesteryear and other accounts
used between us weeks beforehand.

I was on the arm of my father as I walked up the aisle to the strains of 'Here comes the bride', and as our slow walk along it began I was amazed to 'hear' a silent voice say: 'Are you sure you are marrying the right man?' It pulled me up, not literally of course, in that it had me wondering, is this a warning to me at this so late a stage? But long before I had reached Gordon's side I had dismissed such thoughts. However, I never told him of the incident. Much later in my married life I was to be reminded of it.

My four bridesmaids were: Barbara Burtwell (later Spong), friend; Janette McHugh (later Edwards), friend; Sandra Robson (later Holland), Gordon's sister; and Margaret Jane Talmage, daughter of my employer and his wife, Frank and Nora Talmage. Two of the bridesmaids were in pink and two in mauve ensembles. I made their shoes match their dresses by squeezing raspberry and blackberry juice – as appropriate – on to the white satin. (Years later my idea was featured in a published letter in a national newspaper, I was paid for.)

At the reception in The Social Club, now Parish Hall, in Heath Hill Road (where my parents' and sisters' wedding receptions were held also), Mr Talmage and his other staff joined his wife, Nora, who had been at the church ceremony too, for the evening's activities. Amongst the speeches was one by the landlord of the Prince Alfred pub, George Pinchin (who attended each part of the wedding with his wife, Rene). In his speech George highly praised our family, to the embarrassment of us all – especially Dad, a Saturday night regular in "The Prince". Whatever came over George to do that I do not know. We were never as good as George made out!

One of the telegrams read at our reception was from one of my 'old-flames' (an ex-boyfriend), Ivan, who was still a friend of mine in a sense. The telegram, which caused laughter at the event, but slight embarrassment to me, read, 'Once a king, always a king, but once a knight is enough' – and was signed by his name. I still have it (see Page 196) and all our wedding telegrams and cards.

The reception continued until 11.30 p.m., but Gordon and I left it an hour earlier to head for our 'Bramlea' flat. However, thinking some of the guests might be up to some tricks, we diverted our route to there, making it a roundabout one. What happened next caused us merriment. We became ourselves lost in a wood and couldn't find our way out of it for some time! I said, "Fancy us getting lost here, in the dark, now that we are married, *that's* no good. If we weren't married, I would have welcomed it though!" He said he would have done as well!

My Memories of Crowthorne Yesteryear and other accounts

The next morning one of our neighbour male guests appeared at my parents' home (Gordon and I were at 'Bramlea' until the Monday – when we went to the Isle of Wight for our ten-day honeymoon) and asked if he could go back in the Parish Hall for he had lost his false teeth. Mum, puzzled, replied that they wouldn't be in there. He said, he thought they would be! So, together, they went to the caretaker's home and soon they were let into the hall. The wedding guest said, "I'll have a look in the gents', I was sick in one of the lavatories." Mum followed him in, where he looked into the relevant toilet pan and said, excitedly,*"There they are – look!"* She didn't, but he put his hand in the water and pulled out a plate of his teeth, put them straight into his mouth, and said, "I didn't think I was wrong! That's better! Let's go!" Mum, and the caretaker nearby, were speechless.

Left, Shirley Woodason, aged 21, a bridesmaid in a turquoise-coloured dress at the wedding of her sister Glennis and Roy Gibbons in St. John the Baptist Church, Crowthorne, in June 1955. (Photo - Ron Francis.) Right, Shirley, aged 23, the only bridesmaid at the wedding of her sister, Virginia (Virgy) and William (Bill) Fairless, in St. John the Baptist Church, in July 1957 (a sudden gust of wind had just blown up the left-hand side of the large collar of her pale-turquoise dress). (Photo - H. Dawson.)

Left to right, Shirley, Glennis and Virginia (Virgy), née Woodason, in Romsey, Hampshire in 1981.

My Memories of Crowthorne Yesteryear and other accounts

Shirley Woodason arriving at St. John the Baptist Church, Crowthorne, on August 29th 1959, on the arm of her father Dudley ('Syd') Woodason for her wedding to REME Corporal, Gordon Robson. (Photo - Ron Francis.)

My Memories of Crowthorne Yesteryear and other accounts

Corporal Gordon Robson leads his bride Shirley along the aisle of St. John the Baptist Church, Crowthorne, following their wedding on August 29th 1959. (Photo - Ron Francis.)

My Memories of Crowthorne Yesteryear and other accounts

Gordon and Shirley Robson being greeted by Crowthorne British Red Cross members, after their wedding in St. John the Baptist Church, Crowthorne, on August 29th 1959.
(Photo - Ron Francis.)

My Memories of Crowthorne Yesteryear and other accounts

REME Corporal Gordon and Shirley Robson outside St. John the Baptist Church, Crowthorne, following their wedding on August 29th 1959. (Photo - Ron Francis.)

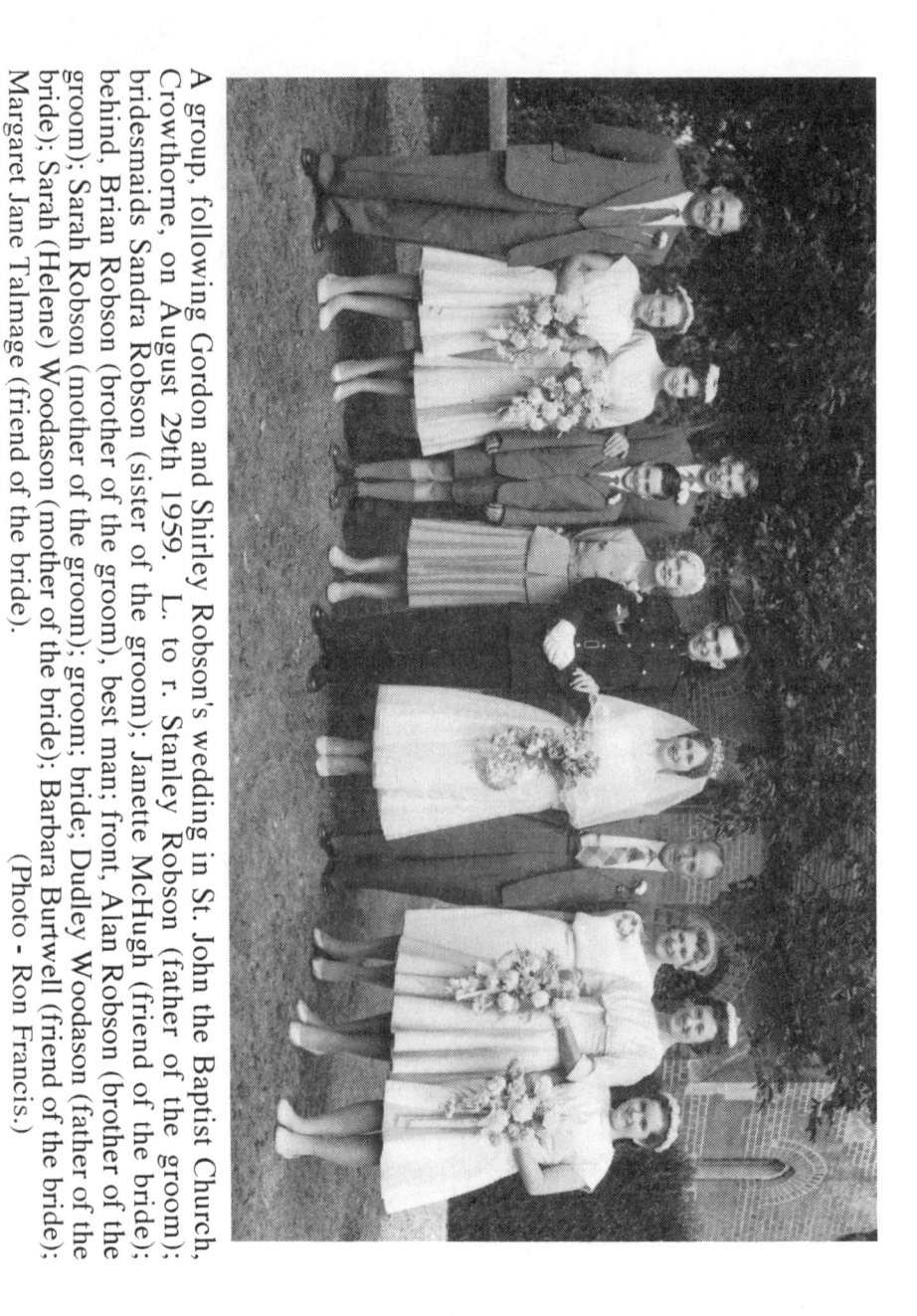

A group, following Gordon and Shirley Robson's wedding in St. John the Baptist Church, Crowthorne, on August 29th 1959. L. to r. Stanley Robson (father of the groom); bridesmaids Sandra Robson (sister of the groom); Janette McHugh (friend of the bride); behind, Brian Robson (brother of the groom), best man; front, Alan Robson (brother of the groom); Sarah Robson (mother of the groom); groom; bride; Dudley Woodason (father of the bride); Sarah (Helene) Woodason (mother of the bride); Barbara Burtwell (friend of the bride); Margaret Jane Talmage (friend of the bride).

(Photo - Ron Francis.)

My Memories of Crowthorne Yesteryear and other accounts

Gordon Robson, REME corporal, and his new bride Shirley leave St. John the Baptist Church, Crowthorne, to join their car for the short drive to their reception at The Social Club (now Parish Hall) in the village. (Photo - Ron Francis.)

My Memories of Crowthorne Yesteryear and other accounts

Shirley and REME corporal, Gordon Robson, prepare to leave for their reception, following their wedding on August 29th 1959, in St. John the Baptist Church, Crowthorne.   (Photo - Ron Francis.)

My Memories of Crowthorne Yesteryear and other accounts

Corporal Gordon and Shirley Robson, are ready to cut their three-tier wedding cake, at the reception in The Social Club (now Parish Hall), Crowthorne. (Photo - Ron Francis.)

My Memories of Crowthorne Yesteryear and other accounts

Mr. & Mrs. D. A. Woodason
request the pleasure of the Company of

....

on the occasion of the Marriage of their daughter
Shirley Enid to Mr. Gordon Robson,
at St. John the Baptist's Church, Crowthorne,
on Saturday, 29th August, 1959, at 2-30 p.m.,
and afterwards at The Social Club, Crowthorne

Wedding Greetings Telegram

Shirley & Gordon
Social Club
Crowthorne.

Once a King always a King,
but once a Knight is
enough.
    Ivan.

CHAPTER TWENTY-SEVEN
OUR HONEYMOON AND FIRST HOME

OUR HONEYMOON. On the Isle of Wight, this was at Freshwater, in an hotel where my mother had once stayed. She had recommended it and advised us to write to the manager there, book it, and say that she had said how nice the place was. I did this and purposely did not mention that we were honeymooners in my letter, and I asked Mum to promise that she would not contact the hotel herself to say we were.

So everything seemed fine over that, but then I had another concern. My family and friends talked of playing a prank – possibly involving tampering with my suitcase to cause me an embarrassment on my honeymoon! I therefore decided to get rid of my case of clothes days before my wedding, to try and prevent this. On the previous Monday I sent it to the hotel address, by rail from Crowthorne Station, and felt very relieved when it had left my hands. The thought crossed my mind though, that there was the faint chance the case would not be at the hotel when Gordon and I arrived there. But I dismissed this. All was well in the outcome, for it *was* there.

We had a very happy honeymoon, spoiled a little for me though, from my discovering that Gordon, behind my back, had arranged with two elderly friends of his parents (a couple), at our wedding, that we would meet them two days after our arrival on the Isle of Wight. I barely knew the couple and at our foursome meeting Gordon played outdoor bowls with the man, while I sat with the woman bored to tears watching their activities. I told Gordon later that I hadn't thought much of this on our honeymoon and he replied that he couldn't see what was wrong with it!

When we left the hotel, at the end of our ten days, the manager drove us to catch the ferry during which we thanked him for our good stay at his hotel. Then I added, "We don't mind you knowing *now*, we were on our honeymoon."

"Oh, I knew *that!*" he responded, "We *always* know them!" Perhaps the fact that Gordon and I were in bed with a 'Do not Disturb' notice hanging on the door, during some of our honeymoon afternoons, helped him to realise this!

We quite enjoyed our six months in 'Bramlea' (our first home, in Crowthorne), before moving to Anglesey, but had some problems concerning our tenancy. None were serious though and we were glad to have had the chance to live there at the start of our married life.

My Memories of Crowthorne Yesteryear and other accounts

Above, Shirley Robson, left, with her husband Gordon and Mrs Lily Griffin, at the front door of Mrs Griffin's home, 'Bramlea', Wellington Road, Crowthorne, February 1960. (Shirley and Gordon rented the top-floor of the house for the first six months of their marriage.) Below, left, 'Bramlea' and Shirley Robson (left), Mrs Lily Griffin (back) and friends of Shirley and Gordon, 1960. Below, right, Shirley Robson, with friends, outside 'Bramlea'.
(Photo's below - Gordon Robson.)

CHAPTER TWENTY-EIGHT
CHANGES

THE TALMAGES LEAVE CROWTHORNE. It seemed almost unreal when, in September 1959, less than a month after my wedding, the Talmage family, on his quite sudden retirement, left their home and shop (they had sold to a Mr R. H. Larby) and moved to Cold Ash near Newbury and their new home. This was Cold Ash Farm, where Frank was to take on dairy farming.

Before they left Crowthorne they invited Gordon and me to visit them at the farm, whenever we wanted to, without necessarily letting them know of this in advance – such as if ever we were that way and liked to drop in on them.

It was in the following January that we drove there, on an afternoon after snow had fallen overnight. The place, farmhouse particularly, looked picturesque clothed in a light covering of snow. Nora, alone in the house, was pleased to see us. She made us very welcome and served us tea and homemade cakes. The coal fire burning in the grate of the nicely-furnished room made it cosy and warm. Frank, she said, was in the cow-shed. She told us of how well they had settled in their new home and enjoyed the quieter life.

When we saw Frank in the cow-shed, where he was hosing it down with cows looking on, he too was glad to see us. And when I asked him how he felt in his new role, he replied, "Oh, I'm very pleased with it and it's good to no longer have Mrs Brown, Smith and Jones breathing down my neck." Yet he used to have plenty of men customers in his shop too! Presumably *they* had been less of a pain to him than the female ones, generally speaking.

ROY LARBY. Our new boss at the shop, Roy H. Larby, was totally different from Frank. He and his wife, Betty, with their several young children, had come from Kent and had accents that sounded cockney to me. Mr Larby was very much easier to work for than his predecessor, but for a long time from his arrival I was still on my guard nevertheless, as I could not get used to Frank not being in the shop. Both Roy and Betty Larby, especially Betty, were quiet-natured with ever-ready smiles and congenial dispositions. What I particularly remember about my early weeks with Roy was, he would forever say, "Right, let's have a cup of tea, shall we?" or similar, which seemed to be happening all day. On one occasion I replied, "We've not long ago had one!"

My Memories of Crowthorne Yesteryear and other accounts

"What does that matter?" he returned, "Go on, put the kettle on, there's nothing like a cup of tea!"

I always obliged and had one myself every time this happened, as did all the other staff. Once I counted how many cups of tea I was having each day, in my new situation – at the shop and away from it. The total was eleven!

My days working for Roy Larby were numbered, for several months after his arrival at the shop Gordon learned he was to be posted to Anglesey, North Wales, and I, it was expected, would be going with him.

I, TOO, LEAVE CROWTHORNE. I was just getting used to running my new home and looking after my new husband when the posting order came through. Gordon was content enough about it, being used to moving about with the army, but I had mixed feelings. Did I mind the idea of leaving Crowthorne and my family? Well, to do so would be a sort of adventure and I would like to have the experience of living in a different place many miles away from my home village and roots. I began to feel keen about the move, while considering I could write to my family and friends and see them sometimes.

However, on Gordon checking, he discovered that we hadn't enough 'points' for army accommodation for us in Anglesey. This meant that if I was to go there with him we would have to find our own place to live on the island. We eventually, by way of correspondence, acquired rooms for ourselves in a bungalow (in which the owners, a middle-aged married couple lived) situated in Trearddur Bay, near Holyhead. The bungalow was spacious and we took three rooms and would share the bathroom and kitchen.

By the time I left my job and we set off for Anglesey I was ready for the move and change, but deep down did not want to leave my home village and family.

BACK FOR A SPELL. We settled well in Anglesey and, in 1962, after we had had some short visits there periodically, to my old family home, I returned to Crowthorne with our first child, few months old, Michael, for a few weeks. We stayed with Mum and Dad. Gordon was working for the army in London then.

FILMING AT WELLINGTON COLLEGE. An Associated British, Warner-Pathé film was in part being made at Wellington College at the time (late summer 1962), this being 'Tamahine', starring Nancy Kwan, John Fraser, Dennis Price, Derek Nimmo, Justine Lord

My Memories of Crowthorne Yesteryear and other accounts

and James Fox, among others. Several hundred boys were needed as 'extras' in the film and a large number of boys from Wellington itself volunteered to return from their holidays and the balance was made up of boys from neighbouring schools, mostly in the Reading and Henley areas. Two of the masters at the college acted as technical advisers.* I joined the crowd of villagers who had gathered to watch the filming taking place, near some of the college buildings. It was good fun. The stars and possibly the filming crew lived in caravans in the college grounds during their days and nights there.

During this happy summer, when Gordon joined us every weekend, I would take walks round all my old local haunts. This included pushing Michael in his pram in the college grounds, with my oldest sister Glennis and her young baby Caroline accompanying us sometimes. On one occasion my one-time school friend, Joan Burton (now Mrs Franklin), joined us, pushing her baby daughter Sara in her pram.

Such lovely, happy days ... forever in my heart, as dear Crowthorne itself.

The second home of Shirley and Gordon Robson, 'Pyracanth', Trearddur Bay, near Holyhead, Anglesey, they shared with the owners, a Mr and Mrs Griffiths. The large bungalow enjoyed an elevated position, overlooking the bay and surrounding countryside.
(Photo - Shirley E. Robson.)

* Information from the British Film Institute, London.

My Memories of Crowthorne Yesteryear and other accounts

Shirley and Gordon Robson embrace, high up a tower near windswept Menai Straits, Anglesey, in 1961.

CHAPTER TWENTY-NINE
MY MEMORIES OF VARIOUS CROWTHORNE SHOPS

FOOD SHOPS. Apart from our family's regular custom at the local **Co-op** store, (where Abbotts health food shop currently is), managed in my childhood by Bill Hitchcock of Ellis Road, we liked to go into **Thame's** grocery shop opposite the Prince Alfred, where Lloyds Bank stands now. Items for sale were stacked on the floor as well as on the shelves and counters, and an overall pleasant smell drifted from the open sacks.

Staunton's grocery store was a shop and house combined (where Circle C supermarket is now in the High Street). Mrs Staunton had a son, Bob, with Down's syndrome.

Halfway along the High Street was **Sworder's**, where fruit, vegetables and flowers were on sale. Much of the produce was displayed outside under a canopy, above both sides of the corner shop.

Like Sworder's, **Dorrell's** fruit and vegetable shop, in Duke Street, next to the Post Office, did brisk business. There I was served by Wilf or Eileen, or José Stonebridge (née Daniel). The Dorrells came to take over the sweet shop, **Maynard's**, which was on the corner of Duke's Ride and New Road.

Abbotts dairy shop, in the High Street, was opposite Sworder's while Mr **Dray** (Edwin, known as Ted or Bill) had a small grocery shop, **Senior Supply Stores**, next door.

In Church Street, near the Lych Gate of St. John the Baptist Church, there was **Douglas's Stores**, grocer's, which was less busy than, but similar to, Thame's. We took our tin containers for paraffin to the Misses Douglas for refilling. They sold a lot of it, also candles. The shop is currently (in 1995) The Last Shoe restaurant.

On the corner of the High Street and Church Street was the **International Stores** (now Watts the Furnishers). The mother of my friend Jeanette Hatt took us with her each week to the 'Inter'. A regular item on her shopping list was a jar of Shippam's paste, as well as one or two packets of a good quality brand of tea, which kind varied.

Opposite **Pearmain's Garage** was the brimful of provisions grocery shop **Lake Stores**, where the smell of fresh coffee filled one's nostrils. At Christmas time we bought more exotic items there – crystalised fruit, nuts, boxed dates, non-alcoholic fruit wines, etc. Whole hams hung temptingly from the ceiling.

As a child I was sometimes sent to the **fish-and-chip shop** next to I. V. Scott's ironmonger's shop and house, in the High Street, with a note from Mum detailing our requirements. (I never knew the fish-and-chip shop owners' names, but in the accounts of Beryl Day and Hilda Butler in *Our Memories of Crowthorne Yesteryear*, the respective owners, or managers, are given as Mr and Mrs Finch, Mr and Mrs Rushent and Mr Frank Knight.) The tall counter was very high for me, I had a job to see over it, and I always had to queue there on Saturday lunch-times.

Despite my working at Talmage's, Mum saw no reason to change her patronage of **Anstee's**, butcher's and fishmonger's, in Church Street (for she and Frank Talmage rarely saw eye-to-eye), even though Anstee's was further from our home. There was also in the village High Street, opposite Wellington Road, another meat/fish shop, **Swain's**, later **Money's**.

Marder's, grocers, in Pinewood Avenue (halfway down, on the right-hand side), was popular with us, being the nearest shop to our home and very convenient. Although most of our grocery shopping was carried out in the Co-op, we also gave business to Marder's. Mr and Mrs Marder, Lionel and Florence, served in the shop – who were the parents of one of our playmates, Derek whose account is in this book. Sometimes there was a bran-tub just inside the door of the shop, with children's cheap toys and so on hidden in the bran. For a few coppers we would excitedly have a go! On the Marder's ground, at the side of the shop, the frontage of which came to Pinewood Avenue itself, there were a number of geese behind, I think, chestnut fencing. One day I saw a woman talking to another by the fencing, when a goose's head and long neck came through an opening in the structure and without hesitation the goose took a section of calf of one of the woman's legs between its beak and applied pressure. She yelled and drew back, looking shocked. The goose released its beak and I saw the woman's calf had turned blue. "Cor!" she said to her companion, "That damn well hurt!" (The motto – don't trust geese!)

Finally, on the subject, there was also a grocery shop in Old Wokingham Road, very close to its junction with Hatch Ride, which I only went into once and have no memories of it otherwise, nor of its owners, the Muir family (previously Reeves). It kept busy, I believe.

SWEETS AND CAKES... A popular shop on the corner of the High Street/Lower Broadmoor Road was **Bon Marche**, selling sweets, ice-creams and drinks. **Rogers Bakery** was nearby, where bread and cakes were sold and some were delivered to customers by Mr Rogers, a quiet, fairly tall man of stocky build. I recall Mr Rogers having an operation on his sinuses. Mum made most of our cakes, rock ones, especially, but some were delivered with our bread from Napper's Bakery in Sandhurst.

Ice-cream, bottles of cold drinks (such as Corona 'fizzy-pop', at 6½d a large one, and 1d, maybe ½d, refund on each empty one returned), and other similar items, could be bought at **Home Dainties**, in Duke's Ride, the cafe run by Cecil Reason and Miss Maud Crane. Both wore white-bibbed aprons and appeared to work well in partnership together. Customers in the annex of the cafe had a good view of the outdoor display of **Teakle's Monumental Masons**! Nobody seemed bothered by this and it certainly did not put me off the superb dinners I had there. My only complaint about Home Dainties was being forced to observe the old, scabby ginger cat that slept, mostly, amongst the sweet jars in the window of the shop part of the premises.

There was a small tobacconist's (possibly also sweets) shop of **Mr Prior**, between those of Douglas and Watts, in Church Street, where elderly, short and slightly stocky, he served his customers. Today it is a Chinese takeaway-cum-fish-and-chip establishment.

OTHER SHOPS. **Watts**, the **furnishers** in Church Street, was a fine, large shop, the size of several shops in one, which it probably was. **Macey's** (like Armitage's), of Church Street, was another **drapery** store (of two long, equal-size sections). Next to Swains, the butchers (in the High Street), was **Fred Long's** small outfitter's shop (later he moved to a large one, now C. T. Bell's Electrical, corner of Heath Hill Road). Our shoes were bought from **Newman's**, near to where their shop is currently (in 1995). This was the only shoe shop in Crowthorne and of course widely used. Wool and haberdashery could be bought from **Beatrice Bell's** shop – together with sundry horticultural items (seeds, bulbs, etc.) – or from **Mrs Spring's** lingerie shop. The latter also sold nylon stockings when available. When they weren't, young and not so young ladies would apply a brown chemical preparation from a bottle to their legs and draw seams down the backs of them, giving the appearance that their legs were clad in fully-fashioned stockings. My mother was one. I would watch her preparing her legs, when she would say, "Make sure I haven't any streaks." Fascinating! When it rained, she and others concerned found it exasperating!

In the converted church (before St. John the Baptist's was built, now Country Wares) was **C. T. Bell's** High Street shop, where radio sets, batteries and other items were sold by quiet-natured and quiet-voiced Mr Charlie Bell. I was particularly fascinated by the large

My Memories of Crowthorne Yesteryear and other accounts

advertising cut-out of the dog and gramophone for His Master's Voice he had by the counter in his shop. **Mr I. V. Scott and Mr Bert Bartlett** ran separate High Street ironmonger's shops, that were 'choc-a-bloc' with tools and similar paraphernalia. There were also two jewellers – **Mr Fred Hare's** tiny shop was to the right of the Plaza cinema – an extension of the foyer – now the right-hand side of C.O.A.T.S. charity shop (the remainder *was* the foyer portion, while the rest of it was where a car park now stands) and **Mr William (Billy) David's** jewellers shop was at the High Street/Wellington Road junction.

I bought my only ever new bicycle from **Hatfield's** cycle shop (opposite what is now Gale's bakery, which, in my young life, used to be **Nora Lawrence's** newsagent's shop). Tom Hatfield and his wife Phyllis served me congenially in their shop, where I also bought accessories for all my various bikes. On identical cerise-coloured bikes, our first ever brand-new ones, bought at Hatfield's, a friend and I (aged about fourteen) went for a ride in the stony Addiscombe/Grant Road area and, from her mishearing an instruction of mine, we crashed into each other. I said, forlornly, "We have christened our bikes now! It had to happen sometime and at least we needn't worry so much about scratching them in the future. Also it means we can distinguish between them, as the scratches are in different places!" But this did not brighten her doleful face. Luckily, we were barely hurt ourselves.

George Armitage ran his large department store next to Talmage's, where men's and women's clothing and household items could be bought. Customers were allowed to take clothes home 'on appro' and Mrs Doughty ran the ladies' section.

At the barber's (opposite Newman's), with its red-and-white-striped pole projecting from the front of the building, **Mr. J. Bennett** took in also, for repair, folks' 'unhealthy' umbrellas, a very worthwhile service in those days. We seemed to have long dry summers, and sometimes, when rain came at last, householders would come out of their homes and shout, "*It's raining, it's raining!*" then cheer.

Where Old Pharmacy Court is now (one of the flats being my mother's last home, for 3 1/2 years, in the 1980s, following Dad's death and after she had sold our family home 'Sydellen') was **Knight's** Pharmacy. But my family frequented **Dring's** Chemists (later **Connock's**) in Duke's Ride, more often, as it was nearer to our home and the Post Office.

And there were the village pubs (still in the High Street today): the **Prince Alfred,** the **Crowthorne Inn,** and the **Iron Duke Hotel**. Away from the High Street, twixt Waterloo Road and Duke's Ride –

also as now – was the **Waterloo Hotel**. The four have always been affectionately known as The Prince, The Crow, the Duke and The Waterloo. By the railway station was the **Wellington Hotel Tap**, as the pub section of the hotel was termed.

SHOPS, ETC., BY THE STATION. Also by the railway station, in Duke's Ride, the shops and other businesses in my memory: (on the station side of the road) **W. H. Smith**, Bookshop; **C. T. Hunt**, Printers and Bookbinders; and on the opposite side of the road, **Metalair**, the small factory, as described by Michael Ifould in his account in this volume; **David Greedy**, funeral director; **Burlton's**, sub Post Office and wireless items; **Fairman's**, ironmongers; **Strudwick's,** barber's (men's hairdresser); and the garage, **Crowthorne Motors**.

SERVICES. **Ted Noakes and his wife Lilian** were in charge of the main Post Office (where it still is, in Duke's Ride), and for a time from leaving school my cousin, the now late Valerie Evans (in marriage Mrs Chick) worked there under them. She was the sister of my cousin, Denis Evans, who still lives in New Wokingham Road with his wife Diane (née White). Greta (née Woodason), Denis and Valerie's mother, was first married to Sid Evans, and then to Tom Partner. (She was a Crowthorne W.I. member, and well-known in the village for community activities as well as for her skills of flower arranging. Greta was often concerned with the latter in St. John the Baptist Church. As a W.I. member, in April 1972, she was awarded the Morrell Cup for the highest number of points gained during the year.)

The front part of the Post Office dealt with sales of miscellaneous stationery and a metal grill separated customers from staff at the post office counter. This did not apply at the parcels counter, which was 'open'. I remember Ted as a somewhat disgruntled character, while Lilian was quiet and pleasant.

Near the Iron Duke Hotel was a sub-branch of **Barclays Bank**, open on weekday mornings only. In my early days at Talmage's, Dorothy used to send me there for change for the shop's till. Later I banked the shop's takings there. Mr 'Bob' Brooker, a retired local policeman, stood guard, as I saw it, in the front (customer section) of the bank; he knew all the locals apparently and had an interested, friendly and jovial approach.

My Memories of Crowthorne Yesteryear and other accounts

CHAPTER THIRTY
SOME CROWTHORNE TRADERS OF 1948

The following details reflect the exact wording from local trade adverts in a copy of the brochure of the Crowthorne, Finchampstead and St. Sebastian Horticultural Society's 44th Annual Show, held on the Derby Field on Wednesday, July 21st 1948:

Home Dainties, Duke's Ride, for Home-made Cakes, Confectionery, jam, etc., Luncheons and Teas, Meat pies a speciality. Everything made on the premises. **E. Palmer**, the Crowthorne Valet Service, Duke's Ride, your Local Dyer and Cleaner. **The Cafe**, High Street, For Good Lunches and Teas, Home made Cakes and Pastry. **Swain's**, Butchers and Fishmongers, High Street and Duke's Ride. **T. A. Hatfield**, The Motor and Cycle Depot, High Street, Cycle Repairs, Accessories, Petrol, Fishing Tackle and Sports Goods. **F. H. Dring**, M.P.S., Family & Dispensing Chemist, Duke's Ride, National Insurance Dispensing a Speciality. **V. B. Elston**, Newsagent, High Street, Books, Games and Toys for children. **J. Huntley**, Florist, Fruiterer & Market Gardener, Floral Tributes made to order. **R. E. Macey**, Ladies & Gents Outfitters, Church Street. **Reading Co-operative Society, Ltd.**, High Street, High Class Groceries & Provisions. The Dividend is an "Extra". **Crowthorne Motors**, Duke's Ride, Prompt Service, Repairs promptly executed. Cars for Hire. **F. J. Hare,** Watchmaker and Jeweller, Repairs a Speciality. **C. G. Daniel**, King's Road, Corn, Seed and Potato Merchant, Dog & Poultry Foods, Patent Manures. **W. Newman & Sons**, Saddlers and Boot makers, High Street and Yateley Green, Trunks and Bags, Boots and Shoes. **Fairman's** (W. H. Fairman, late W. J. T. Williams, Ltd.) Everything for the House and Garden, Ironmongery, Radio and Cycles, Duke's Ride, near the Station. **T. Knight**, M.P.S., Pharmacist and Dispensing Chemist, The Pharmacy, Crowthorne. **Lending Library** – 2p per volume per week. **S. Townsend**, Automobile Engineer, The Garage, Crowthorne, well appointed Cars and Coaches for hire for all occasions, Day and night service and Sundays, Repairs and overhauls, Furniture Remover and Haulage Contractor, Cycle Agent and Repairer (and beside the phone number is the message Telegrams "Townsend," Crowthorne. **Oxbridge**, Crowthorne Nursery, Sandhurst Road, Specialities – Tomatoes, Cucumbers, Bedding Plants, Vegetable Plants, Fresh Cut Chrysanthemums. **Pinewood Nurseries**, C. G. Andrews, Specialities - Wreaths, Bouquets, Cut Flowers, Bedding and Vegetable Plants, Salads, etc. **A. J. Bennett** (late W. E. H. Thomas)

My Memories of Crowthorne Yesteryear and other accounts

Gentlemen's Hairdresser, Toilet Requisites. **The Hygienic Dairy** (Proprietor: J. Abbott) "Grade A" (Tuberculin Tested) Milk Supplied, Fresh Butter, New-laid Eggs and Pure Rich Cream, High Street. **C. T. Bell**, High Street, Electrical and Radio Engineer, Television Demonstrations Daily, Lighting and Power Installations, Radio Sets, Components, and all Electrical Accessories, Public Address Equipment, Accumulators re-charged, collected and delivered, Gramophones & Records, All Electrical & Radio Repairs. **W. Pearmain & Sons Limited**, Central Garage, Motor Agents and Engineers. The Finest Hire Service in the District, Oxy-Acetylene Welding, Cellulosing, A.A. & R.A.C. Repairs. **J. Mason & Sons**, Coal and Coke Merchants, Motor Haulage Contractor, all kinds of carting done, all kinds of coal and anthracite in stock. **Lakes Stores**, The Crowthorne Grocer, High Street, and Yorktown Road, Sandhurst, we specialise in our own roasted Coffees which have no parallel in the District, For Provisions – Have no doubt – Just get them here, Wines and Spirits, Ales and Stouts. **J. & A. Blunden**, Carpenters and Builders, Old Wokingham Road, Plumbing, Drainage, Decorating, Haulage. **B. N. Bell**, Nurseryman and Seedsman, High Street, Horticultural Sundries – Fertilizers etc. **Katrina**, Duke's Ride, Ladies & Children's Hairdresser, Permanent Waving a Speciality. **F. Bell**, Baker and Confectioner, Duke's Ride, Families waited upon Daily. **Crowthorne Motors Ltd.**, Next to Crowthorne Station Post Office, The Garage with Modern Equipment, Official Repairer to A.A., Cars for Hire. **D. R. Rogers & Son**, High Class Bakers, Pastry-cooks and Confectioners, High Street. **E. W. Dorrell**, High Class Fruiterer and Florist, Duke's Ride, Wreaths and Floral Designs made on the premises. **Wilfred Newman**, High Street, Plumber and Heating Engineer, Furnishing Ironmonger. **G. F. Bell**, Upholsterer and Furnisher, High Street, Bedding Re-made, Suites Re-covered, Good range of materials in stock, Furnishing Sundries.

(Supplied courtesy of Peter Ratcliffe)

Peter Ratcliffe also showed me an admission ticket on which is printed: Crowthorne Warship Week   Opening Ceremony   Plaza Cinema Saturday, February 21st (1942) 11 a.m.   Admission by ticket.

(There is no mention of a price, so possibly there was no charge).

TAYLOR & WHITLOCK JEWELLERS

The shops at the railway station end of Crowthorne have seen many changes over the years, with all types of business coming and going – some through choice, others due to the turbulent financial climate.

One recent addition is the jeweller's, Taylor & Whitlock at 170, Duke's Ride, which in 1989 replaced the gent's hairdresser's, Strudwick's. Many will recall Dennis Strudwick, who traded in the village for many years.

The previous jeweller in business in Crowthorne, before Taylor & Whitlock opened, was Mr Fred Hare, who enjoyed a very long period of trading, from his small shop in the High Street (being part of the now C.O.A.T.S. charity shop), until closing circa 1970.

Mike Taylor and Glenn Whitlock, who, before opening their Crowthorne shop, already had an established jewellery business in Camberley, felt the freehold shop in the village offered them an ideal opportunity to control the spiralling rental situation, in the late 1980s.

From small beginnings, their business expanded and the retail side proved to be a huge success, with an enormous amount of support from the local community.

In July 1991 the partnership was dissolved and Mike Taylor took over the business, which today has become one of the most comprehensive jeweller's in the area, offering not only jewellery products and all the associated services, but also sports trophies of every description for awards, ranging in many different materials, from wood to lead crystal.

The success of the business, though, has not been without its problems, and in the seven years that the shop has been open it has been the target of no less than four vicious robberies, the most recent in February 1995. Happily, no one was hurt, and as the business was well-insured, no financial damage was suffered. However there was the urgent need for additional security and another revamp of the shop is due to take place in 1996.

My Memories of Crowthorne Yesteryear and other accounts

My Memories of Crowthorne Yesteryear and other accounts
MICHAEL IFOULD
(late of the Waterloo Hotel, Crowthorne)

I am the son of the late Maurice and Winifred Ifould (they had no other children), for many years of the Waterloo Hotel in the village. And I believe I am the last surviving member of the Ifould family, who seem to have been established in Crowthorne for some period before the building of Wellington College.

The original family came from Wokingham, where they were butchers, to take over the shop they came to name Ifould Stores, on the corner of the High Street and Church Street, near the Iron Duke Hotel. They were established there in 1867. This general store (now occupied by G. M. News) later became a Post Office as well, and is reputed to have been the oldest shop in Crowthorne.

The Ifould family's butcher's shop in Wokingham was near (as far as I know) to the Town Hall, by the side of a road, which was called Ifoulds Lane, that runs east from it. The shop is now a supermarket.

During the family's early period in Crowthorne, they started to hold lectures, or church services, in their kitchen, and later, when this was not big enough, in the loft over the shop, that was later bought by Over (in some books on Crowthorne the loft is referred to as a bakery – Editor). Then an actual church was built further up the High Street, on the opposite side of the road, where the Fire Station is now.

Later, the church building, which was wooden, was moved across the road on rollers, and later still (after St. John the Baptist Church was built in Church Street, in 1872/'73) the wooden High Street church became C. T. (Charlie or 'Teddy') Bell's electrical shop, where he sold and mended radios, charged accumulators during the war, and so on.

The building, far more substantial than then, is currently, in 1995, occupied by Country Wares (cafe, and cakes, bread and gift shop).

The Ifoulds came to move to their Waterloo Road house (that later became the Waterloo Hotel) from their shop, but I have no date as to when this was. However, it was before Wellington College was built (the foundation stone for the college was laid by Queen Victoria in 1856 and the college was opened in 1859 – Editor), and the architects concerned with the building of the college used to walk across to the Ifould's house (using it as a hostelry) at lunch-times, for their cheese and beer. I have seen a photograph somewhere of these rough architects sitting outside the Waterloo having their refreshments.

There was a mystery surrounding Mr Ifould (whose Christian name was unknown to me), who used to spend a lot of time up in Newcastle and come home only on occasions.

My Memories of Crowthorne Yesteryear and other accounts

Mrs Ifould (whom I only always knew as "Old Granny Ifould") had a son, Harry (H. E. Ifould), and two daughters, Emily Gertrude and May. Edward White Benson, the first Master of Wellington College (who came from Arnold's Rugby in 1858, and later, after 14 years at the college, became Bishop of Truro and Archbishop of Canterbury – Editor), somehow set Mrs Ifould up to provide accommodation for bachelor masters (this when the Waterloo was not an hotel as such). I am not sure why Mr Benson did this, though have some thoughts on it. The arrangement continued right through the war.

Some very well-known masters of the college stayed there, who still visited years after the house became an hotel. One of them was Mr R. Timberley, the college's Director of Music, who right through the war occupied two rooms above the front door of the building, being a sitting-room and a bedroom.

After Mrs Ifould died (I am not sure when) what had become the hotel passed to her two daughters, Gertie (as she was always affectionately known) and May. There was always a mystery surrounding May, who I feel probably committed suicide. No one ever mentioned her.

Gertie was born in the hotel and lived there all her life. She died in 1971 at 99 years in the same room that she was born in, right in the roof of the building. Throughout she must have been a wonderful woman, who ran the hotel, was renowned for her cooking, and was very well known by many of the pupils of Wellington College, who became famous people.

Harry (my grandfather) ran the bar at the Waterloo. He married Emily Gertrude Chaplin, daughter of one of the Broadmoor attendants. For a time he was the laboratory assistant in the Wellington College science laboratories, carrying out experiments for the boys. He would sit at the back of the room, listening to the instructions and absorbing everything he heard. He was a clever, very competent man by all accounts, who in his spare time used to install electric door bells in big houses in the area. These were worked by zinc accumulators, on a bellboard (stars flashed backwards and forwards) with his name, H. E. Ifould, on. And he used to mend clocks and watches.

He also applied for and obtained the first licence in the area for all Kodak equipment, followed by the first licence for Ever Ready batteries and torches. Sometime later he gave the licences to Tommy Knight, of Knight's the Chemist in the High Street, as a gift, which then made T. Knight the only agent in the area for these.

For a period early in the era of which I write, the Ifould family ran the tuck shop (The Grubbies) at Wellington College.

My Memories of Crowthorne Yesteryear and other accounts

Famous people came to the Waterloo all through the 1930s and '40s – so, including through the war – to see and talk to Gertie about old times. Gertie always read the Daily Telegraph every day and would go through the marriages, births and deaths etc., columns – to keep up with all these people, as it were. And when they came to see her she always knew who had got married, engaged, given birth, and so on.

One of the famous people who used to visit the Waterloo quite often – and a great friend of "Auntie Gertie" – was Rudyard Kipling, the well-known and famous author, who used to call her "My dear Gertie" and give her a hug and a kiss when he visited.

Likewise a man called Alan Murray stayed from time to time at the Waterloo, who was also a great friend of my aunt. I think he composed the song 'I'll Walk Beside You' which, as far as I know, was composed at the Waterloo.

During this time it became a custom for Wellington College to have a Speech Day every year, which was always a great occasion. On the lawn beside the Waterloo Hotel a huge marquee would be erected and a lot of the parents of the boys at the college used to walk through the woods from there and come to the hotel for luncheons and dinners. These were served both in the hotel and in the marquee. Always traditionally served were cold salmon, cold chicken and asparagus.

Crowthorne, of course, used to be packed full of these "posh people", as they were known, who lodged in people's houses around the village and came to the Waterloo for their meals. As a very young child I went to help (along with all the family) and one of my jobs was "popping peas" – involving sacks of peas that had to be shelled. Also I would help with all the lettuces, some 200 of them, that had to be washed, put in little metal baskets, then taken outside to be shaken. These tasks constituted a major event!

Naturally, the Wellington Hotel (licensee Mr Lester and his wife), then opposite Crowthorne railway station now demolished (which was the better of the two I suppose, it being a 3-star one, whereas the Waterloo was only ever a 2-star hotel), was doing the same sort of thing. And they built a huge 'glasshouse' (like a conservatory) onto the side of their hotel. This was rudely called by people "the monkey house", in which their customers were seated for their meals.

There were all sorts of famous people who used to visit Wellington College during the long period of the Ifoulds involvement with the Waterloo Hotel, besides the parents of the college boys (and very often the same parents came back because their sons went on to the Royal Military Academy, at Sandhurst, and the brothers of those sons then came to the college, sometimes whole families being concerned).

My Memories of Crowthorne Yesteryear and other accounts

My Great-aunt Gertie knew them all very, very well indeed, by name. They were mostly army people.

Visitors fairly regularly were from the Arab world, who were spending quite a lot of money on the education of their boys by sending them to Wellington College and the Royal Military Academy. These people used the hotel, rather than the pub, or licensed part of it.

During the entire period between the two World Wars, and maybe for a time during the first, the Waterloo had the only off-licence and was the only deliverer of wines and spirits in the area. And until the Common Room in the college obtained a licence, we used to supply all the college – the Common Room and all the masters' houses – with liquor. It was more-or-less the work of two men (well, boys) to deliver all the wines and spirits around to these houses.

Some of the amounts delivered to two of the houses seemed extraordinary. We found that the orders and bills at one stage, when I took over the hotel in 1968, involved deliveries of 6 bottles of Gordon's gin, 6 bottles of White Horse Whisky, 2 kegs of Worthington beer, and so on. And within a fortnight there were further deliveries of the same amounts. It seemed impossible, but they must have had it.

In about 1940 Harry died, who incidentally had had the nickname of "Bumpy". Apparently when a youngster he was dropped and broke his back, though was not a hunchback. I believe at school he was called Bumpy, which rather stuck, and he was often called this by his friends.

Harry's son, Maurice (my father), then took over the hotel, and ran it in conjunction with Gertie. Also, my mother, Winifred, moved in and helped my father with the running of it. This was continued right through the war.

After 1950 I left Crowthorne to go in the RAF, where I served my national service and became a pilot. Then I came home, before going away to work in the hotel industry.

I returned to the Waterloo in 1968, for a five-year period. Gertie and my parents retired and I, together with my wife Joan, took over the Waterloo from my father, who was then old and poorly.

My memories of Crowthorne during the Second World War include the day war broke out. I used to live at the top end of Napier Road with my parents in those days, at a house called 'Brackenmount', and I remember that everybody was terribly upset and crying all over the place. But I thought it was wonderful, because I found it very exciting! People were being evacuated and all sorts of things like that were going on.

It was then we learned that the St. Paul's School, Hammersmith,

My Memories of Crowthorne Yesteryear and other accounts

was being evacuated to Crowthorne and was to move into Lord Devonshire's mansion at Easthampstead Park. All the boys had to have bicycles and a lot of them rode down from London on them in a big convoy.

They all met at Pinefields, the little hall down Church Road (it is actually in Waterloo Road, near its junction with Church Road and is still there, in 1995, but not used for anything public now – Editor). Pinefields used to be the gymnasium, with the swimming pool next to it, of the preparatory school of Wellington College, Crowthorne Towers. (This had been across Waterloo Road from Pinefields before demolition in 1938 – Editor).

Pinefields was taken over in the first instance to accommodate many of the St. Paul's School boys, because initially billets could not be found for them around the village. Later, they *were* all placed there. We had four billeted with us and, by odd chance, two of them were my cousins from London, who had come down from Acton. I thought this quite good and it was great fun having all the boys living in the house, which made life very exciting indeed!

But there was shock and horror when the boys (in total) first arrived, because the only things they had to sleep on were palliasses. These were distributed to them at Pinefields by the ARP (Air Raid Precaution) unit, who used the hall throughout the war. All the boys came from good homes and for them to have to sleep on these straw mattresses on the floor, all over the village, was very hard!

However, latterly, Dunlopillo Lilos were produced by the government and to my knowledge all the boys slept on them around the village for the duration of the war.

It used to be quite a sight in those days when all the boys of the whole school (who had to be up at the mansion at Easthampstead Park ready to start work at 9 o'clock in the morning), cycled out onto the Old Wokingham Road for there. I used to see them in the wintertime.

Also, the boys used Crowthorne (St. John the Baptist) church for their chapel. So Sunday services then were very busy indeed, because all of them used to go to church.

It was very good of Wellington College to have lent St. Paul's School a lot of their facilities during the war, such as their swimming pool, playing fields, gymnasium and, in particular, their science laboratories; also a scout hut.

St. Paul's School had a junior school, called Collet Court, the boys of which came down to the village as well. They were all accommodated in one of the college houses, Wellesley House, situated at the east end of the college drive, or "the kilometre", as it is known.

My Memories of Crowthorne Yesteryear and other accounts

Wellesley House had been one of the college boarding houses for the Wellington College boys, and likely is today.

All the St. Paul's Collet Court boys went to school, and there were some boarders, in Wellesley House. They also, like the senior St. Paul's boys, were allowed the use of the college grounds and a lot of the college facilities that were enjoyed by the Wellington College boys themselves.

It was to Wellesley House, when known as Collet Court, that I went as a day boy – from the age of nine or ten – having previously, from the age of 5, been educated in Wokingham, at the Presentation Convent, also as a day boy, which had a reputation of being a very, very good educational school.

I used to cycle to school at Wellesley House every day – right through the war – until I left there and went away to school.

At the outbreak of war all the young men in the Crowthorne area were called up and, with a lot of the others in the village, were formed into a Home Guard unit. They had no weapons as such and were to be seen parading around Crowthorne with broomsticks and pitchforks. While *they* provided the latter, the government, I believe, provided the broomsticks.

My Memories of Crowthorne Yesteryear and other accounts

The Home Guard platoon were led by the then local Barclays Bank manager, Mr F. J. W. Girling, who lived in accommodation that formed part of the bank building, near Crowthorne Station.

Mr Girling was an amazing character, who was about 6ft 6 inches tall and as thin as one could possibly be. He used to march out in front of his troops and was bent to almost leaning backwards, like a stick, which caused a lot of derision amongst the youngsters at the time.

In about 1940 there was a big exercise involving the Home Guard, as well as the Officers' Training Corps (OTC), of Wellington College, the St. Paul's School, and the Sandhurst Cadets. They all wore what uniforms they had and rushed around Crowthorne when the exercise was underway. One or two boys had motor bikes, for which they were given petrol for them to act as despatch riders. The police joined in, as did the air-raid wardens, and all the citizens were supposed to stay indoors, for this very important occasion.

In the throes of the exercise, they were bombarded. I believe it was a Lysander aircraft that came over and 'bombed' some of them at Crowthorne. But instead of bombs, bags of flour were dropped on them, which caused an awful mess all over the railway station yard. One of the sacks, I think, fell on the roof of the nearby printer's, Hunt, and the bookshop that later became W. H. Smith's shop. In particular, another bag fell on the station roof and broke the glass. The Stationmaster there at the time was very cross indeed and considered it "a lot of lunacy."

My Memories of Crowthorne Yesteryear and other accounts

The huge playing field between the railway line and the (Lower) Sandhurst Road, was that of the Derby Field, because it was given to Wellington College – before the war, of course – by Lord Derby, I understand in the year that he won the Derby. The field, with the footbridge across the railway leading to it, was, and still is I feel, for the college boys to play their games on.

On 'high days and holidays', before the war, there was a flying circus that used to visit there and fly aircraft in and out. At the beginning of the war big banks were ploughed in the middle of the field, so that it could no longer be used for aircraft to land or take off.

Also in the village (and of great importance, I suppose) was a post of the Observer Corps. This was a little way along Bracknell Road, on the right-hand side and had to be manned twenty-four hours a day, seven days a week, including on Christmas Day, etc.. It was made of sandbags and there was a sort of dug-out on one side of it. Within was a paraffin stove for the men to try and keep warm by, and in the middle a little telescope which ran around on Meccano wheels.

There were always two men on duty, who had to try and identify and record, day and night, all sounds and sightings of any aircraft and report on them by telephone to headquarters. This went on to the plotters at Fighter Command, for the defence of Britain. The call sign of that particular corps was N2 (or Nuts 2) and they used to call up and say such as, "Nuts Two calling, Nuts Two calling. One Spitfire flying south-west," and so on. All the Crowthorne men, either in protected work or who were too old for the forces, were in the local Observer Corps.

My father, Maurice Ifould, was a member, as were practically all the other men in the village in their forties and fifties. Such men as Arthur Hook, who managed The Grubbies in those days. And I think Ted Anderson was another, who, if I am right, had only one leg and used to cycle up there on a bike with a fixed pedal.

I believe they used to do 4-hour shifts, including the "graveyard shift", which was from midnight till 4 o'clock and again from four till eight in the morning, the situation being that they were mostly shopkeepers.

It was from there that they saw London burn and had reports of all the aircraft. I think in some ways they had a very interesting time, for they at least knew all of what was going on.

They had to wear tin helmets and uniform, which looked like an RAF uniform; also they were armed – *really* armed! Although important people in the war, they had only one rifle and five rounds of ammunition to protect their post in the event of an invasion.

My Memories of Crowthorne Yesteryear and other accounts

Also in the war, all the roads – the Wokingham Roads, the Bracknell Road, as well as up to Caesar's Camp, and so on – were lined on both sides with low Nissen huts, that were filled to the brim with shells and cases of ammunition.

And about every 1/4 mile along the road there had been built what looked like small concrete swimming pools, which were filled with what appeared to be land-mines. These had netting across the top to stop people, including youngsters of course, from falling in.

I was amazed that there was all this ammunition lying around there, yet it was never guarded or touched (I never saw anyone, soldiers or others, guarding it). The situation, apparently, was that it was left to people's goodwill not to go there, and I am sure that children, myself for one, usually complied. However, I used to go and peep under the sacking, placed for protection over the entrance to one of the huts, where I saw all the shells piled up.

Crowthorne was bombed during the war on two occasions, in my memory. One was when the enemy tried to bomb Broadmoor at seven o'clock one morning. Luckily, the bombs straddled the wall. One fell near the gasworks and I think two fell inside the wall, in the gardens of the female wing. So no real damage was done, except for there being a lot of dirt thrown about and everybody being rather frightened.

The really bad bombing that Crowthorne suffered concerned, in October 1940, the stick of four or five bombs that fell across Wellington College and killed the then Headmaster, Mr R. P. Longden, who received a direct hit as he came out of the front door of his house, The Lodge. (He died under fallen masonry of the collapsed porch – Editor.) All the senior boys at the college had to do ARP duties and the Headmaster was just leaving the house to go round and inspect the boys and make sure they were at their posts, when there was a direct hit in front of his house which was badly damaged and later demolished. (His car was blown into the top of a tree. Another house was subsequently built, in replacement of the original. See Page 239 first and then Page 70 – Editor).

Another of the bombs fell close to The Grubbies, a further one close to the old indoor swimming pool of the college, a fourth in the playing field between The Grubbies and The Lodge, and there might have been a fifth which, if so, would have landed down by the laundry (Wellington College had a very modern and efficient laundry at the time). Certainly some of the Chapel windows were broken by the bombing and had to be replaced.

During the war there was a famous local character called Captain Parker. I think he was probably an army captain, or a retired one, and prior to the war he was very interested in following the hounds, in particular the foxhounds and the guard hounds. To do this he had a rare old Trojan car, which had solid wheels and ran on 2-stroke petrol and oil mixed, having a 2-stroke engine.

The captain lived permanently at the Waterloo Hotel and kept his old Trojan in a garage there. All through the war he obtained a petrol allowance to go all around the area picking up sacks of waste paper, he collected for recycling. I do not know where he took it to. He was quite a sight in his old car and used to wear a bowler hat, if I remember rightly, when he was driving around and picking up the waste paper.

The wartime generally was very busy indeed, and after school in the evenings all the children went into people's gardens to 'Dig For Victory' (quoting the slogan of the time). They planted carrots, turnips, potatoes and so on, and I believe they all had to participate as part of the war effort.

Pinewood Hospital, between the wars[*1] (see footnote on Page 223) had been built by the London County Council (the LCC) as a TB Sanatorium, out in the country, for, as far as I know, TB patients from the London area. This was kept on and used throughout the war.

My Memories of Crowthorne Yesteryear and other accounts

In the woods alongside it the Canadian army built a major hospital*2 with a most up-to-date operating theatre and the facilities of the time, with a view to casualties from Europe being brought there for treatment.

I cannot quite remember how many men were involved, but there were certainly a lot of patients in the hospital during the war, who all wore white shirts, light-blue suits and red ties.

They were allowed out of the hospital to go on walks and could be seen doing this, from Nine Mile Ride crossroads, along the New Wokingham Road to "Dr Chapman's Corner" (as it was sometimes known, close to his house Quatre Bras), and up Duke's Ride to the village, to buy toothpaste and that sort of thing.

Every Christmas the hospital staff used to give a superb party for all the local children, when they also gave them chewing gum, sweets, maple lollies, and so on. Also, they put on all sorts of entertainment for the children, and very good it was too.

Likewise, they used to give a party once a year for all the local residents wanting to attend, where there was Canadian whisky free to drink, and suchlike. I used to hear all sorts of tales of the parties themselves and of the results of them, either on the same night or the following morning!

Meanwhile, almost opposite the Waterloo, in Duke's Ride, at Edgcumbe Park (where they've built a sort of housing estate, mostly, I think, for the likes of airline pilots and the kind from Heathrow Airport), there was a property called Edgcumbe House. This was occupied by, first of all I believe, the Free French, for some training scheme, then by Australians and New Zealanders.

I particularly remember the Australians being there. They used to come across to the Waterloo and were regular customers during the

---

*1   In *'The Crowthorne Chronicles, The Formative Years 1700 –1939'*, by Roger Long, the following appears: quote – '1911 This was probably the year that the Pinewood Sanatorium opened in St. Sebastian's. It was originally called the London Open Air Sanatorium and was designated for the use of the capital's tuberculosis sufferers, the surrounding pine trees thought to be conducive to recovery.'

*2   Marcel Messier (French Canadian who was a patient there – now deceased) said in his account in *'Our Memories of Crowthorne Yesteryear'*: quote – 'I arrived with other French Canadian soldiers at Pinewood on the 10th September 1942, though there was a Canadian hospital there before then, I think the Cana-dian 15 General Hospital with English Canadian staff. We took their place and they went to another part of England. Then the name was Canadian 17 General Hospital, with all French-speaking staff.'

My Memories of Crowthorne Yesteryear and other accounts

war. I think perhaps they were all dentists, or similar. It was very sad, as they all went to war, on D-Day, and I believe every man was killed, for we never came to hear of any of them surviving.

They were a terrific bunch of fellows, particularly one who used to visit the hotel very regularly called "Shorty". He was getting on for seven feet tall. During the war clothes were rationed, as is widely known, so were difficult to get. I was ten years old at the time and growing up, and Shorty came into the Waterloo one day and asked my mother, "What does your boy wear in bed at night?"

She replied that I wore pyjamas and he went on, "Do you have a job to get pyjamas to fit him."

She responded, "Yes, because he is growing up and I have insufficient coupons to buy pyjamas for him."

He then told her that there had been a "big joke" across the road, because "being Canadians we don't wear pyjamas, we all wear nightshirts. I put in an application for nightshirts and don't know how it came about, but they sent – from Canada – my allocation of these (and he showed my mother some nightshirts only big enough to fit a boy of twelve). It was obviously some kind of joke," he concluded, "because I'm called Shorty." So for the rest of the war I slept in flannelette nightshirts!

My Memories of Crowthorne Yesteryear and other accounts

Over at Owlsmoor during the war there was a gypsy encampment and, from then until 1955, I was never allowed to cycle through Owlsmoor. This was because, with all the gypsies out there, they could drag me off my bike and ransack me. However, all the heathland on Owlsmoor, which was very boggy, was used right through the war as a training ground for tank drivers and tank crews.

It used to be quite a thing for us youngsters to go off the Sandhurst Road, particularly to the big mound there, on the right-hand side (part of the Wellington College grounds in fact), and out towards Cock-a-Dobby and the Treacle Mine, from where we used to be able to watch the tanks practising and firing. There would be two or three old derelict tanks in the middle and we used to watch the other tanks roaring round and across Owlsmoor firing on the derelict tanks.

In the same way, as we were not far from Blackbushe (Yateley), which was a major airport during the war from where, I believe, mostly Hudsons were flown, we would watch when the planes were coming in to land. This was when all the runways were alight with twinkling, coloured lights. We mainly saw it from a relative's, Mrs Brady's, house in Pinehill Road, from where we could see right across Owlsmoor to Blackbushe. And of course we children, who had never seen coloured lights at night, considered this a wonderful and spectacular sight!

Naturally, the lights were only on for a short time because the enemy aircraft used to hang around these places and wait for the runway lights to come on, before trying to shoot the aircraft down as they were landing.

Certainly Blackbushe was a terrific place during the war and the Ely Hotel, nearby, was noteworthy and popular. The hotel, where it appeared they always served steak of some sort, even if only whale steak at times, never seemed to close!

Also in wartime, because the Waterloo was a Free House, we had two or three suppliers, in particular H & G Simmonds Ltd., of Reading, and also the Henley Brewery Company (later Breakspear Henley), of Henley-on-Thames – which is still in existence today (1995). We had a full quota from both breweries which constituted six times that of other pubs.

And we had a full quota of spirits, which meant we had whisky (whisky being a great thing in the war) and, particularly from the Henley Brewery Company, we used to get our spirits in carboys (big round jars in a basket of straw with metal bands around them), right through the war.

We could not possibly serve the whisky, gin – or rum, in those days, as well – from the big carboys. So, one of my jobs was to help my father in the afternoons, when the pub was closed, by pouring the whisky (which was not named at all, just called whisky, and came to us as 'a carboy of whisky' from the brewery) into already used, from memory, Black Horse, Black and White, John Haig, and Vat 69 whisky bottles, for dispensing in the bar. Nobody seemed to mind in those days.

We also had barrels of beer sent direct by train from Worthington (originally Bass Ratcliffe Gretton), of Burton-on-Trent. These used to arrive at Crowthorne Station and 'Ticker' Lovick, of Lovick's Garage in the High Street, used to go there with a lorry and then deliver it to us. Finally on this, we obtained spirits from the Aylesbury Brewery Company, of Aylesbury, in Buckinghamshire. I don't know how, but we did. I think we remained open for virtually the whole of the war, while other pubs closed for one day a week.

A big problem, amongst others, we had was, glasses could not be bought during the war, when the Waterloo was very short of them indeed. During the summer the business was so great that people used to come along with jam jars to drink out of, and I used to see some of them sitting around on the roadside by the hotel and on the lawns at the back of it – well, all over the place – drinking beer out of their jam jars, because we had not been able to serve it in anything else.

Also during the war, it is probably little known that Crowthorne used to supply Spitfire parts, which were made in several small workshops around the village: in a hall beside the Iron Duke Hotel; in a hall behind the Prince Alfred pub; and there was also a factory down by the station (near where 'Tommy' Hunt's the printing works and stationer's were). Later, this little factory was demolished. All the factories, or workshops, came under the firm, Metalair, of Wokingham. Metalair was actually making Spitfires and farming out some of the work to these smaller factories.

In Wellington College, the old indoor swimming pool, no longer in use because in about 1939 they had built a new outdoor pool, was also used as a workshop for making Spitfire parts.

So Crowthorne was in fact producing quite a lot towards the war effort.

Several of the men of Crowthorne used to go every day, early in the morning, to spend time at Farnborough in the RAE (Royal Aircraft Establishment) experimental factory, where they carried out high security jobs, experimenting on various German captured aircraft. Also, they were trying to perfect British aircraft, as well as stress factors in Lancaster wings, and that sort of thing.

My Memories of Crowthorne Yesteryear and other accounts

My father (Maurice) was given a petrol allowance to take himself and three others by car to Farnborough, as their work there was considered "high priority."* And Doug Spear (not the one of the Crowthorne building company) was a toolmaker at the RAE, which allowed him to be exempt from war service.

It was also at Farnborough that two of the Crowthorne men experimented with the first doodle-bug, and found out how the engine worked and what fuel it ran on. They were also involved later with the first propeller-less aircraft, that to everyone's amazement (because no one had seen an aircraft that did not have a propeller) was seen flying around in about 1943.

Another of my memories of wartime is, we seemed to have a lot of snow, which was quite a thing. And 1940 seemed to be a very snowy year when Napier Road where, at the top of the hill, I lived at the time with my parents (before we went to the Waterloo), was famous with all the local children as a tobogganing hill.

It used to be a great place for this. And I remember, particularly, that the best toboggan in the area was owned by Brenda Jaycock (now Mrs Body) and her two brothers Cecil and Denis (Jim) of the Crowthorne Inn. They had a very nice proper Canadian sled, that went much faster than anyone else's. I was very, very pleased when I was offered a ride on their sled, sitting behind Brenda, who really had 'the works' there!

We obviously saw all the local characters in the Waterloo throughout the war, and after it. We also saw quite a lot of the life of the village through people who visited us.

I remember a 'Snowy' White and his wife – no, girl friend, I think – named Doreen. He was famous for digging drains, a wonderful drain digger. When anyone had problems with drains (they were not running away, as it were, or anything else was wrong) he never seemed to have to worry about checking levels and things, but just went and dealt with the situation and always knew what was on and managed to sort it all out. Snowy was a very hard working bloke and a hard drinking man too!

---

* My father went into the Merchant Navy at the age of fourteen, where he remained throughout the First World War. He was torpedoed twice, became a captain and was considered brave and courageous. He left the navy in 1930. Then he volunteered for "the real navy", but was too old. They said they would only employ him as a stoker. So instead he joined the Royal Observer Corps.

My Memories of Crowthorne Yesteryear and other accounts

I also recall Wilf Newman, the local plumber, who used to come into the Waterloo quite regularly. I am sure lots of people knew him; he was related to the Newman family that had the saddlery in the village, and had a sister Nell, who had the shoe shop in the High Street which I believe is still there. But I don't think the saddlery is still going.

Just after the war we used to have Hugh Myers come into the Waterloo. He was of the well-known and wealthy Myers family of Wiltshire Avenue, who were very strong Catholics. Hugh was a war correspondent of a kind, I believe, during the war. Then, soon after the war, the BBC took him on and he was a European announcer on, I think, the World Service. He was very well-known in those days as a BBC announcer.

There was also a fellow called Brian Clayton who would come to the Waterloo, being, I believe, one of the two sons of Lt. Colonel Clayton. Brian was a magical man, I felt, who used to go off on a push-bike to do landscape gardening at Bagshot and places like that.

He also ran a superb Crowthorne Scout group and I believe they achieved five King's Scouts in a year with Brian Clayton – the highest number there had ever been in one troop.

Brian Clayton did a lot of good work around the village, including as a member of the choir of the St. John the Baptist Church.

A family who visited the Waterloo, whom I found very interesting, were the Hawkins. They, or some of them, should still be around in Crowthorne. Just after the war Harry Hawkins and his wife Emily took over Pinefields (the little hall, as mentioned earlier, in Waterloo Road), as caretakers. There was a house on the side of the hall, which the couple occupied. After the war Pinefields became the venue for dances and that type of thing.

Harry had been in the First World War and had a bit of asthma. He used to puff and grunt and come down to the Waterloo for a pint. At the end of the war his two sons, Albert (Bert) and Geoff, returned from war service. Albert was a very, very good cabinet maker, or joiner, and Geoff was a mechanic who went to Woodley to work in the aircraft factory there.

Very regular customers of the Waterloo, they were great fun. Geoff, the younger of the brothers, always highly amusing, with a good sense of humour, married Nora Newman, the eldest of two daughters (the other being Hilda). Her family of Newmans (no connection with the aforementioned Newmans) included her father Albert and mother Ella. Albert Newman was the manager of the Wellington College farm. Besides the Hawkins being a great family, very nice to know and always great fun, so too were the Newmans, and Nora was a very nice girl indeed.

Also among those who visited the Waterloo Hotel was a man called Albert Noblet (pronounced No-bley), a Frenchman and the languages, particularly French, master at Wellington College. (He is named in a document I've seen from the college as M. Noblet – Editor.)

His wife and family lived on the Cherbourg Peninsula and became very famous during the war, because they had billeted on them the senior German officers guarding the Cherbourg Peninsula and all the time they were working for the Underground.

While the German officers were being billeted and staying with his family in France, the family were hiding RAF pilots and other Underground agents waiting to be picked up and brought back to England.

They were also going into Cherbourg itself – the daughter in particular, I believe – with vegetables for sale in the market there, and were taking messages hidden in the vegetables. They all survived the war.

I would not say Albert Noblet lived in the Waterloo, but he spent a lot of time there. One of our most regular customers, he was both a jolly little Frenchman and a great character, who was very friendly with a senior master at Wellington College – Gerry Roy – who ran the Officers' Training Corps there.

Gerry was also a very great character who visited the Waterloo a lot and was renowned because he had a glass eye, having lost an eye in the First World War. He used to fix his glass eye on someone or other and frighten them. But he was charming and so was his wife Eve.

Unfortunately, soon after the war, when he returned to France, Albert Noblet died very suddenly from shingles.

Another regular customer of ours after the war was a man called John Price. John ran the gardens at the college, those down by the fives court and those by the lower gates, and used to produce the vegetables for use in the college kitchens.

John Price was also responsible for the swans on the college lakes, which of course were drained in the war, but there were still some swans around there that I used to see.

John did not come on the scene till after the war, when all the swans were back, and sometimes they used to leave the lakes and go and sit in the main road, or similar, when the police used to get John out of bed! He would then go on his push-bike to pick them up, before being seen peddling back down "Knight's Path" (opposite the then Knight's the chemist in the High Street), with a swan under his arm

My Memories of Crowthorne Yesteryear and other accounts

and its head going round to stick out in front.

A famous character, John Price had been a captain in the commandoes, who were dropped at Arnhem. He came back from there, although I understand from knowing him very well indeed (he was a personal friend of mine), that he was mentally damaged by the war and not quite the man he was beforehand.

Just after the war, before Edgcumbe Park was built, Edgcumbe House on the site was occupied by a man called Duncan Hamilton and his wife. He became a famous racing driver and used to come in to the Waterloo a lot. On occasions, he used to bring his friends there for a drink, being other famous drivers of those days – people like Louie Chiron, Reg Parnell and Bob Gerard.

Duncan Hamilton gained his popularity from winning the Le Mans twenty-four hours race in a Jaguar. I cannot remember what year it was. His cars were maintained by a mechanic, Jack Cotterell, employed near Crowthorne Station at the garage I think called Crowthorne Motors, close to Pat Burlton's (sub) Post Office and who was the radio man there (who sold, and possibly mended, radios – Editor.).

Jack was a brilliant mechanic, who used to prepare and do all the work on Duncan Hamilton's cars, when he owned his own racing pantechnicon, in which they used to load the racing car concerned and take it to the various circuits for Duncan Hamilton to drive. I sometimes used to go into the pantechnicon and down to the garage too, where I would watch Duncan Hamilton driving, help him polish the car, push it out and so on.

We also had less well-known people, or perhaps well-known ones in some other ways, in the Waterloo, Christine Keeler being one. It was she who was caught up in the Profumo case and nearly caused the downfall of the government.

Her mother used to live along the Nine Mile Ride and, after the Profumo case, Christine Keeler stayed for quite a long time with her, when she used to come into the Waterloo. She would walk up to the village to do her shopping and on her way back to Nine Mile Ride call into the Waterloo, have a shandy and buy cigarettes. And a very charming young lady she was at that!

Another famous person who visited the Waterloo quite a lot, both before it became famous and afterwards, was a gentleman (I think, Christopher) Kerrens. His mother lived locally and it was when he visited her, while on leave, that he would come into the hotel. He was noteworthy as Commander Kerrens who took over the Amethyst in the Yangste River escapade, got the Amethyst out under the Chinese guns, and saved all the crew and the ship. He became a highly-decorated hero in, I suppose, the 1950s.

There were three brothers who used to come in to the Waterloo (they visited all the local pubs). Named Walt, Tom and Shan Wheeler, they lived in Pinewood Avenue and were popular and humorous. Well known locally they were all part of the scene, as it were.

But regularly, nearly every Saturday night, the brothers would have too much to drink and, usually outside the Iron Duke, would start fighting, or two of them, Tom and Shan, would, when Walt used to try and stop them. However the pair concerned had apparently always fought, since they were kids, and as soon as they had a couple of drinks in them they would fight. They went on a sort of round, visiting pubs in turn, and from the Waterloo would go back to the Iron Duke, having already been there earlier.

There is a famous story relating to a public building in Crowthorne, in the 1930s, that goes like this. Some building work was going to be carried out, where unfortunately there was a big rubbish tip that was infested with rats. There was an attempt made to get rid of the creatures before building work could commence, but this failed.

But there was a local rat man around (I do not know what his name was, but he was known as "The Rat Man") who was quite

My Memories of Crowthorne Yesteryear and other accounts

name was, but he was known as "The Rat Man") who was quite famous because he used to earn pints of beer in the Iron Duke pub on a Saturday night by taking a live rat out of a bag and biting its head off! It was pretty disgusting. However, this was his trick and he said that for a sum of money he would get rid of all the rats from the area.

No one really believed him, but eventually he was told that, "Yes, all right," if he could do it they would pay him a certain sum. I feel the amount wasn't very much.

The story continued that he went and saw the rats and on the night in question led them, like a Pied Piper, with them all following him, out to Owlsmoor somewhere and got rid of them. I remember talk of the event, in or about 1939. It was quite a thing!

Another person who used to come to the Waterloo fairly often was Teddy (Edward) Jones, who had the sawmills in Pinewood Avenue. He was a Welshman, with a very strong Welsh accent I found interesting. I used to think he was fantastic. Teddy Jones had a very modern tractor in those days, and a special trailer. He used to buy standing timber and, with wedges and two men using two-handle cross-cut saws, saw it down. They then lopped them, burned all the branches and, using the tractor and a winch, picked them up, put them on the trailer and take them back to the sawmills.

At the mill they had a big saw bench, where the wood was sawn into planks. The saw bench was powered by an old steam locomotive that had been put there permanently, still standing on its wheels but had been lifted up with jacks and things. Beside the locomotive, there was a long leather belt that ran round to power the saw.

The steam locomotive had to be kept steamed up every day of the week and, of course, all night as well, to enable it to be working during the daytime.

It was of great fascination to us children to go round there, because the boiler fire of the steam-engine was alight and Mr Jones used to have an old man on the site, a Mr Cotterell, as a watchman and to keep the fire stoked up. He lived in a shack-type caravan, and unfortunately only had one arm, so had a wooden arm with a steel hook on the end of it.

We boys used to go there to try and pinch bits of wood to make rafts and also – which we used a lot – for barrow-loads of sacks of sawdust to take home for the bedding down of our rabbits.

However, we were mainly on our best behaviour when we went there and would ask "Old Hookey", as the old man was usually called, for the sawdust. But first, when he appeared before us, he would ask gruffly, "What d'you boys want now?"

My Memories of Crowthorne Yesteryear and other accounts

"Ple..ase Mister, do you thi..nk we cou..ld have some saw..dust for our rab..bits?"

"Yes, right, but you'd better not take anything else and don't get burned on the fire."

The best sawdust was just underneath the saw bench, in a big pit. We literally had to go down into the pit to get this and put it in the big sacks we had, before taking them away in barrow-loads to the rabbits.

He was quite a frightening old man, "Old Hookey", who used to come forward and shake his hook menacingly at any of us he thought were pinching pieces of wood or anything like that. We all used to run away screaming, for he was just like the pirate in Captain Cook. I am sure he never washed, because he looked a dirty old devil, who wore awful, dark old clothes.

A lady, always welcome at the Waterloo for as long as I can remember (whom I always knew as "Auntie Louie", though she was no relation to me at all) was Miss Louie or, to be precise, Louise Goddard, the famous teacher at Crowthorne C. of E. School for many years and so highly respected.

She was of the same age as, and very, very friendly with, old Miss Ifould (Gertie, my great-aunt). And during the 1920s, just after the First World War and through that period, these two girls used to go away together a lot, just the two of them. They would travel to such places as Rome, Pisa to see the Leaning Tower, Edinburgh, etc..

This must have been pretty brave in those days because, if one thinks about it, even to go to Europe necessitated going to one's railway station, that of Crowthorne in this case, get the train into Wokingham, or wherever, and then up to London, stay the night there, then get the train (boat train, I suppose) to Paris, before travelling across Europe, to Pisa, and so on.

My Aunt Gertie had a most wonderful collection of photographs from all the famous cities and other places they visited in Europe and Britain, including Scotland, Wales and Ireland.

Louie Goddard was a great friend of the Ifould family and a permanent guest with us at the Waterloo every Christmas. She lived as part of the family for much of the time and was always treated as such.

Another Crowthorne character who was in operation right through the war (I don't know when he retired, but it must have been sometime in the fifties) was 'Bobby,' real name Robert, Brooker, the village policeman. There was another policeman there too, whom I cannot really remember.

Bobby Brooker lived in Cambridge Road and what a character he was – he was big, he was fat, he was pleasant, he was jolly. He had bad asthma, so wheezed, puffed and groaned. Everybody said they could hear him coming, as of course he only had a bicycle for getting around.

He used to ride about on his big, double-crossbar (because of his weight) bike, over the handlebars of which he had his cape with a strap round it to keep it from falling off, and one could hear him peddling up the hills around, when all the time he was wheezing. The children used to call him "Fat guts Brooker."

But he was as all a village policeman should have been, an ideal village policeman, who knew everything that was going on in the village and had no intention or wish to ever leave it and get promotion – being quite content to control it and all that went on.

And provided the local poacher just poached a few rabbits, and kept it down, also I presume gave him the odd rabbit, and people otherwise kept within bounds, Bobby Brooker was a great friend to all – he really was – and a great friend to the village.

He kept control of Crowthorne too, also of the local boys who could be a bit naughty at times. Although they called him "Fat guts Brooker" and used to make faces behind his back, and go puffing and wheezing at him, they had great respect for him. As they grew up, I think this was even more so. Quite a few of them, I believe, had a cuff round the back of the neck from him, but were certainly not cheeky to his face.

Yes, a great Crowthorne character indeed was Robert (Bobby) Brooker, who was so very, very well-known and very popular with all, and when he retired he went on living in Crowthorne, in Church Road, until, I think, he died.

Father Marshall Keene, of the Roman Catholic Church, then a tin chapel, in New Wokingham Road, is in my memory as a fine figure of a fellow, who was well up to six feet tall. He had a booming voice and was a great man's man.

He would drink draught Worthington from his own cork beer mug and every Sunday, at 12.10 p.m., following the mid-morning service, would take off his surplice, leave the church and stride down to the Waterloo with some of his male supporters, who had been at the service. There, from a leather bag strapped round his waist, he would tip out all the money from the offertory (which *was* all for him) and ask for his mug to be filled up. Sometimes he would also buy drinks for his friends and they would do so for him.

Father Keene lived in the vestry, where of course he did all his cooking, but not on Sundays for the smell from it would not have been welcome in the chapel.

It was said, and I believe it to be true, that every Friday without fail he would lock all the doors, strip naked, then scrub the church and the vestry.

This was before the time of Canon Boyle's long period (1947-'63) at what became the brick-built Catholic Church there. After leaving Crowthorne, my memory tells me, Father Keene went to Jersey for three months rest, where he stayed in a nunnery (or convent) and was the only man there. Then he took the oath of silence and went to a monastery in, I believe, Asia.

I have here related quite a lot about Crowthorne, from hearsay and personal knowledge, concerning mainly the period just before the war, (though a long time before that in relation to the Ifould family and the Waterloo Hotel), throughout the war and up to about 1950.

After my wife Joan and I took over the Waterloo we built the hotel up, developed the bars, and became famous, or infamous perhaps, for having penguins in the garden, which was a great attraction to children and their parents. Through the attraction we made the hotel into a very busy and successful establishment. So much so that it really became too much for me and, when I came to have medical

My Memories of Crowthorne Yesteryear and other accounts

problems, my doctors advised me to do something different.

So we sold out to Courages and then Joan and I, with Jane our young daughter, born in 1971, and my parents, Maurice and Winifred, moved to Cornwall to live, where I intended having a much quieter life running a family holiday hotel. But in fact it did not quite work out like that, because once there I was soon working again, running a very busy hotel indeed.

As a result, seven years ago, doctors advised me that I would have to take early retirement and sell out, which is why I am now retired while still living in Cornwall.

I find it interesting when I think some of the people who visited Crowthorne. One of the main reasons we were given a terrific boost, when Joan and I had the penguins, was from the television and radio personality (just radio then, I believe), Jimmy Savile, coming into the hotel one day.

This was when we were just getting going quite well with the Waterloo, had the penguins and were fairly busy. On the particular lunch-time concerned, one of the staff said to me, "Would you believe it, there's a big yellow Rolls Royce outside?"

"A yellow Rolls Royce?" I replied. "Good heavens! Whatever next?"

The next thing was, somebody came up to me and said, "Do you know what, we've got Jimmy Savile in the bar!" Well I did not know about him, for I never listened to the radio, so responded, "Jimmy Savile, who's Jimmy Savile?"

The fellow replied, "That's the bloke who's on BBC radio (and he named the programme, I cannot recall now), every morning from ten to twelve. Everybody listens to Jimmy Savile."

Well, besides this, Jimmy Savile was (and still is probably) one of the Friends of Broadmoor, who had come to visit Broadmoor. And during the lunch interval there he had heard about the Waterloo and the penguins, so had come down for some lunch and a beer.

When he had had these, I saw this amazing character with his dyed blond hair (well, perhaps it wasn't dyed, but it looked it to me) who came up to me and said, "My friend, are you the landlord?"

I replied, "That's right. Mr Savile, isn't it?"

"That's right, that's right, it is, yes. You've got a wonderful pub here and I understand you've got penguins in the garden."

I told him, "Yes, that's right."

"Can I meet them, go and see them?"

"Of course, Mr Savile," I replied, "we'll go out and see them."

Well, there were a few kids out in the garden and when they saw

My Memories of Crowthorne Yesteryear and other accounts

Jimmy Savile they knew him instantly, began talking to him and I must say, he was very, very nice while chatting to them.

I brought out some sprats and Jimmy Savile came into the penguin compound with me, where I introduced all the penguins to him by name. He fed them all and talked to and stroked the little friendly one, Tiddy. As he was leaving, he put an arm round my shoulder and said, "My friend, I think you're doing a fantastic job here. And I think you have a super pub. I don't know of another one like it and I will do everything I can to help you."

"Well," I replied, "that's very nice of you Mr Savile, thank you very much." And we said our goodbyes.

A couple of days later, on the Monday (I did not hear it), Jimmy Savile, on his radio programme, apparently told his listeners, "My friends, over the weekend I have been to the most fantastic pub. The place is called the Waterloo Hotel at Crowthorne. Mine host there has everything, including penguins in the garden that talk to the children and it is a fantastic pub. And their food is good."

Well, he did this twice a morning for about three or four days, with a result that over the weekend following we had never been so busy and could never have imagined being so busy.

People were driving out from London, they were coming from Reading, from Pangbourne, from Basingstoke ... They were coming from Aylesbury, they were coming from every direction one could possibly think of. Hundreds of people were visiting us.

The police had to come and sort out the traffic problems on the roads about Crowthorne, from all the people trying to get to the hotel to see this pub and the penguins. And I must say, thanks to Jimmy Savile, *that* really put us on the map and made the Waterloo such a busy place from then onwards.

I now relate a VE Day memory concerning Nora Lawrence, the one-time popular pianist of Crowthorne, being driven around the village on a Ford coal lorry (along with others in the procession), while she played. The lorry was driven by 'Ticker' Lovick and the piano was placed on the lorry with its back to the cab, and tied to the cab with a rope. Nora sat on her own piano stool, while the piano was from the British Legion Hall.

As the vehicle moved along, the strains of 'We'll Meet Again', and so on, came from it. There was also a saxophone player and drummer on board to accompany Mrs Lawrence, and the noise was quite deafening at times.

The lorry had many stops and, at 4 p.m., when it had returned to the B. L. Hall, where the core of activities (as well as across the road

My Memories of Crowthorne Yesteryear and other accounts

on the Morgan Rec.) were going on – there was a sudden downpour. This brought a rush to get the piano, etc., off the lorry, and Ticker Lovick, who had a leg over the side as he tried to manhandle one end of the piano to get it onto the footpath, came to put his foot through the drum that someone had already put there!

I am sorry to have been a bit vague on dates, but the stories of the people around and of the particular characters, etc., were more-or-less timeless, that just sort of went on ....

Editor note: Sir Jimmy Savile's secretary, Janet Rowe, said recently (after he had read the piece concerning him in Michael's account), that he has never had a yellow Rolls Royce (presumably also not ridden in one). So whose was it, I wonder, in the Waterloo car park that day? Sorry, there's no prize for the answer!

Michael Ifould lives in St. Mawes, Cornwall, with his wife, Joan.

My Memories of Crowthorne Yesteryear and other accounts

The Master's Lodge, Wellington College, after severely suffering bomb damage, in October 1940, from which the Headmaster, Mr R. P. Longden, was killed. (Photo - Wellington College.)

The Waterloo Hotel, pictured from Waterloo Road, in 1991.
(Photo - Shirley E. Peckham.)

My Memories of Crowthorne Yesteryear and other accounts

Jimmy Savile, O.B.E., K.C.S.G., LL.D., on September 13th 1987, after participating in the New Forest Marathon, an annual charity event, then organised by the Lions Club of New Milton, at New Milton, Hampshire. The event is now organised by the New Forest Marathon Association, in the town. (Photo - Shirley E. Peckham.)

My Memories of Crowthorne Yesteryear and other accounts

ALAN BUTCHER
(ON THE HISTORY OF HUNT'S ONE-TIME PRINTERS AND BOOKBINDERS BY CROWTHORNE RAILWAY STATION)

Early in the life of Wellington College, The Master, Edward White Benson, appointed Mr George Bishop in charge of writing and music. Music was not Mr Bishop's strong point however, and he was consequently appointed College Bookseller in a shop near the railway station (then Wellington College for Crowthorne station), which became the College Press. As the business increased, a manager was sought and Mr Thomas Hunt was appointed.

About 1902, Mr Hunt bought the business and carried on a very successful printing and bookbinding business. Although he had several men on the printing side, more were employed bookbinding.

He supplied the College with most books, but also when boys left he purchased their old books and re-bound them. These were then sold to new boys at a reduced price. Many of the early apprentices started as paper boys at the shop and were taken on to become 'journeymen', remaining with the firm all their working lives and some well past retirement age.

Upon Thomas's death, in 1921, his son, Charles Thomas, took over the business. He seemed more interested in selling books, and as the bookshop had been let to W. H. Smith and Son and he did not get the opportunity to sell books in the shop, he bought a shop in Reading and only retained the rear premises at Crowthorne. He was able to keep the binders busy with work from his Reading shop and the printers with work from Wellington College and many local firms. During the Second World War, St. Paul's School was evacuated from Hammersmith to Crowthorne and this was another useful customer, especially as paper was on 'ration', but school work warranted an extra allocation.

Partly due to the connection with the college and also by reputation, several rather special organisations became very good customers. These included the Free Foresters Cricket Club, the Butterflies Cricket Club, many local boarding schools and there was a lot of Masonic work.

Upon Charles's death, in or about 1937, his wife Gladys took over and ran the printing business until 1963, when it was bought by Butcher of Ascot, a well-established, family-run printing firm.

I became the Managing Director of this and in 1976, due to the termination of the lease and the need for more advanced machinery, it was decided to close down the Crowthorne business and transfer the work back to Ascot, but in order to retain part of the name it was re-registered as Butcher, Hunt Ltd.

Alan Butcher lives in Sandhurst, with his wife, Jean.

CYRIL OWEN

I was employed at C. T. Hunt Printer's and Bookbinder's, by Crowthorne Station, for 35 – 40 years, six years of this serving my apprenticeship. When I first joined the firm, in 1930 or '31, Mr Charles Russell was foreman, and Cyril Barton of Sandhurst and Ron Austin of Forest Road in the village, also worked there. Bill Castle was an apprentice, who was employed there for a short time. I took over from him as an apprentice.

My first weekly pay was eight shillings (40p), in my second year it was nine shillings (45p), in my third year, eleven shillings (55p), in my fourth year, thirteen shillings (65p), and in my fifth year, fifteen shillings (75p). After six years it was still under £1-0s-0d a week.

The firm did a lot of Wellington College work, as well as posters, handbills, etc., which was their main work.

Charles Hunt took over the firm from his father Thomas Hunt, after Thomas died in 1921. In the 1930s Charles died too. His wife Gladys subsequently took over, almost immediately after her husband died, and ran the business until 1963, when Butcher, printers of Ascot, bought it.

When Butcher took over the firm, I helped them a lot as I knew all the contacts.

My late sister Evelyn worked in the office at Hunt's, having taken over there from Mrs Hunt after *she* became widowed, and previously in the office at Talmage the butcher's, in the High Street, where she had taken over from a Miss Morse.

In 1961, I married my wife Connie and we celebrated our Silver Wedding Anniversary in 1986, with a party for a hundred people in the Parish Hall. We are Life Members of the Crowthorne Musical Players.

Cyril Owen lives with his wife, Connie, in Church Road in the village.

My Memories of Crowthorne Yesteryear and other accounts
PETER RATCLIFFE
(who was an apprentice at C. T. Hunt.)

C. T. Hunt Ltd. was a small traditional printing firm situated close to Crowthorne Station. Originally called the Wellington College Press, it is perhaps remarkable that it managed to survive for so long in that location.

Tucked away behind a newsagent's, it was never the most accessible place. A flight of shallow steps led down an unlit passage way to the main door. Behind this door to the left was the machine room, housing three machines plus a guillotine. One of the machines, a cumbersome-looking Heidelberg Cylinder, had to be brought in through the window when installed.

A flight of steps went up and curved sharply to the left, to enter the composing room and manager's office. It was extremely cramped. Most of the space was taken up by about 200 cases of lead type. There were frames used for typesetting, a proofing press and storage areas for completed jobs ready for the machine.

These days there is a faint whirring and the sound of fingers moving rapidly over a keyboard. In minutes another page of typesetting, complete with headlines, borders and possibly photographs, has been produced. Within a few years the computer or word processor had practically eliminated five hundred years of printing skills.

The letterpress process had been introduced to England in 1476 and was still in force at C. T. Hunt Ltd. in the mid-seventies. The hand compositor held an adjustable 'composing stick' in his left hand, whilst his right hand gathered characters from a case of type, arranging them against the setting rule. Varying the space between words enabled the line to be filled out and placed on a metal tray called a galley. It would take about five minutes to set each line. Any logos or photographs would be sent away to be made into metal plates. Having made the page to the right depth, it would be tied up and stored on a galley until required.

Organising a major job, such as a carnival programme, could take several weeks or more to prepare. Once the pages were ready, they would be locked up in a special frame called a chase. This assembly then became a forme, a term still used today. Depending on the size of the job, as many as sixteen pages could be printed at a time. Being made of lead, these formes were very heavy. Probably the greatest challenge was lifting them off the stone, then negotiating the steep descent to the machine room below.

In order to learn about printing skills, an intensive five-year apprenticeship was served, at the end of which a City and Guilds

My Memories of Crowthorne Yesteryear and other accounts

examination would be taken. If passed, the title Craftsman would be bestowed upon the apprentice. Before that, other skills had to be mastered: making tea, sweeping the floor, burning the rubbish, unfreezing the toilet in winter, all done with varying degrees of enthusiasm. It was also the tradition that the apprentice supplied a cake at Christmas and on birthdays, a tradition upheld to the end.

Various circumstances, mainly technology and a reducing work load, eventually led to C. T. Hunt amalgamating with Butchers of Ascot, to become Butcher, Hunt Ltd.

The Crowthorne works closed in 1980. A small amount of type and one machine were transferred to Ascot, where even today the old skills are occasionally put into practice.

Peter Ratcliffe lives with his wife, Louise, at Owlsmoor.

Sections of the interior of C. T. Hunt Ltd. printing works, just before it closed down in 1980. (Photo's - Peter Ratcliffe.)

My Memories of Crowthorne Yesteryear and other accounts
LILY CAMBAGE (née REASON)

I was born in Cambridge Road, Crowthorne on July 31st 1909, being one of twins, the other being my brother Cecil (later known as "Son"). I came to move with my family to a semi-detached house in Pinewood Avenue, now No.40.

My mother and father, Rose and Harry Reason, who had thirteen children, were well liked in Crowthorne and were good friends of Mr and Mrs Jaycock, Bill and Harriet, landlords of the Crowthorne Inn. Also, they were good friends of Mr and Mrs Lovick, Charlie and Kezia, who were Harriet Jaycock's parents, of Lovick's Garage in the village.

Cecil (Son), my twin brother, and I were named after Mr and Mrs Lovick's twins, Lily and Cecil. We always used to call Cecil Lovick "Ticker" – a name many knew him by. He was a great pal of my brother Ernest, whom we called "Tubby", or "Bubbles".

Cecil and I were the first babies put on Mr F. Knight's (the Crowthorne High Street chemist) baby food. I don't know if it was actually his food or not. We were pictured on the labels that were around the food tins (see below).

Lily Reason (later Cambage) left, had a pink sash around her waist, and her twin brother, Cecil, wore a blue sash around his waist.
(Photo courtesy of Lily Cambage.)

My Memories of Crowthorne Yesteryear and other accounts

Some of my parents' thirteen children were: Joe; William (Wit); Ernest (Tubby); Lily (myself), my twin brother, Cecil (Son); Georgina (known as Paula); Mary; and Jim. The others died, two as babies, of consumption (TB), one of whom was known as "Little Eva".

Living next door to us in Pinewood Avenue were Mr and Mrs Charlie Cripps and Bert Butcher, who lived with them.

An old Mr Mundy used to come round at Christmas time with his horse and carriage, bringing food gifts for the elderly.

I went to Crowthorne C. of E. School and loved my school teachers very much: Miss L. Goddard; Miss M. Green; Miss D. Hunt; and our beloved Headmaster Mr H. J. Sharpe, succeeded in 1925, on his retirement, by Mr A. C. Goodband. Miss Green was very strict.

On May Days we always had a lovely time, singing in the playground a song I loved, called 'England My Homeland', and of course dancing around the May Pole.

Mr Sharpe (the Headmaster) caned a boy in my class, whose name was Max Dewdrey. When Mr Sharpe brought him back in the classroom afterwards, he said, "Max, what I have done has hurt me more than it did you." Max had sworn at Miss Hunt, our teacher. I never heard of Mr Sharpe caning anybody else.

When Mr Sharpe retired and went to live in Camberley, I used to visit him, also Miss Goddard, we knew as Judy, who lived in Wellington Road.

Another person I loved was Canon Coleridge. In wintertime he used to come into our classroom and stand right in front of the fire, warming his back. He was a lovely man.

Before I was born my father worked for Mr Lovick (Charlie), driving his horses and carriages, used for weddings and transporting people about. Later, on Sunday mornings, he used to bring a horse-drawn waggon down from Lovick's to take all us children to Bracknell, to see his mother and father, my Gran and Grandad Reason, who lived next door to a public house called The Running Horse.

After leaving his job at Lovick's, my father worked on the East Berks Golf Club course and stayed there until he retired. He kept the course greens looking like velvet and was well liked.

There was a well, dug for sewage, and my father fell into it and had to stay there until somebody found him, while he was crying out for help. Good job the well was dry! (Lily did not say where this was – Editor.)

My mum looked after the cleaning of the small school building in Cambridge Road. The building was used by Crowthorne C. of E. School for the girls doing cookery on Mondays and Tuesdays, and for

My Memories of Crowthorne Yesteryear and other accounts

the boys doing woodwork on Thursdays and Fridays.

Mum did a lot of nursing in Crowthorne. She helped bring babies into the world and attended Greta Woodason, who was then Mrs Evans (later she remarried to Tom Partner – Editor), when she had her two children, Denis and Valerie.

Greta was a daughter of Shirley Peckham's gran and grandad, Ada and Jim Woodason, whom I knew well. I spent many happy hours with them and used to call them "Aunty Ada" and "Uncle Jim". I really loved them.

My memories of Ada's and Jim's other children are of their son Victor, their eldest, who made lots of model planes, Syd (real name Dudley, Shirley's late father), and the youngest in the family, Maurice.

My mum also attended Mrs Maud Rowe, when she had her children, at her then home in Pinewood Avenue (later the family moved to Manhattan Place, in the High Street). Mrs Rowe had quite a family, of ten children.

Mum also nursed Bert Butcher, her next door neighbour, when he was very ill, and used to spread goose grease onto brown paper, then onto his chest, which saved his life. She was not a nurse as such, but helped people a lot and was often called out in the middle of the night to nurse somebody, then stayed with them until they were better. Besides those incidents and others mentioned here, Mum laid out the dead. She also carried out a lot of washing and ironing for the 'well-to-do', and would sometimes be ironing up until 3 o'clock in the morning.

Among others too, she nursed Frank David's mother, Elsie. Mrs David and her husband William (Bill)) owned a jeweller's shop in the village High Street and carried out repairs to clocks and watches.

An occurrence in the First World War, my father and mother used to talk about, concerned the Blair Nursing Home that was over or behind the Post Office, in Duke's Ride (opposite the Prince Alfred). A young girl had a broken love affair and got out of the home, in her nightdress, and ran down to the Wellington College lakes in the snow, where she threw herself in one of the lakes and drowned. I am not sure what her name was, but she was found the next day as people skated over her.

We used to go down to King's and Queen's Mere (the two lakes) on moonlit winter nights, to skate. And to the college lakes for the same reason, when there used to be car lights shining all around the lakes and a man with a stand of hot chestnuts.

I loved my walks, particularly going up to Finchampstead Ridges, which was always a carpet of bluebells in the spring.

Mrs Adelaide Ward, who lived with her husband Walter in the last

My Memories of Crowthorne Yesteryear and other accounts

house on the left at the bottom of the hill in Pinewood Avenue, opposite Circle Hill Road, was a midwife, whom we knew very well. One of her daughters, Marie, known as Billie, married our milkman, Billy Gear, of Birchin Inhams Farm, near Wokingham. (The Wards also had a daughter, Kathleen, and two sons, Bob and Tom – Editor.)

A Mr Cooper lived opposite our house. He had a lot of land, on which he grew fruit trees and vegetables which were sold by his daughter in her little shop in Church Street. (Apparently one of the Cooper daughters, maybe this one, often used to wear a straw hat decorated with roses – Editor.) Mr Cooper's son used to drive a van, taking parcels to and from Reading.

At the time I was working at Edgcumbe Mount, in the village. It was lovely when the foxhounds used to meet at the front of the house. When the hunt was on, my mother, my sisters (Paula and Mary) and I would follow them.

My sister Mary was very friendly with May and Annie Watts, who later became Mrs Townsend and Mrs Cripps respectively, and every year May spent her holiday with Mary, at Eastbourne.

I used to love going to Southsea by Sid Townsend's (May's husband) charabanc. It was an open-top one, from which we enjoyed the scenery as we were going along.

As a child I used to line up with others to go to our village cinema (St. George's, later the Plaza) on Saturday afternoons. We would never miss the serial that was on, called The Green Archers. The first talking picture at the cinema was called The Big Pond.

Mr Bert Harvey (who was a postman – Editor) and his wife Liz, of Pinewood Avenue, had a daughter, Phyllis, who went to Canada and married. I knew all the people down our road, Pinewood Avenue.

I often went to Little Sandhurst after my childhood, as my sister Mary lived there. They called it Cock-a-Dobby.

There is so much to say of all the people in Crowthorne: Mr Fred Long, of the clothier shop, Mr Talmage (Edwin, then Frank, his son), the butcher, all the Donnelly family ... And when the fair people, Whittles, were there, I courted one of the sons.

In Pinewood Avenue Mr Harry Over had a little shop which sold everything. He was a very jolly and kind man. His son, Ken, was friendly with my brother William (Wit), who was killed while serving in the navy.

Sometime after leaving school I worked for Miss Booth, the one-time school teacher of Crowthorne C. of E. School. Also, I worked for Mrs Wotherspoon, in her home 'Cawsand', Pinewood Avenue, she shared with her husband.

My Memories of Crowthorne Yesteryear and other accounts

I also worked for a time for a lady in a house called 'Woodside', in Pinewood Avenue, whose name was Mrs Beecher. Her husband was a jockey who rode in the Grand National. When jumping the Brook, as a rider, he had a fall and broke his neck and that is how Beecher's Brook got its name. They had a picture of it hanging on the dining-room wall.

As the old lady got older she used to walk down to the village in her nightdress and dressing-gown, sadly, and often the police brought her home. The house was just past where the Donnelly family (the coal people) lived. My twin brother Son and sister Mary worked at Woodside as well.

My parents lost two boys, William and James, in the navy. William (Wit) lost his life on the Curacoa, in 1942, along with Mr and Mrs George Watkins son, Arthur, as detailed in *Our Memories of Crowthorne Yesteryear*. This was when he was aged thirty, and James (Jim) suffered the same fate, on H.M.S. Suffolk* (see footnote on Page 251) when he was twenty-one. It was a big loss to the family, particularly to my mother. Wit and Jim I considered to be my two best brothers. Thank God they were not married. Also, a son-in-law of my parents was killed in Burma in that period.

My father died of cancer, sadly, in approximately 1947, after he had retired, and my mother died in about 1955.

My twin brother, Son, was in the Merchant Navy in the war. He came to help Miss Maud Crane run the cafe, Home Dainties, in Duke's Ride. Beforehand, in wartime, they worked together at Wellington College.

Before having Home Dainties they had a cafe in the High Street, near to Mrs Beatrice Bell's woolshop. (This later became the cafe of a Mrs Young – Editor.)

The cafe in Duke's Ride (Home Dainties) belonged to Reggie Chowings, whom my brother used to give a dinner to every day and, when he died, Reg left his house to Son, who sold it to a fellow working at Broadmoor. Reggie Chowings had the cafe built, which was a sweet shop originally, onto the side of his house for his sister Winnie, who was a cripple. Winnie's and Reg's father, Samuel, was a stonemason, who displayed his work on the front of his house. When Winnie died and Miss Crane took over the shop, it was first used as a fish-and-chip shop, then turned into a cafe.

Folk who used to visit inmates of Broadmoor Asylum (later Hospital) always stopped at the cafe to have their lunch. The cafe was badly run. Miss Crane got past it and went into a home in Reading. While in Crowthorne she lodged with my mother.

My Memories of Crowthorne Yesteryear and other accounts

Cecil (Son) Reason, circa 1980. (Photo courtesy of Jackie Watson.)

When I married my husband, Leonard Charles (a Londoner, I met while working there in service), and went to Chiswick to live, Fred McHugh, the Crowthorne taxi firm owner, used to come and fetch me to drive me to one of my sister's. I was so pleased to read of him and that he is still alive, in *Our Memories of Crowthorne Yesteryear*, also the same of George Daniel.

I spent such happy days in Crowthorne and *Our Memories of Crowthorne Yesteryear* brought back to me so many happy memories of so many people I knew.

---

* The Suffolk had just docked and a big oil tanker rammed it. In a pub called The Waterloo, at Huntingdon, Cambridgeshire, where my sister Shirley used to live, there was a picture of HMS Suffolk on the wall. The owner of the pub was on the Suffolk, but was on leave at the time the ship sank – Jackie Watson (née Cambage), daughter of the late Lily.

My Memories of Crowthorne Yesteryear and other accounts

Sisters, Lily Cambage, née Reason (left) and Paula Browne (née Reason), circa 1983. The sisters passed away, a week apart, sadly, in June 1995.   (Photo courtesy of Jackie Watson.)

Editorial:- Sadly, Lily (widow of the late Leonard Charles Cambage, of London), who was living in Mablethorpe, Lincolnshire, with her daughter Shirley, passed away in June 1995, within a few weeks of writing her account. Her death followed that of her sister Paula, who died just one week before her. They were the last of the family of Mr and Mrs H. Reason. Lily was very upset by Paula's death.

I was in touch with Ken Over, mentioned in Lily's account, recently, who said that old Mr Reason (Harry, Lily's father) was quite a character, a very big man weighing around 17 stone. During Jubilee celebrations for King George V a sports day was held on the Morgan Recreation Ground, and when it came to the Tug of War there was one team short, so, said Ken, "One or two of us got together and raised a team, with old Mr Reason as anchor man." Ken went on to say that my father, Syd Woodason, was in the team and although this was one of "outsiders", they got to the final, and to the surprise of everyone including themselves, they beat Broadmoor in the final. Afterwards they said it was due to old Mr Reason "whose weight won the day!"

My Memories of Crowthorne Yesteryear and other accounts
LAURA (BABS) HILL (née BENNELLICK)

My home, 'Kyrtonia', in Addiscombe Road, Crowthorne originally belonged to my parents, Frederick John and Laura Bennellick. They came to Crowthorne in about 1908 from London. Originally they lived, met in their school days, and were married in Crediton, South Devon. They left there in about 1900. Kyrtonians is the name applied to the people of Crediton, hence the choice of my parents' house name.

They bought the piece of land on which the house, No.28, stands through Brake's, the local land agents of the time. This plot, 20-ft wide and 200-ft long, cost £20-0s-0d. The house was built in 1914, by a Sandhurst builder named Dalley, at a cost of £258-10s-0d (I still have his receipt), and after he had had to clear the plot and all about it of trees and gorse bushes. It was the first house in the road to be built, which was then an area of gorse-covered gravel. The fence that now runs between Addiscombe and Lower Broadmoor Roads is a comparatively recent addition. There was nothing like it, dividing the roads, for years.

When my parents first came to Crowthorne from London, with my four brothers and sisters, they rented a semi-detached house in Cambridge Road. The eldest in our family, my sister Elsie, and my brother Frederick, were born in Crediton. After my parents moved to London, my sister Nellie and brother Richard were born. I was born in Crowthorne, when we lived in Cambridge Road.

In London, Dad worked for a big leather-goods firm, Pocock's. The firm recommended Dad for the role of boot and shoe maker in Broadmoor (then Asylum), after suggesting he try it and if he did not like the role he could return to working for them. So that is why he and the family moved to Crowthorne. Dad became the bandmaster of the Broadmoor (patients and staff) Band, in which he played the cornet. This involved the patients taking part in concerts, put on for the other patients first and the staff later. These occasions were long before the Broadhumourists concert parties were set up, which were also performed to the general public in the Central Hall of the men's wing.

Dad's work at Broadmoor involved his measuring the inmates, possibly the staff as well, for the boots he made for them. He settled well there, liking his work, and remained so employed for approximately 26 years (1908 – 1934).

A keen musician, Dad was also the bandmaster of the Sandhurst Brass Band, which he helped form. Later, when it became a silver band, he was still the bandmaster. And he played in them both.

At first in Kyrtonia, the only house in the immediate area (although there were a few in Pinehill Road nearby), we had no gas, no

My Memories of Crowthorne Yesteryear and other accounts

electricity and no mains drainage laid on. And during the First World War my parents could not get coal. All our water had to be heated by the fire and our food had to be cooked on our kitchen range.

Coal in those times, when available, was 2/6 (12½p) a hundredweight bag. We would go wooding (collecting wood) and gathering fir-cones in the nearby woods for our fire.

My father bought two goats from someone in or near Eversley, and he and my oldest sister Elsie walked home with them on leads. They were called Sally and Martha and were tethered in the woods, as our house was on a large woodland plot. My friends and I used to take the goats for walks up towards Broadmoor, along the main roads, and they would stop and eat bits and pieces by the roadside.

The children of the Broadmoor attendants (who today would be nurses, from the institution being renamed a hospital) were given a wonderful tea every summertime in the Central Hall, and sports on the cricket field were laid on. In the evening the staff (male and female attendants) had races, tug of war contests, and then dancing to the music of the band.

During the First World War there was a very large common fire, which started at the holly hedge near Broadmoor School that ran along Gordon Road. The fire came very close to our house. I was very young, five or six years old, and frightened. In those days when a wood fire started people came from the village to see it, and they were saying in this instance, "Bennellick's ought to take their furniture out in case their house goes on fire." Then an army officer on horse-back

My Memories of Crowthorne Yesteryear and other accounts

arrived with German prisoners of war and the officer asked my parents if the Germans could go in the house and get water to make a bucket-chain to the fire, which they gladly agreed to. If anyone called a fire engine in those days they had to pay for it.

My sister Nellie and her husband, Jack Osborne, came to live next door to us in 1932. Their house was built on a plot of land just over 20 ft wide x 200 ft long, close to ours. A smaller plot was between the two. Their plot, like ours, was bought through Brake's, the local land agents, and I think for the same amount, £1-0s-0d a foot. Jim Blunden, the Crowthorne builder, built Nellie and Jack's house. We were very fond of Jim Blunden and his wife Vera, who did most of their courting at our house.

Dad took over from Captain F. G. Robertson as Secretary, and was also Treasurer of the Crowthorne British Legion Club, until 1959, when his son (my brother), Frederick W. Bennellick, took over the role, until 1974. (Captain Robertson was a founder member, who was secretary from 1929 until 1937 – Editor). The President at the time, or some of it, was Lt. Colonel A. B. Clayton. When he completed his service, Dad was presented with a chiming clock bearing an inscription on the front of the case: 'Presented to F. J. Bennellick by the Crowthorne British Legion Club in appreciation of his valuable services as Secretary and Treasurer'.

My mother, also Laura, like me, was a very kind and loving mother and very hard-working, which she had to be with a family of five. She did not go out to work. Mothers did not go out to work much in her day. She had plenty to do with the family and the house.

We did not go far in those days. We went to Reading about three or four times a year, when we walked to the station to catch a train and would put a penny in the machine at the station for a bar of Nestlé chocolate.

My mother went to the shops in the village, where all the shopkeepers had time for friendly chats.

I attended Crowthorne C. of E. School, which I found to be a fine school, and consider myself better educated than many of the children today.

I quite liked going to school and remember most of the teachers. In the Infants there were Miss Blanche Annetts, Miss Nellie Smith, Mrs Sutton. In the "Big School" (I cannot recall the Class 1 teacher) there were, Class 2, Miss Hawes (or something like that), Class 3, Miss K. Stevens, Class 4, Miss M. Green, Class 5, Miss Dorothy Hunt (whom I liked very much), Class 6 and 7, Miss Louise Goddard (who had a sister, Alice), and Mr H. J. Sharpe was the Headmaster.

My Memories of Crowthorne Yesteryear and other accounts

I was a Brownie and a Girl Guide, and also a Puck Dancer (the Puck Dancers were run by Miss Napier-Jones in the village). I used to like running relay for Crowthorne C. of E. School, and won prizes. I did not go out to work when I left school, but did a lot of dressmaking for friends and relatives and later went to Sworder's, the florist and greengrocer in the High Street, to help in the shop and do flower work: wreaths, etc., and holly wreaths at Christmas time. They were very happy days in that shop.

My husband James (Jim), whom I married in 1967, was a Berkshire man (of Hampstead Marshall), who later lived in Lincolnshire. He was a groomsman in the First World War and the brother of a dear friend of mine. Jim was of a large family of nine children, seven boys and two girls. We were married for nine years before I sadly lost him.

All my life I have been a gardener and still enjoy it very much. Writing in May 1995, I recently entered both the Wokingham Horticultural Society Spring Show and later the Crowthorne and District Horticultural Society one. In the Wokingham show I had ten flower entries, from which I gained three first prizes, one second, and four third ones.

In the Crowthorne show I had twenty-nine flower entries and a pot of marmalade one, altogether winning ten or eleven prizes. For the second year running I won the silver Twinkle Star cup, for the most points in the daffodil class. The cup was given by a Mr Starr who was one-time secretary of the society.

I have been entering exhibitions in the local shows for about sixty years. For eleven out of twelve years I won the cup at the Broadmoor Horticultural Show, in the name of Bennellick (my maiden name).

I enter the local shows at the Morgan Centre, Wellington Road, in the spring, at Wellington College in the summer and at Finchampstead in the autumn. My flowers are usually auctioned at the end of the day, the proceeds each time being for the relevant society's funds.

Laura (Babs) Hill lives in Addiscombe Road, in the village.

'Kyrtonia', Addiscombe Road, built in 1914, pictured in 1995, long-term home of Mrs Laura Hill (née Bennellick), previously that of her parents, Frederick and Laura Bennellick, and family.
(Photo - Shirley E. Peckham.)

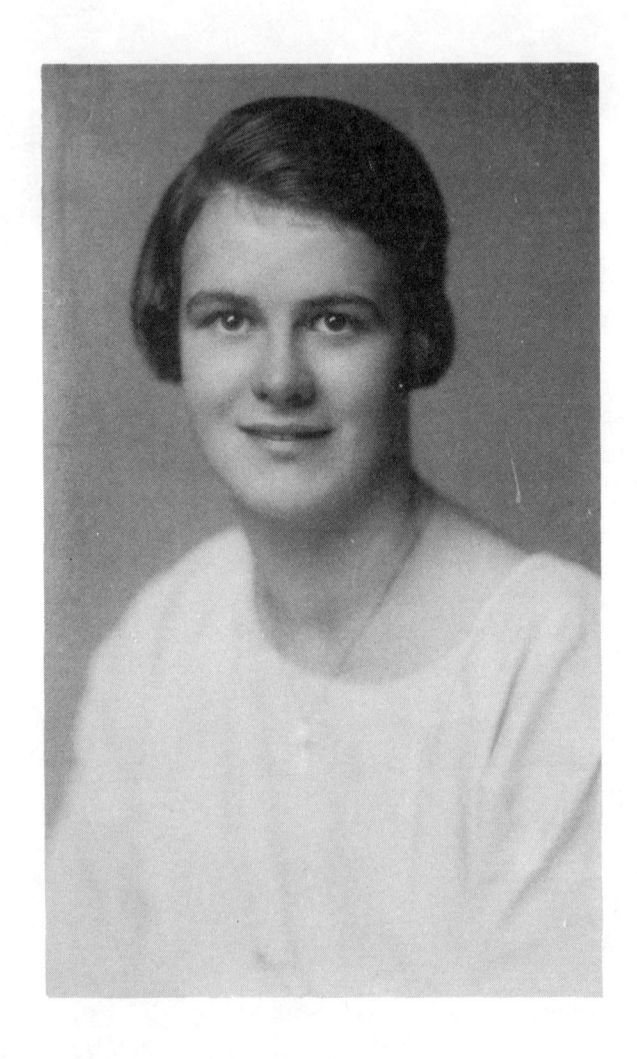

My Memories of Crowthorne Yesteryear and other accounts

Laura Bennellick (later Hill), when aged about 15, in the 1920s.
(Photo courtesy of Laura Hill.)

My Memories of Crowthorne Yesteryear and other accounts

Frederick John Bennellick and his wife, Laura, parents of Laura Hill, on holiday in Exmouth, circa 1939.
(Photo - Remington's Photo Services, courtesy of Laura Hill.)

My Memories of Crowthorne Yesteryear and other accounts

Frederick John and Laura Bennellick, parents of Laura Hill, July 1954. (Photo courtesy of Laura Hill.)

My Memories of Crowthorne Yesteryear and other accounts

Page
246   Account of Lily Cambage:

Harry and Rose Reason, parents of Lily Cambage, with two of their grandchildren, Jimmy and Shirley Cambage, in the back garden of the Reason family home, 40 Pinewood Avenue, Crowthorne, in 1940. (Shirley is now Mrs Brooks.)
(Photo courtesy of Jackie Watson.)

My Memories of Crowthorne Yesteryear and other accounts

ADDENDUM

Page

26   Footnote to the photograph should refer to Daphne Robertson's *older* brother, Ian.

104   Footnote to the top picture:
Reference to Daphne Robertson should be Jennifer Robertson (now Mrs McQueen).

207   Add the following:
Another service in the village, in the High Street, that lay back off the road, opposite the Prince Alfred pub, was G. R. Vaughan, Blacksmith, and then Lawn-mower Repairs, in business from 1919 to 1972.

210   Taylor & Whitlock, jeweller's. 2nd paragraph.
Dennis Strudwick and his wife, Barbara, owned the property that is now the jeweller's, but *did not* occupy this shop as his gent's barber's, but *the one next door,* that is now a fancy dress hire shop. The Strudwicks originally, many years ago, bought what is now Taylor & Whitlock's shop, from a Mrs Walmsley, who, said Barbara, sold children's clothes, mainly, and some ladies wear. The Strudwicks then let the shop as a D.I.Y. one, followed by an antiques one (run at one time by David Greedy, the local funeral director). Then, for a while, it was a sports goods shop, but latterly – before it became the jeweller's – was a cafe, that also sold bread, cakes, etc.

235   Michael Ifould account: 13th line down from top, should read:

He would drink draught Worthington from his own quart beer mug

276   Jones' Sawmills, now Edward Jones (Crowthorne) Ltd.
The last sentence of the picture caption should read:

Machine in background was apparently a Garrett Compode Portable Engine.

279   Jones' Sawmills, now Edward Jones (Crowthorne) Ltd. The last sentence at the bottom of the page should read:

Until then, the timber was always bought in the 'round', some times being already felled, or felled by the workforce of Edward Jones.

The Bennellick family bandsmen, of Sandhurst Silver Band (probably 1953-54), l. to r. Frederick William Bennellick, Thomas Laurie Bennellick and Frederick John Bennellick (Frederick John was the father of Frederick William, while Thomas is the son of Richard Walter and Elizabeth Anne Bennellick. Richard, in turn, was the son of Frederick John and brother of Frederick William Bennellick, in photo).
(Photo courtesy of Laura Hill.)

My Memories of Crowthorne Yesteryear and other accounts

Cornet player member of Sandhurst Silver Band, Thomas Laurie Bennellick, aged 9 or 10 (in the fifties), son of Richard Walter and Elizabeth Anne Bennellick (who lived at 'Leeston', Ellis Road, in the village) with a cup he won in a contest. He regularly entered contests for his playing, in and roundabout Crowthorne, and won many times.
(Photo courtesy of Laura Hill.)

My Memories of Crowthorne Yesteryear and other accounts

Above, Sandhurst Brass Band, in 1908 or '09, before they had uniform, the first time being in 1912. L. to r. ? ; Harry Gore; Mr Austen; ? ; Mr Dalley' ? ; ? ; Frederick W. Bennellick, bandmaster; Frederick John Bennellick (father of Frederick William); Albert Johnson (other names also unrecalled). Below, Sandhurst Silver Band (previously Brass Band), sometime between 1912 and 1916. Back row, l. to r., Mr Final; Mr Johnson; F. J. Bennellick; Cliff Clarke; Mr Evans; Middle row names uncertain. Front row, l. to r., ? ; ? ; Mr Jeffries; 'Teddy' Tims.   (Photo's courtesy of Laura Hill.)

My Memories of Crowthorne Yesteryear and other accounts

Frederick John Bennellick (father of Laura Hill), Secretary and Treasurer of the Crowthorne Royal British Legion Club 1939 – 1959, at an awards presentation function combined with the Annual Dinner in the British Legion Hall in the village, date uncertain. Mr Bennellick was to present the Bennellick Shield (pictured) given by him, for the successful billiards player in tournaments at the club, this being an annual event, with the shield each time passing to the winner.
(Photo courtesy of Laura Hill.)

Broadmoor Hospital, previously Broadmoor Criminal Lunatic Asylum. Picture shows the main entrance, more-or-less how it looked from the establishment being built and opening in 1863, to some eight years ago when the hospital was altered significantly, both constructionally and operationally. In part, the former brought a change of siting of the main entrance. This is now situated some 100 yards from where the original one was. See also picture on Page 337.

(Photo loaned by Bernard Fourness.)

My Memories of Crowthorne Yesteryear and other accounts

A hunt meet at the Iron Duke, Crowthorne, date uncertain but believed to be in the 1920s. (Photo courtesy of Laura Hill.)

My Memories of Crowthorne Yesteryear and other accounts

Laura Hill (née Bennellick), in 1995. (Photo - Shirley E. Peckham.)

My Memories of Crowthorne Yesteryear and other accounts

MARTHA ORAM (née FLOODGATE)

I came to Crowthorne from Southwark, S. E. London, in April 1918, with my parents, Marion Hannah and Arthur Floodgate, and my brother, Arthur George Michael Patrick. I was ten and my brother was twelve. We moved into one of the Stroud Cottages, Broadmoor Road (now Upper Broadmoor Road). The village was very small then. It has grown a lot.

We came to Crowthorne to escape more of the bombing in London, but seven months later, in November 1918, the war ended. The early shops were Hatfield's (cycles, etc.), Bell's (radios) and Rogers (baker's). Also Pearmain's garage was there from the early days.

My brother and I attended Crowthorne C. of E. School, for four years only, leaving at fourteen, and we were quite happy there. In fact I liked school, while a lot of children did not, and was never absent and never late.

Miss L. Goddard (sometimes known as Judy, as well as Louie) took Standards 6 and 7, two classrooms. I remember her teaching me. She would have the tallest in class sitting at the back of the room, and Lily Donnelly and I were concerned when, in winter weather, snow would sometimes come in the window and down our necks. Miss Goddard would invite us to come up to the front of the class and warm our hands by the fire. Sometimes she would get those of us who were cold to run around the playground two or three times to warm up. This often meant a number of children were out there doing this at once, who would then play tag to make fun of it.

Shirley Peckham's late father, Dudley Woodason, was at the school and in my class when I was there.

Mum had to go out to work as Dad did not work very much. He had a right hand deformity, but was good at doing things with his left hand. He had been a bookbinder and packer for a London firm while we were there, then was a kitchen porter at Wellington College and afterwards at the Wellington Hotel, near the station. Mum did domestic work. In High Holborn, London she was an office cleaner.

I remember Sarah (Ellen) Laybourne (later Woodason when she married Dudley) coming to Wellington College to work as parlourmaid at the Master's Lodge. Several young women from the north of England came there to work in service.

My first job from leaving school was as housemaid at 'Heathcote', Sandhurst Road, for £1-7s-6d (£1.37½p) per month. This was for Colonel William Henry Hinde, an Old Wellingtonian, and his wife. It was hard work, where altogether three servants were employed: a cook, a housemaid, and a parlourmaid. Colonel and Mrs Hinde had one son, Cyril, who was lost in the war. The Colonel caught 'flu and died, and is buried in the north of England.

I later worked at the Wellington Hotel, then, for 9½ years, at the Waterloo Hotel. At the former, Mrs Lester, the owner, would put on big dances in the glass lounge, where I served teas. Parents of Wellington College boys would collect them from the college and take them to the Wellington Hotel for tea.

In the Second World War the Headmaster of Wellington College, Mr Longden, was killed outright by his front door. The siren had gone and he was on his way to make sure that 30 or 40 of the boys had gone to their air-raid shelter. He was by his front door when a bomb dropped nearby causing the porch to fall in on Mr Longden. The Germans likely had the college as a target, possibly being aware that the boys were being trained there to eventually be officers in the army after also training at the Royal Military Academy, Sandhurst.

I left my job at the Waterloo sometime after my marriage, having mostly enjoyed the work, in a general capacity in the kitchen. Miss Ifould (Gertie), Maurice's sister, used to push work onto me. She lived to a good age, 99. I did not see a lot of Mrs Ifould (Winifred), who lived with her husband Maurice at the top of Napier Road.

Ellen Laybourne (being Sarah Ellen 'Helene', Shirley Peckham's mother – Editor) also worked at the Waterloo Hotel. She waited at tables in the marquees on the lawns, specially erected for the Wellington College Speech Day weekends every June. I knew Ellen well and liked her very much. She was great fun. I cannot be certain, but she may have worked with me at the Wellington Hotel as well.

I remember Michael (possibly Michael John) Ifould, son of Maurice and Winifred, as a lovely baby. He later went away to boarding school.

Daisy Wheeler, of Pinewood Avenue (who came from London), also worked at the Waterloo Hotel, in the kitchen. This was some years after I had left there.

Ron, my husband, and I met at Longmoor Lake (California-in-England, Nine Mile Ride). He was an Eversley man.

After we married we moved straightaway into our bungalow 'Peacehaven', in King's Road, which I had had built. It has remained solely mine. When we moved in, it was small, with only three rooms. I had it improved and enlarged several times.

Ron was employed at Broadmoor for twenty-three years, working on the boilers and in the grounds. He does our gardening and was employed as a jobbing gardener when I met him.

My Memories of Crowthorne Yesteryear and other accounts
We had three children, Ralph, John and Marion.

Martha Oram and her husband Ron live in King's Road, in the village.

" ... in winter weather, snow would sometimes come in the window and down our necks," said Martha, talking of her school days.

My Memories of Crowthorne Yesteryear and other accounts
JOHN (JACK) H. LECKENBY

I was born in 1916, in Rampton, Nottinghamshire. At the time of my birth German Zeppelins were bombing Retford Gasworks.

My parents and I moved to Broadmoor in 1918. My father, Thomas William, was the Asylum baker and confectioner. My mother was Bridget. I was an only child. We lived at No.100, the first house on the left after the sequoia tree, on the road between the High Street and Broadmoor School (Lower Broadmoor Road).

I attended Broadmoor, Crowthorne C. of E. and Ranelagh (Bracknell) schools, successively. Broadmoor was my home until 1941, when I was conscripted into the RAF. I could not volunteer, because I only had one eye, a birth injury.

After a six-week Officer Training Course at Cosford, Cheshire, I came back to Crowthorne. When a parishioner, Mrs Lushington, saw me in my uniform, she exclaimed, "My God, we must be in trouble!" She did not know how right she was!

Reading *Our Memories of Crowthorne Yesteryear* brought back fond memories, so much so, that I contribute as follows:

I remember helping the installer when a refrigeration unit was installed in Mr Swain's butcher's shop (in the High Street), in 1929 or 1930.

I loved the muffin man. He usually came on Saturdays. The arrival of onion men was also an annual event. Their headquarters were in the Aldershot area and they would walk to Broadmoor and Crowthorne carrying strings of onions on their shoulders.

Wally Mothersele (the bookmaker) lived at 99 Broadmoor, next door to us. My mother often gave him a 'couple of bob' (two shillings, now 10p) to put on a horse. She would say to me, "Don't tell your father." He was not a gambler.

George Vaughan, besides many other things (some listed in *Our Memories of Crowthorne Yesteryear*), made the iron work for the main distribution frame of the dial telephone equipment, when the local exchange (behind the Post Office, in Duke's Ride, I believe), changed from manual to auto.

Before Jones' Sawmills used the tractor (mentioned in *Our Memories of Crowthorne Yesteryear*), the pole waggon was drawn by two horses, together with a driver and a helper. They would go to the woods beyond the Broadmoor Farm in the morning and, around 4 p.m., would return with two or three tree trunks. When asked, the driver would deliver a tree limb to my mother, who would pay him sixpence (2½p). Sometimes the driver was the man with the hook (as a hand replacement, he being a Mr Cotterell).

My Memories of Crowthorne Yesteryear and other accounts

At the Plaza cinema (previously St. George's) we paid 'tuppence' (about 1p) to see such films as 'Dr Fu Man Shu'. When I went to Ranelagh (secondary school, at Bracknell), I graduated to the "four-pennys" (now 2p). When 'All Quiet On The Western Front' came to the village, the price of a seat increased to sixpence. I wanted to see the film, but my mother said I had to choose between the film and a new crystal for my radio. I chose the crystal.

Several bombs fell in the region of Broadmoor Farm. It was later learned that the cowman had a shaded lantern and, if he stumbled when on his way to the cow barn, at 4.30 a.m., the lantern would rock and the light became visible to a German plane on lone patrol many thousands of feet above.

Ted Stokes was, in his day, a genius. An acting vet, in the village, he would neuter a cat for sixpence (2½p). I never heard that he ever lost a patient!

Harry Over (grocery shopkeeper, first in the High Street and then in Pinewood Avenue) was also well known for his tea-blending expertise. I would get the plywood chests, lined with tinfoil, that the raw tea came in, and try to make models. The plywood was of such poor quality, that I seldom found material suitable to work with.

I agree with Ken Over (son of Harry) that Crowthorne C. of E. School was an excellent school. We could do with a few more Judy Goddards, Miss Greens and Mr Sharpes (Headmaster before Mr Goodband), with their benevolent discipline, in our schools today.

George F. Robertson's (a one-time steward of the East Berks Golf Club) son was a pilot. He was shot down when attacking the German battleship, Scharnhorst, when it was escaping up the Channel.

The Revells (who lived in Duke's Ride, next to what is now Lloyds Bank) had two sons. One, Tony, came to America. He worked for the General Dynamics space programme in San Diego, California. I saw him in 1976, when he came to the East Coast for a vacation.

There was a Crowthorne Cricket team. I played a few games with them. A list of the following week's players was usually posted in, I believe, C. T. Bell's (radios, etc.) shop window, in the High Street. The matches were on Wednesday afternoons and were played on the Polo Field, by the railway station. I do not remember the names of the opposing teams.

One event that caused a lot of controversy was a football match played on the Morgan Recreation ground. The home goalkeeper was hopelessly out of position and "Ponny" Tailor stepped in from the sidelines and saved a certain goal. *Was* it a goal, even though the ball never crossed the goal line?

My Memories of Crowthorne Yesteryear and other accounts

Fred Cripps was an excellent long jump athlete. In, or about, 1928 he won his way to the county meet, but unfortunately fell back in his achievements after making a record jump.

There was the Wheatley store, next door, in the High Street, to the International Stores – this being on its corner with Church Street. A sub-branch of Barclays Bank was on the other side of Wheatley's (these premises forming part of Waterloo place – Editor). Wheatley's was the mealiest store in the village, with masses of china and tinware on the floor. When one opened the door the place reeked of paraffin, which was sold by the gallon. Most of the items on sale there were of tin plate: candlestick holders, paraffin cans, tin cups, tin kettles, etc.

Miss Wheatley taught piano playing and I was one of her worst pupils. I have been told that I have perfect pitch and that under an expert tutor I would have become a decent pianist.

Sometime in the 1930s, the Thames Valley buses (serving the village) changed over to diesel. I can remember going into Reading one afternoon, sitting behind a driver who had never driven a diesel bus before. It jerked, the gears rumbled, as the driver tried to master the new technique. The redeeming feature of these buses was the temperamental heater mounted on the wall behind the driver.

Shortly after transferring to Crowthorne C. of E. School (from Broadmoor School), I slipped and broke my arm. Ruby Hills, another pupil, walked me home. Later Dr Chapman and another doctor walked to our house and set my arm in the front bedroom. My arm has never given me any problems since.

My father loved green bacon. On a Saturday, if the weather was good, my mother would tell me to cycle to Wokingham for a pound of this delicacy. The grocery shop was almost opposite the Town Hall on the left hand side of the Wokingham-Bracknell Road. I can't remember if the price was fourpence or sixpence (2 or 2½p) a pound.

Several times I cycled from Crowthorne to Hayling Island, on my trusty 26" Raleigh three-speed bicycle, for a swim in the Channel. I would leave at six in the morning and arrive home at ten o'clock at night.

For some years I cycled to work in Reading. On the way I would meet several Broadmoor employees, who lived in Reading, cycling to their work. One winter I was taking three night classes a week at Reading University. Cycling home at 9 p.m. and having to get up at 6 a.m., to go back to work in Reading, was too much. So I graduated to a motor bike.

My Memories of Crowthorne Yesteryear and other accounts

John (Jack) H. Leckenby lives with his wife, Helen, in East Greenwich, Rhode Island, USA., and will be pleased to write to anyone who cares to drop him a line (care of the publisher).

John (Jack) Leckenby.
(Photo courtesy of J. H. Leckenby.)

My Memories of Crowthorne Yesteryear and other accounts

John (Jack) Leckenby, with his wife Helen (left) and their grandchildren, Robin, and in the front, Denise, an excellent swimmer now training for the 1996 Olympics.
(Photo courtesy of J. H. Leckenby.)

My Memories of Crowthorne Yesteryear and other accounts

A RÉSUMÉ OF THE HISTORY OF JONES' SAWMILLS, NOW EDWARD JONES (CROWTHORNE) LTD. OF PINEWOOD AVENUE

Compiled by Shirley E. Peckham from material written by Susan Parkinson and supplied by Jeff Gibson, Managing Director of Edward Jones (Crowthorne) Ltd.

The original sawmills were owned by Mr Edward Jones, who lived with his family opposite to it, from sometime in the 1920s to 1957. Then the site and the business was sold to a Mr Irving. Timber was brought from local estates. According to documentation for 1956 on the mill: nineteen fir trees were purchased from Wellington College for the sum of £29-0s-0d; one spruce tree was bought from R. Clarke (no address available) for £3-3s-0d (£3.60); and twenty-one fir and two beech trees were bought from Broadmoor for £35-0s-0d.

There is no other documented evidence, apparently, of the history of the mill during its first some thirty years, but the photo's of it that follow (and on Page 313) indicate how it looked and operated then.

The team, employer and staff, of Jones' Sawmills in Pinewood Avenue. Date uncertain, but possibly in the 1930s or 1940s. L. to r., ? , Ted Jones, Bert Dale, Ernie Fisher, Frank Milam, Tom Day and Jim Herridge. Identification of machine in background uncertain, maybe a Fowler Traction Engine.   (Photo courtesy of Jeff Gibson.)

My Memories of Crowthorne Yesteryear and other accounts

Above and below, sections of Jones' Sawmills, Pinewood Avenue, in possibly the 1930s or 1940s. (Photo's courtesy of Jeff Gibson.)

My Memories of Crowthorne Yesteryear and other accounts

Further pictures, above and below, of Jones' Sawmills in possibly the 1930s and 1940s. (Photo's courtesy of Jeff Gibson.)

My Memories of Crowthorne Yesteryear and other accounts

During the latter part of 1957 the mills were enlarged at the rear, from the purchase of additional land from a Mrs Miles and a Mrs Bissell, who lived in New Road. Their gardens backed on to the mills.

In 1958 additional office accommodation was erected, requiring the installation of electricity.

There was very little change in working conditions for the staff at the sawmills until early in 1969, when it was decided to modernize the mill. But delays over planning permission caused problems and concern for Mr Irving. They were overcome and in June 1971 a construction company, Hewitt, of Cranleigh, Surrey, having won the contract with their figure of £7365.00, was invited to go ahead with the work. This they did in the following August, when also all the necessary fire safety precautions for the new construction had been passed.

Meanwhile, for the duration of the new construction, planning permission had been given for a temporary wood storage building to be erected along the front of the site, backing on to Pinewood Avenue.

The excavation and building work, for the erection of a two-storey modern building for the mills, was beset by problems encountered by the contractor. These concerned the ground being far too wet for them to be able to comply with the planning permission stipulation that concrete blocks, 10' x 10' x 10', had to be used for supporting the precast columns of the two-storey framed structure. So the situation had to be rectified and work ceased until this was resolved.

Eventually, piling had to be used to give the structure sound support, which cost the company as much as the completed building.

In March 1972, land lying adjacent to the sawmills, that which held a former pumping station, was acquired by what had become Edward Jones (Crowthorne) Ltd., on a five-year lease, at a cost of £1,972.00, and remains in occupancy of the company today.

THE PRODUCTS. There is no evidence, in the records available, that Edward Jones bought any imported timber until 1967. It is therefore assumed that the company only dealt with the home grown market.

The earliest recorded evidence of the purchase of timber states the year 1956, when the mills were under the ownership of Edward Jones. The early part of 1957 shows a pattern of purchases of wood similar to those of 1956. However, by 1961/'62, records show that, though still from the home grown market, timber came from further afield within the home counties.

Until then, the timber was always bought in the 'round', sometimes

My Memories of Crowthorne Yesteryear and other accounts

Prior to the Second World War, much of the timber was axe-felled.

Payment for timber was generally based on its cubic capacity. The measurement of timber bought in the round has never been easy. Rarely was it weighed, considering weight was computed from volume by conversion factors that varied with the species of trees. However, there is no constant relationship between the size of green timber and its weight, as the latter decreases as seasoning proceeds.

The capacity of timber in the round was achieved by the men of Edward Jones measuring its length and girth, and then using Hoppus's measurer, a table devised by Hoppus in 1936.

IMPORTED TIMBER. In 1967 the company began buying imported timber, while still continuing its purchase from the home grown market, until 1985. The decision to purchase imported timber was based, originally, on the company's breakthrough into the housing construction industry, in which high quality, strong material is necessary.

In 1985 the company ceased purchasing timber from the home grown market. Storage of the product was 'untidy' and wasted space. Instead it was decided to use the area to support a Builders' Merchant's, which would sell bricks, blocks, sand and cement, and compliment and add some diversity to the timber trade. This has been a successful project, even though the prime business remains with timber.

In 1986 the sales area and DIY shop was expanded to 1000 sq. ft, offering a much larger selection of goods. During 1989 an additional DIY shop was opened in the High Street, in Crowthorne. The shop came to be sold (as a running business) as part of a long-term plan.

PLANT AND MACHINERY. During the 1920s the men at Edward Jones used traction-driven circular saws. Nothing further is known about the machinery used at the mill in that period, except that the company has safely stored away an American Inserted Tooth-saw.

In 1957 the company introduced band saws. These were used for cutting large pre-sawn planks. As an example, reducing an 8" x 4" one to 4" x 4". Among others, the company has continued to use this type of saw, only replacing them with updated machines as and when necessary, such as in 1971.

During the years from 1958 to the present, the company has increased and updated its machinery on a regular basis, in order to maximise production. Edward Jones (Crowthorne) Ltd. currently uses a Stenner band saw.

In 1967 the company purchased new planing machinery.

The equipment used at present is called a Weinig Four Spindle Moulder and planes timber on all four sides in one pass through the machine.

In 1973 sawdust extraction machinery had been installed. The sawdust is extracted from the saws by an electric, motor-driven fan impeller, which then forces the sawdust into the cyclone and into a huge crate below.

TRANSPORT. The pole-waggon was always the traditional timber carriage in Britain, the original ones being horse-drawn before becoming mechanised.

Until the middle of this century, trees were loaded on to a pole-waggon, usually by rolling up simple ramps of short logs. This being a process called cross-hauling or parbuckling. The hauling ropes were then passed around the log in such a way that the horse or tractor, working on the far side of the waggon, could pull the log up the ramps and so on, to the bed of the waggon.

Until 1960, Edward Jones owned and used a Foden tractor to haul the pole timber. It was replaced by a Unipower tractor and, eventually, by an ex-army Bedford lorry.

The timber was loaded and unloaded by crane until 1979, when the company purchased their front-loading forklifts. Side loading forklifts were purchased in 1986 and these proved more efficient for stacking the timber.

Today the company has its own fleet of lorries for delivering timber and other goods to its customers. It employs nineteen staff, with Jeff Gibson heading the team as Managing Director.

Jeff Gibson and his wife, Heather, live in Wokingham.

My Memories of Crowthorne Yesteryear and other accounts

Above, the sawmills, now Edward Jones (Crowthorne) Ltd., early in the 1970s, in its modernization stages. Below, work in progress for the mills on spare land to the right of the site, Devil's Highway, 1971 or 1972. (Photo's courtesy of Jeff Gibson.)

My Memories of Crowthorne Yesteryear and other accounts

Above, work in progress for the modernization of the mills. Below, the newly-erected two-storey building. Early 1970s.
(Photo's courtesy of Jeff Gibson.)

My Memories of Crowthorne Yesteryear and other accounts

CLARE MUNDY (née PRICE)

My mother, Gladys Clara Price (née Hook), was born in Longdown Road, Sandhurst in August 1896, a daughter of Albert and Clara Hook. Mother had a brother, Victor, and two stepsisters, Edie and Lottie Annetts, who were from their mother's first marriage.

Mum met my father, Francis (Frank) Price, who was from Gloucester and had come to Crowthorne in 1920 to work at Wellington College as a porter in the Porter's Lodge, after he was invalided out of the Grenadier Guards.

They married in 1922 and set up home at 'Recview', Wellington Road (from where there is a view of the nearby Morgan Rec ground), opposite the home of my grandmother Clara Hook, who was then a widow. Our home was one of four cottages owned by a Mrs Dean. The other three cottages were occupied by Miss Louise Goddard, Mr and Mrs (Sid and Win) Rixon, a Miss Kelsen, a Mrs Pearson and Mrs Dean (the latter three residing in the same one).

I had two brothers, Geoff, born in 1923, who died many years ago, sadly, and Philip, born in 1926. My sister Margaret was born in 1930 and I was born in 1934.

While we were children we moved as a family across the road (Wellington) into Gran's house – Oak Cottage – where Mum nursed her for a number of years through ill health.

Some of my memories of my childhood include seeing two of the Crowthorne policemen going about the village on their bikes. These were Mr Robert (Bob) Brooker of, at one time, Cambridge Road, and Mr Robert Bates of Church Road. Mr Sam Ward was a Special Constable who ran Anstee's butcher's shop in Church Street, opposite to Macey's (and Cain's) department store. I was stopped while riding my bike without lights in Church Street once, by Mr Ward, who said, "I did not expect *you* to be riding your bike without lights." I failed to get into trouble, though never did this again!

There was a small bookshop, named the B.C.M. Library, in Church Street, run by Miss Rachel Cornish. Here there were Enid Blyton books in stock. I used to read them and loved the stories. The shop was where the sports shop is now (early 1995).

Thinking about my school days at Crowthorne C. of E. School, I have sharp memories of Mr A. C. Goodband, the Headmaster, and during part of my final year at the school, Mr R. E. Butcher, the Head after Mr Goodband retired. I did not particularly enjoy school. Of the teachers, I especially recall, Mrs E. Hallett, in the infants; Miss M. Green (in the main school), whom I found terrifying, and also in the main school, Mr Holley; Miss G. Burton; Miss Goodyer;

Mrs Luckock; Miss L. Mohr; and Miss Kinley. There were all lady teachers there until after the war, Mr Holley being one of the post-war ones.

The school had terrible toilets, never clean, with green doors.

I left school at fifteen and went to work at A. H. Bull, Broad Street, Reading, a departmental store. It was a John Lewis store and they bought Heelas, whom I also worked for. I was in the soft furnishing workshop for six years. However, I found working for Heelas not as likeable as previously and then went to work at Holmes, the furnishing store in St. Mary's Butts, Reading.

I met my husband, Cyril Mundy of Sandhurst, when I was twenty-two. We wed in 1956 at St. John's church in Crowthorne and began married life in the top-half of my parents' house in Wellington Road, made into a flat. We remained there for two years, before moving to College Road, College Town, Sandhurst.

Our son, Andrew, was born while we were living there and we moved to Addiscombe Road in 1965, when he was 2 1/2 years old. In 1966 our daughter Diane was born.

In 1971 my father died, and the entry in the Wellington College Year Book that followed read:-

(Headed *College figure.*) 'A Porter at Wellington College for 39 years, and known to generations of Old Wellingtonians, Frank Price, died in hospital in Reading last week at the age of 82.

'Mr. Price (he was Mr Francis Price) lived at 53 Wellington Road, Crowthorne. He joined the Grenadier Guards in 1910, becoming a sergeant, but his military career ended in the First World War when he lost a leg in the Battle of Loos in 1916.

'He went to Wellington College as Assistant Porter in 1920, later succeeding his father-in-law, Albert Hook, as Head Porter, and retiring in 1959, the year of the College centenary.

'During those celebrations he was presented to the Queen, and he was also presented to the Queen Mother when she visited Wellington to unveil the Chapel's stained glass windows in 1952.'

Also following my father's death, the Rev. Michael Campling, then vicar of St. John the Baptist Church in the village, wrote in the Parish magazine of him:

'I mention Frank Price who died in January. He had served his country as a Sergeant in the Grenadiers, losing a limb in the First World War, and then had served Wellington College for very many years. Considering the fact that he had been confined to his house for so many years, it was heartening to see the great number who turned

My Memories of Crowthorne Yesteryear and other accounts

His wife, Gladys, has looked after him so wonderfully these last difficult months, many kind neighbours and relatives have helped to share her burden and care for him, and the Clergy have been glad to take them the Holy Sacrament many times. It is most fitting that at his funeral we sang the epiphany hymn, of which the last verse is:

> In the Heavenly country bright,
> Need they no created light;
> Thou its Light, its Joy, its Crown,
> Thou its Sun, which does not down;
> There for ever may we sing
> Alleluias to our King.'

My husband's father, George Thomas Mundy, was the verger at the Royal Military Academy, Sandhurst for 19 years till June 1968, and his mother was Irene May Mundy (née Franshaw).

Clare Mundy lives with her husband, Cyril, in Addiscombe Road in the village.

Francis (Frank) Price, front right, when recovering from First World War injuries, pre-1920 (location uncertain, possibly Roehampton Hospital, where he spent some time).
(Photo courtesy of Clare Mundy.)

My Memories of Crowthorne Yesteryear and other accounts

Francis (Frank) Price, right, porter at Wellington College, and his father-in-law, Albert Hook, the Head Porter. Frank Price also became Head Porter, although he had an artificial leg from war injuries sustained in the Battle of Loos (France) when serving with the Grenadier Guards.
(Photo Wellington College, courtesy of Clare Mundy.)

Wedding group photo of Francis and Gladys Price (née Hook). Front row left, Albert Hook and his wife Clara, parents of the bride. Front row right, Levi Hook (brother of Albert) and his wife Alice, of The Grubbies, the Wellington College tuck-shop. Behind them is Miss Winifred Hook, daughter of Levi and Alice. Next to the groom (Francis Price) is his sister, Miss Annie Price, (Later Mrs Rhymer) and on the right of the bride (Gladys née Hook) is a Miss Goddard (not Miss Louise Goddard, well-known school teacher in the village, and no connection with her), who at the time had been a maid in the Matron's department at the College for a number of years, and George Binfield (best man), who will be remembered by some as the Lynedock Dormitory man, at the College. (Photo courtesy of Clare Mundy.)

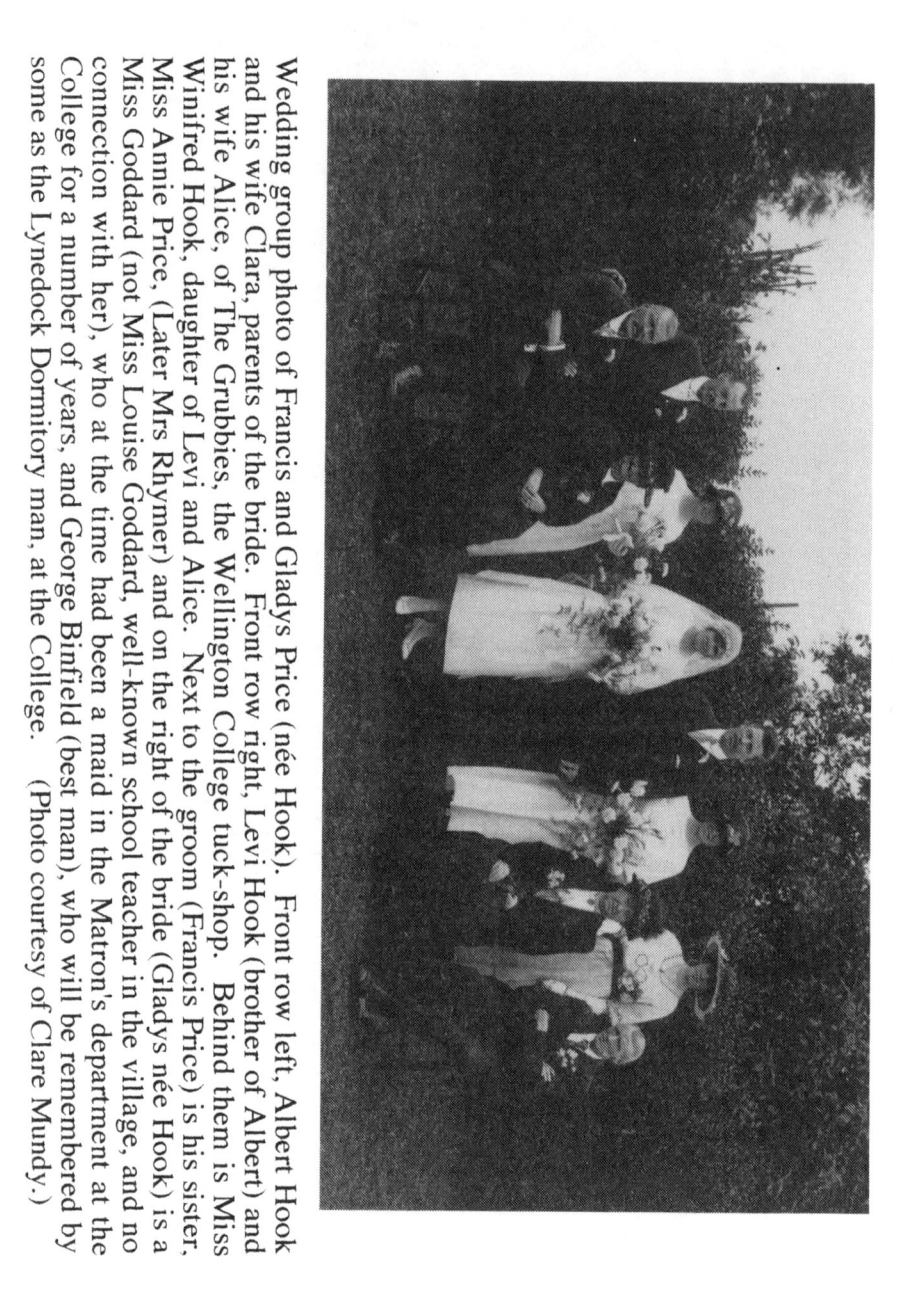

THE WOODAGE FAMILY BUSINESS IN CROWTHORNE

(By Shirley E. Peckham, based on information supplied by the family.)

Sidney J. Woodage was born in Crowthorne in May 1921 and attended Crowthorne C. of E. School. He was also for a time a choir-boy at St. John the Baptist Church. From the age of eleven he was an errand boy working for Staunton's grocer's (previously C. Harvey's), in the High Street, and would cycle laden with heavy groceries on his deliveries. From this the idea evolved for him to have such a business of his own.

Eventually, at Easter 1949, after leaving the RAF, Sid with his wife Doris (née Pearce, of Wokingham), whom he had married locally in August 1941, bought the very shop, near the Prince Alfred in the High Street, now Circle C, where he had worked as a child, naming it S. J. Woodage, Central Stores.

Together the pair built up the shop, measuring 200 square feet, from what was virtually only the front room of a house. After considerable changes and expansions, the shop, by 1972, was 2,000 square feet, had been changed in form to a supermarket with an off-licence, and had a brand new image.

After being closed for a spell to allow for the main part of the work to proceed, the store, with Malcolm, the eldest son of the family (born in 1947) as a partner, re-opened as a supermarket bearing its new title of S. J. Woodage and Son. Sid and Doris, in declaring that Malcolm had already, by then, been a mainstay in their business, was 'given' his new position as a surprise from his parents on the re-opening day.

Now with Malcolm an important figure in the shop, Sid felt easier about having to rush from it from time to time when demanded by his role in the village as a fireman for the Crowthorne brigade. At this time (1972) he had been in the brigade for seventeen years and its Officer-in-Charge for over two years.

The supermarket, that came to be Londis, had two full-time members of staff besides the Woodage trio to run it and by 1975, Neil, the youngest son (born in 1957), was also employed there, completing the family involvement.

Sid Woodage was proud of the fact that he had provided a service to the local community. During the time he and his family had the shop, they experienced enormous changes in the methods of selling, and enjoyed meeting people which the business gave him every opportunity to do.

Sadly, Sidney J. Woodage died in December 1976 and the family sold the business in December 1989.

My Memories of Crowthorne Yesteryear and other accounts

Doris Woodage now lives in Cambridge Road, while Malcolm lives in Lyon Road and Neil in Upper Broadmoor Road, in the village.

The small grocer's shop, Staunton's, in the High Street, Crowthorne, in 1935, decorated for the Silver Jubilee of King George V. Standing outside the door in one picture is Bob Staunton (who suffered from Down's syndrome), son of Mrs Staunton, who ran the shop. In 1949, the shop became that of Sid Woodage and his wife, Doris, and was named S. J. Woodage, Central Stores.

(Photo's courtesy of Doris Woodage.)

Above, S. J. Woodage, Central Stores, High Street, Crowthorne, soon after the family took the shop over from Mrs Staunton in 1949. Below, the same shop in the severe winter of 1963.
(Photo's courtesy of Doris and Malcolm Woodage.)

My Memories of Crowthorne Yesteryear and other accounts

S. J. Woodage & Son, Londis, supermarket, in the High Street (now Circle C), as it was from 1974 – 1989.
(Photo courtesy of Malcolm Woodage.)

(L. to r.) Sidney (Sid) Woodage, his wife, Doris, and their son, Malcolm, in their supermarket, S. J. Woodage and Son, High Street, Crowthorne, at the time the premises re-opened from their refurbishment, in 1972. (The store is now Circle C.)
(Photo – courtesy of the Evening Post, Reading.)

My Memories of Crowthorne Yesteryear and other accounts
REVD. PETER BURTWELL

All my Crowthorne years (1932 – 1945) were lived by the station. My parents, Stan and Kathleen Burtwell, had been summoned from Cambridgeshire to look after my maternal great-granny's (Mary Dean's) bakery shop, when her younger son, Wade, and his wife had died young. I always felt that Crowthorne Station was a village in its own right: the big houses between the station and the village along Duke's Ride holding the two parts of the village together.

Our Memories of Crowthorne Yesteryear testifies to the quality of Crowthorne C. of E. School in those days, which I warmly endorse. Any school today that had such a team as Arthur Goodband had, would reckon itself in clover! I remember the Wilding boys, Reggie and Philip, particularly Reggie. I was neither strong nor courageous, but I could carry Reggie on my back and go into battle on the playground trying to dislodge other riders. Despite their physical disabilities they were brave and good-humoured lads.

Every week the Wellington College carter, Mr Carter by name, who lived in a cottage by the lower gates of the college, brought his heavy horse to Mr George Vaughan's workshop (in the High Street, opposite the Prince Alfred) to be shod. His return along Duke's Ride coincided with the end of school and we used to scramble aboard the heavy four-wheeled cart for a free ride home.

Later, in the war years, some of the older Thames Valley buses were fitted with gas trailers, to save petrol. These were unreliable and unpopular with their drivers and bad timekeepers. Many a time I watched from outside our shop as the bus revved up outside W. H. Smith's shop opposite (now The Book Shop), to work up sufficient power to climb the railway bridge on its way to Wokingham.

But my real joy, living near the station, was to see the trains. The Reading to Guildford line was an anachronism, built in the days when railway companies built lines anywhere to keep other companies out. It had belonged to the South Eastern and Chatham Railway, though it went from west to east, and nowhere near Chatham! There was a regular service at one minute past the hour in one direction and eleven minutes past the hour in the other direction. It was one of very few lines the Southern Railway had not electrified, possibly because of the war, and so had a rag-bag of steam engines representing almost every age of steam except the very first.

In holiday times I would go down to the goods siding, below the railway bridge and on the village side of the line, where the daily 'pick up' goods waited for the passenger train for Guildford to pass at 2.11 p.m.. I made friends with the engine crew, who allowed me to ride on

My Memories of Crowthorne Yesteryear and other accounts

the engine with them, while they shunted waggons, sometimes as many as thirty of them. The engine might have to go beyond the Derby Field footbridge to bring all the waggons out of the sidings. The engine crew and shunter had to work fast to get their train all connected up and in the right order before the next passenger was due. If the rails were slippery, the engine was out of sorts, or there was a particularly large number of 'shunts' to be made, the goods train might have to go back into its siding again at Crowthorne to let the 3.11 passenger train go through, before it could go on to its next port of call – Blackwater.

The station was a fine building, built to impress visitors to Wellington College, and included a continuous weather canopy on both platforms (removed by the time the drawing in *Our memories of Crowthorne Yesteryear* was made). The station staff included a station master, shared with Wokingham, I think, a full time clerk, a porter, and a signalman. Charley Scutter was a well-known and popular porter. It was said that when he called out **"Crowthorne, Crowthorne,"** as the train came in, people in the village knew they had missed the train, while those in Sandhurst were warned to leave for their station to catch the train, so strong and clear was his call. Roy Morgan, who was at school with me, was, I think, the last signalman before the box was closed.

My Memories of Crowthorne Yesteryear and other accounts

We were so lucky in those days; we enjoyed a freedom denied to youngsters today. We could roam the 'College Woods', walk along the railway line towards Sandhurst, kick up the beautiful sweet chestnut tree leaves in autumn, behind the Wellingtonia pine trees, go to the 'lakes' in Barkham Ride – all without adult supervision.

My first brush with the law occurred in those days. My companions were Terry Norcutt, who lived at the station, and Frank Watson whose home was down Barkham Ride. If my memory serves me right, an artist had a studio in the middle of King's Mere and we thought it would be fun to chop down the bridge to the studio. We had intended to wait to see how he got off the island, but we took fright and dashed home instead. I was greatly impressed and appalled at the efficiency of the local police force when PC Brooker called at our shop, and told my father what had happened. I got a thrashing from Mr Brooker and no sympathy from my father. If it did not turn me from sin, it made me more careful then about being caught!

Many years later when I was on leave from Zululand, I was invited to preach at Evensong in St. John the Baptist Church, Crowthorne, and discovered that Mr Brooker, by then retired, was the churchwarden and was 'looking after me'. We had a good laugh over the memory.

Crowthorne was very fortunate in its vicars. George Coleridge, Andrew Nugee and Michael Campling, in their turn, were the three I knew, and I found each one to be a real man, and a man of God. My cousin, Adrian Burtwell, became a Franciscan friar and a highly regarded Secretary to the Minister General of the Friars – the top man of the Order. Adrian took the name 'Sebastian' when he became a friar, I always assumed after St. Sebastian's Church – an unusual dedication. I was older than Adrian and beat him to ordination by some years, but while he served the Franciscans in many parts of the world, I travelled only as far as Zululand where I worked for more than ten years, meeting my wife Bridget there, before we returned to England.

Another Crowthorne priest was railwayman Charley Scutter's elder son Jim, who like me became a missionary, but he worked in the vast open spaces of Botswana.

The hustle and bustle of present day Crowthorne makes it a very different place from my childhood home. If it provides as fascinating and encouraging a start to life as I recall, then its residents will be fortunate indeed.

Peter Burtwell now lives in Allington, Salisbury with his wife, Bridget.

My Memories of Crowthorne Yesteryear and other accounts
PAMELA SMITH (née GANGE)

My father, Edgar W. H. Gange, my mother, Ellen E. Gange, my sister Jeanne and I, came to live in Crowthorne in September 1938, when I was 7 and Jeanne was 4. We rented 'Tregenna' in Church Road from the niece of Mrs Childs who lived in Heath Hill Road, for ten shillings and four pence (52p) a week. (Later, my father and mother bought the house.) I had to go to Mrs Childs' house each week to pay the rent money and was scared stiff of her. I thought she was a witch, because of how she looked to me as a child, and she had a large toad under a stone in her front garden she would always show to me, when I could not get out of her garden quickly enough!

We settled into 'Tregenna'. Father had just left the army when we moved there, after doing 25 years in the Royal Hampshire Regiment, and was kept busy painting and decorating the house and cutting back the 6-feet-high holly hedge which surrounded the house and garden. This certainly let in the light and the garden itself was huge, containing apple, plum, greengage and damson trees. Father also kept chickens and as kids we had rabbits as pets.

To go back in time, Father was born and brought up in Portsmouth. He had been left an orphan. His father was a sailor who died at sea. His mother remarried and when giving birth to Dad's sister, she died. The two children were brought up by an aunt.

My Memories of Crowthorne Yesteryear and other accounts

'Tregenna', Church Road, when the Gange family lived there, from 1938 for many years. The house still stands (in 1995).
(Photo's courtesy of Pamela Smith.)

Dad ran away at the age of fourteen to join the army and told the powers-that-be he was eighteen. He went with the army to France, this being at the time of the First World War, where a bomb blew up in front of him. He received dreadful stomach injuries and was shipped back to England, where it was discovered he was only fourteen. After recovery from his injuries, he became a boy soldier in the Royal Hampshire Regiment. On reaching eighteen he rejoined the army and served for twenty-five years.

In September 1939 the Second World War broke out and Father went off to re-enlist, but was turned down as he was then forty-three years old. He was subsequently taken on at Wellington College in the armoury as a Sergeant Instructor. Also in the armoury at the time were Frank Eccles and George Cox.

My father, along with two other men, was responsible for the firing ranges at the college. When they were in use flags were flown and all surrounding areas were cut off and out of bounds to all civilian personnel. All the older college boys were given basic army training ready for their service careers and some went from there to the Royal Military Academy at Sandhurst for officer training. I understand the armoury building at Wellington College is still there.

My Memories of Crowthorne Yesteryear and other accounts

Wellington College, in 1953, showing college boys on parade on the parade ground. (Photo G. W. Cox, courtesy of Pamela Smith.)

I also remember Wellington College laundry and think it was run by Mr and Mrs Faulkner. My sister and I used to go there on Saturday mornings and earn 3d each sorting out the washed socks into pairs. Working there also was a young girl named Netta Taylor. She was a neighbour of ours in Heath Hill Road and I understand still lives in Crowthorne, now at Carlysle Court, King's Road.

Our neighbours in Church Road included two families, members of whom are still there, and I communicate with them. They are Mrs Kathleen Goddard and the Tickners – Mrs Dorothy Tickner and her son Peter. Peter, until October 1995, was a well-known local postman of many years standing. He has a married older brother, John, who has a family. Dorothy Tickner's late husband Harry worked at Broadmoor.

There was also Mr Robert Bates, a policeman in the village, living two doors from us in a police house. He and his wife had one son, also Robert, and known as Bobby. Next door to them was a girl named Shirley Milsom, whose father I understood was a Co-op manager, and apparently the family came to move to Reading. Mr George Wakelin took over as policeman in the village when Mr Bates retired.

Further up the road was the garden of Ruth Priest and her family, who in fact lived in Duke's Ride but their back gate was in Church Road.

On the opposite side of the road (Church Road) lived a lady whom we knew as "Granny Ward". Her late husband, I have heard, was one of the men who came to Crowthorne from Devon in the very early

My Memories of Crowthorne Yesteryear and other accounts

stages of the village springing up, near the end of the last century. "Granny Ward's" granddaughter Evelyn used to come and stay with her.

Opposite to our house (Tregenna) on the corner of Heath Hill and Church Roads, lived Mr Robert Brooker, another Crowthorne policeman before he retired and moved there. He lived with his wife and their only child, Daphne. Mr Brooker worked in his 'retirement' for a time as a bank guard in the front part of the sub-branch of Barclays Bank, close to the Iron Duke Hotel. Daphne took up modelling as a career. The family came to move to Heath Hill Road north, where they had had a bungalow built. This was opposite the home of the aforementioned Netta Taylor and her parents David and Jessie (née Morgan). Netta was an only child, who attended Crowthorne C. of E. School.

Mr Brooker's sister, Hettie James, came to Crowthorne in her retirement to live with the Brookers. She, I understand, had been a senior nursing officer.

My sister Jeanne and I went to Crowthorne C. of E. School in Duke's Ride and being left-handed I was given a very bad time from the teachers, in particular being rapped on the knuckles with a ruler by Miss Green and Miss Mohr.

When I left school at the age of 14, I went to work for Mr Fred Long in his first (little) clothier's shop in the High Street. I earned £2-0s-0d a week and stayed there for two years. Jeanne, when she left school, worked at Armitage's (departmental store), also in the High Street. There she was under the wing of the manageress, I believe a Mrs Doughty.

In July 1955, when I was 24, I married Fred Smith of London in St. John the Baptist Church in the village. The Rev. A. C. Nugee officiated. We recently celebrated our Ruby Wedding Anniversary. We had no children and spent most of our married life in Slough, that was in Bucks., now in Berkshire. My career was nursing, from 1948 to 1963. Now, in retirement, Fred and I live near the New Forest.

Jeanne, who in 1957 married Ken Roberts (not a local man), also in St. John the Baptist Church, Crowthorne, came to settle in Kent. They had five children and Jeanne died, sadly, in 1987, when aged 53, from a massive brain haemorrhage.

After my mother died, Dad, who had become a sergeant, went to live as an ex-long-term-soldier pensioner, in the Royal Hospital Chelsea, in London, where he enjoyed every moment.

Dad too died, on July 2nd 1968, aged 71, ending a very satisfying life right to the last.

Chelsea Pensioner, Sergeant Edgar W. H. Gange, left (other man unknown), in pride of place outside the Guildhall in Portsmouth, in 1967, at a Freedom of the City event (not directly involving them, but to satisfy the request for "two old soldiers from Hampshire" to be present for the occasion, and Sergeant Gange was originally from Portsmouth.)   (Photo courtesy of Pamela Smith.)

My Memories of Crowthorne Yesteryear and other accounts

Pamela Smith (née Gange), in her role as a nurse, circa 1950.
(Photo's courtesy of Pamela Smith.)

Rev. Andrew Nugee, with Pamela and Fred Smith after their wedding in July 1955, at St. John the Baptist Church, Crowthorne, officiated by the Rev. Nugee.   (Photo courtesy of Pamela Smith.)

My Memories of Crowthorne Yesteryear and other accounts

Rev. Andrew Nugee and other guests following the wedding of Pamela and Fred Smith, in St. John the Baptist Church, Crowthorne in July 1955. (Photo courtesy of Pamela Smith.)

My Memories of Crowthorne Yesteryear and other accounts

Jeanne Gange, left, and Joyce Silk (later Bennett), bridesmaids at the wedding of Jeanne's sister, Pamela, and Fred Smith, at St. John the Baptist Church, Crowthorne in July, 1955.
(Photo - Marshalls Photographers.)

Pamela and Fred Smith prepare to leave for their reception, following their wedding in St. John the Baptist Church, Crowthorne, in July 1955. (Photo courtesy of Pamela Smith.)

My Memories of Crowthorne Yesteryear and other accounts
WINIFRED (WIN) RIXON (née ELLIS)

I moved to Crowthorne from Bracknell in 1938, with my late husband Sid. He had been employed by the Thames Valley bus company as a driver, at their Ascot depot.

He then operated from the dormy-shed (a large tin building where four buses were kept and maintained) in Cambridge Road, in Crowthorne, where the Somerfield supermarket car park is now (1995). The bus cleaner was Harry Woods.

Sid very much enjoyed his work on the buses, which he began in 1925 and carried on for thirty-seven years, retiring in 1962. The route concerned was the Reading/Wokingham/Crowthorne/Camberley one; later also the Reading/Windsor (including Ascot and Bracknell New Town) one. The latter, though, for only two years before he retired. Stan Bennett, who lived in Napier Road, was Sid's conductor some of the time. His son, Donald Bennett MBE, now operates a car hire business in Crowthorne. Another of the conductors was Cecil Hayter.

Sid and I were married in Warfield in 1927, when I was in service. Sid lived in Bracknell then. We had two sons, David and Derek. Both boys went to Crowthorne C. of E. School and Derek went on to Ranelagh Grammar School at Bracknell. They joined the local Cubs, Scouts, Army Cadets and did national service in the Air Force.

As a matron's maid at Talbot House, Wellington College, for twelve years, I had a lot to do with the boys. Following this I worked in the college itself for seventeen years as a personal maid to tutors, where I was also involved with some of the boys and was employed for some of the time in the college dining-room, serving the meals and carrying out other jobs that were necessary. I enjoyed this very much and also helped with cricket lunches and masters' parties.

For forty years I worked in the Lady Chapel at St. John's Church in the village, attending to the flower displays, with Miss Louise (Louie) Goddard for some of that time, and was taught how to do this by her. Fresh flowers were given often (and extra ones for festivals) by local people, as gifts from their own gardens in remembrance of their loved ones. We dealt with the flowers as often as necessary, which was mostly more than once a week. Sometimes people gave money for special occasions. Nowadays the Mothers' Union attends to the Lady's Chapel flowers.

During wartime I helped the local British Red Cross Society branch and carried out house-to-house collecting in King's Road for the Agricultural Fund. In charge of this was a Mrs Hayes, a widow who

My Memories of Crowthorne Yesteryear and other accounts

lived in Duke's Ride (believed to be at a house named 'Chippingdene' – Editor). Also, I helped with the refreshments for the Red Cross Cadets in the evenings, and at Long's small clothier's shop in the High Street (then otherwise closed down for he had moved his business to a larger shop nearby) we sold goods made by handicapped people in Reading for the Red Cross. In control there were Mrs E. Moorcroft (who became the local Red Cross Commandant in 1953 – Editor). Another of my involvements was making tea and coffee for the blood donors at the Morgan Centre with Mrs Joyce Hamblin, of Grant Road, when we wore white overalls. I carried this on until I was eighty.

The late Mrs Dorothy Lloyd, of Wellington Road, and I operated the white elephant stall for the church. This was at the annual Summer Fair in The Vicarage garden (later on the Morgan Recreation Ground) and also at the Christmas Fair held at the Church of England school. Mr Fred Anderson, who had a business workshop in Heath Hill Road (previously the laundry premises of Miss Budge of Albert Road) would use his van to help with the moving of goods. Fred lived in The Avenue.

I recall the typhoid outbreak in Crowthorne in 1949 (mentioned quite fully in *Our Memories of Crowthorne Yesteryear* – Editor) and the warnings regularly throughout each day to "boil all your drinking water," etc. The message was relayed from vans, with loud-speakers attached, touring the village and no one could have missed hearing them. A schoolboy living in Wellington Road, Graham Smith, was one of those who contracted the disease. Very ill, he was taken by ambulance to hospital in Winchester wrapped in a blanket. The outbreak was said to have been linked with tinned corned beef sold sliced at the butcher's in the High Street, Swain's, but I did not hear if this was true.

Sid (my husband) was in the Home Guard in the Second World War and had previously served in the army, in the 1914 – '18 War.

The war years were not all gloom. We did things we never expected to, like working into the night putting gas masks together in the British Legion Hall under the eye of Major Lloyd, our Air Raid Warden of 'Hollybank', Wellington Road; practising pulling an unconscious person down a staircase in the home of Colonel Bouchier of 'Birch Knoll', Wellington Road; and learning how to use a stirrup pump for fire-fighting.

I've liked Crowthorne. We had such lovely Sunday afternoon walks up the Ridges, Wellingtonia Avenue, around the Wellington College grounds and the lakes, and had heather, rhododendrons and chestnut trees growing just outside our garden.

My Memories of Crowthorne Yesteryear and other accounts

A neighbour living next door to Sid and me, Miss Louise (Louie) Goddard, had been a pupil, a pupil teacher and finally Head Teacher at Crowthorne C. of E. School for many years. We became friends and in spite of my not having been one whom she described as "my girls", from Crowthorne C. of E. School, we were very fond of each other. Mrs Gladys Price and Mrs Dorothy Lloyd (our neighbours), and I looked after Miss Goddard during her last few years so that she could remain in her home 'Meadside'.

Our neighbours, Frank and Gladys Price, had two sons, Geoffrey, who unfortunately died when young, and Philip. They also had two daughters, Margaret and Clare (now Mrs Bird and Mrs Mundy respectively), both still living in Crowthorne. Miss Maud Green, for many years a teacher at Crowthorne C. of E. School, had also lived there, but moved to Napier Road before Sid and I came to the village. However, she was always coming to visit Miss Goddard so we knew her well.

Probably the last picture of Louise (Louie) Goddard, mentioned above and elsewhere in this volume, at the doorway of her home, 'Meadside', in Wellington Road, in the village, in April 1962. Miss Goddard (sometimes also known as Judy) apparently died in 1965 in Pinewood Hospital.

Winifred (Win) Rixon lives in Wellington Road, in the village.

My Memories of Crowthorne Yesteryear and other accounts
DEREK MARDER

I moved with my parents, Florence and Lionel, to Crowthorne from Acton in London in 1938, when they took over an empty shop in Pinewood Avenue. I was six years old at the time.

My earliest memory is of the sawmills, Jones', at the top of Pinewood Avenue. I was not allowed to go there on my own. However, when I was eight or nine, I started to visit it with other kids, when we climbed over the logs and played on the sawdust. The engine driver's name was 'Tiddler' Cotterell. He lived in a hut at the mills and would chase us off! As I got braver I would go and stand at the door of the engine shed. At first Tiddler would chase me away, but I kept going back! In the end he let me in by the engine, and when he found I was interested, he became more friendly and would tell me all about the engine. This was the start of my love of steam, which I still have today. The rack bench was a Stenner & Gunn, of about 1912, all steel, with a 5ft inserted tooth blade.

The other people I knew in the village included Mr V. Burgoyne, of Crowthorne Farm. He was a brilliant electrical engineer and a keen steam man, having a 9 1/2 gauge railway running around the farm, on which I and a lot of the other kids in the road were privileged to ride. Unfortunately he died at an early age and that ended the railway.

Mrs Burgoyne, who remarried to a Captain Bent of the Canadian army soon after the death of her husband, came to move with him to May Cottage at Sunninghill. The farm was then sold to a Mrs Robson, who remained there until after my family and I had moved to Andover in 1947. She was a kindly lady.

Once there was a glut of apples at the farm and Mrs Robson approached my father, who had recently come out of the army, to see if he would use some of them to make toffee apples for all the kids in Pinewood Avenue and Ellis Road. In those days everything was on ration, therefore Father, who had agreed the idea, had to apply for a sugar permit and was lucky enough to get it. So, with me having made the sticks, all the kids had their free toffee apples.

Now I write of other characters that I recall, in the village. First, George Sharman. George ran the Hand Laundry in Pinewood Avenue. This was from his home. His house was about one-third down the avenue, from the village, and was situated a long way back from the road. George was quite a character. He was invalided out of the army in the First World War and had a steel plate in his head where he had had a shrapnel wound. The laundry was a brick building at the rear of the house. The hot water came from a large, brick-built copper boiler and the smoothing irons were heated on a tall, tapered stove with

My Memories of Crowthorne Yesteryear and other accounts

narrow shelves. The stove was coke-fired and held about twenty flat irons of varying weights. There were several, large wooden tables, used for folding and ironing. All the drying was done in the open air on what was known as "the drying ground", which was a small paddock to the rear of the laundry.

Billy Gear – milkman. When we first moved to Crowthorne, Billy came round in his Austin 10 van, twice a day, early in the mornings, carrying a can of milk and a measuring jug, and would ladle the milk according to one's requirements into one's jug, left on the doorstep. He would then return later in the day with a second delivery. It was quite some time before he changed to bottle delivery. There was also another 'milkman', who used to deliver in the same area, a Miss Lucas, from Barkham Ride. She always used ex-Post Office Morris Minor vans.

The Village Carrier – 'Ticker' Lovick, of Lovick's Garage, High Street, Crowthorne. In my time in the village Ticker used an old Dennis coach, with a rear entry door, in which he carried all the goods from the railway station, a mile and a half from the village. He delivered to all the businesses in the area, and to Broadmoor Asylum.

Among other interesting vehicles locally, was one at Townsend's garage in the High Street, a 1928 Bean Charabanc.

The aforementioned Jones' Sawmills, at the top of Pinewood Avenue, had a new Foden Timber Tractor, with a heavy winch and a Gardner 5 LW diesel engine, circa 1940.

Mr V. Burgoyne, at Crowthorne Farm, ran Packards, one of which he had converted to a pick-up truck by old Ernest Lightfoot (1876 – 1960), local coach builder and wheelwright.

Charlie Mason – barber – in the High Street. Charlie was a kindly old gent, who smoked a pipe and had a lighter made out of a pom-pom shell (type of gun). He used to come around to our back door every Sunday morning and collect an ounce of tobacco. He would also go round to clients' homes, on his bike, on Sunday mornings to cut their hair, these being the ones who were unable to get to his shop.

I remember one incident where a kid, Peter C., of Pinewood Avenue, tried to put one across him. Peter called into the barber's for a haircut on the Saturday morning concerned and, after his hair had been cut, said his mother had not given him any money. Charlie, being Charlie, said "That's all right, you leave that until next time."

When next time duly arrived, Charlie gave him half a haircut, all up one side of his head, then promptly asked him for the sixpence for the previous haircut. 'Nipper' gave him the sixpence and Charlie asked, "What about today's?"

My Memories of Crowthorne Yesteryear and other accounts

The reply was, "I haven't got it." So Charlie sent him home to get the other sixpence. It turned out that the kid had spent the previous sixpence on sweets! While the price of a haircut was sixpence, if you sat still you got 1d back. Even George Donnelly, coalman of Pinewood Avenue, who had been going there all his life and was in his thirties, still got his 1d back.

George sold logs as well as coal. To provide the power to drive his circular saw bench he had an old Bean lorry from which he removed a rear tyre and settled the chassis on blocks. He then drove the saw bench via a flat belt, using the wheel of the lorry as a pulley. This worked quite well for a time. Then he bought a steam engine, which was much better for the job. This was purchased from a Jack Bennett, of Pinewood Avenue, who was afraid of steam.

When I purchased my first steam engine and lit it up for the initial time, Jack, who then had six kids, was running round calling them all indoors and shutting windows, saying the engine would blow up! Jack was a small property developer, and haulage contractor for the Milk Marketing Board. He later went into the furniture removal business and was successful.

Other incidents which come to mind concern "Blowers Fall". Halfway up the hill of Pinewood Avenue there lived a man named Mr Blower. He was not particularly friendly to us kids and one winter, when we had had some snow and ice, we made a wonderful slide right outside his front gate and Tom (I believe his name was) came out of his gate to chase us off and slid up on his backside. This caused roars of laughter from us and thereafter that spot was known as "Blowers Fall".

All the side roads in Crowthorne, as Pinewood Avenue was, were just dirt and gravel, known as "dirt roads". There was water and gas laid on to most of the properties, but some that were back off the road had none and their occupants were still using oil lamps. Drainage was either cesspits or bucket and "chuck it", which came as a bit of a shock to a lot of the evacuees billeted in Crowthorne!

There were several large houses in the Ellis Road area that had soldiers billeted in them during the war and there were a good number of Land Army girls billeted in the same area. There were some real live wires amongst them!

I think one of the most frightening things to happen was when about 70 acres of forest caught fire off Old Wokingham Road one hot summer afternoon, circa 1945. At the time, all along the sides of the road around Crowthorne were elephant shelters that were filled with ammunition, and by good fire fighting on the part of the NFS (National Fire Services) and the army, none of the ammunition exploded.

My Memories of Crowthorne Yesteryear and other accounts

An elephant shelter is like a small Nissen hut. They were about 7ft wide and 14ft long, made of very thick corrugated steel sheets bolted together, and had a canvas sheet dropped down at the front.

I attended Crowthorne C. of E. School and feel the education we received then and there was better in many respects than applies today.

Derek Marder lives in Andover, Hampshire, with his wife, Sandra.

Florence and Lionel Marder, in the front of their Austin 7 car, with their son Derek in the back, outside of their one-time grocery shop 'The Stores' in Pinewood Avenue, Crowthorne. Circa summer 1939.
(Photo courtesy of Derek Marder.)

Jones' Sawmills, in Pinewood Avenue, circa 1940. *The sawmills are still there today, very much modernised and now known as Edward Jones (Crowthorne) Ltd.* (See also pages 276 – 283) (Photo courtesy of Derek Marder.)

My Memories of Crowthorne Yesteryear and other accounts

L. to r. Dennis Mason, Cecil ("Son") Reason, Arthur Priest, and Cecil ("Ticker") Lovick, pictured in playful mood at an agricultural event in the 1950s. (Photo courtesy of John Priest.)

My Memories of Crowthorne Yesteryear and other accounts
KEN PARKER

I was born in March 1939 at my family home, 9 Pinewood Avenue (now No.14), to Beatrice and Arthur (nicknamed "Pake") Parker, and was the third of six children. The eldest was Margaret, who now sadly is deceased.

The next was my brother Dennis, who still lives in Pinewood Avenue, although not in our family home. My three younger sisters were, oldest to youngest, Anne, Kathy and Sylvia.

I attended Crowthorne C. of E. School, as did my brothers and sisters, and the only teachers I can remember there were Mrs Hallett and Mrs Harrington, in the Infants, and in the Big School (as we called it) were Mrs Luckock (in the first class, after the Infants) then everybody's favourite, Miss Burton. Following her, in the next class, was Miss Goodyer, after which came a young lady teacher, Miss Kinley, whom I for one, and many others no doubt, had a schoolboy crush on.

Then came Miss Hardman, followed by Mr Loney. And in the classroom, individual and separate from the other two school buildings (Infants and Big School), was Mr Webb, referred to by some of us as "Willie".

In the latter stages of my school life Mr R. E. Butcher took over as Headmaster from Mr A. C. Goodband.

I will never forget one morning being ridiculed in front of the whole school at Assembly, which used to be held in the top two classrooms with the dividing partition pulled back. Mr Butcher said "We have a young lad who would rather go and work at Thame's Stores (the grocer's in Duke's Ride) than represent his school playing football."

He then proceeded to ask me to come forward in front of everyone and explain why. I tried to explain to him that coming from a family that did not have much money, I was asked by my parents to go out and do a grocery delivery round after school to help with the housekeeping, and that I did not have a pair of football boots to wear except old ones that had a large split in them. Also, that there were a lot more important things for my parents to buy for our home and family before football boots.

This was seen as a great joke by the assembly, who promptly burst into fits of laughter, but unfortunately, as it turned out, Mr Butcher did not see the funny side. He smartly sent me over to my classroom where Mr Webb took great delight in giving me "six of the best" (three strokes on each hand) with his cane.

My Memories of Crowthorne Yesteryear and other accounts

My younger days, when not at school and before I started working part-time at Thame's Stores, were one big adventure with hardly any houses about compared with today to spoil the wasteland and commons we children used to play on and where we built tree cubbies and underground cubbies.

We would think nothing of trudging nearly a mile to the Palmer's Park woodlands (at St. Sebastian's), sawing down some of the straight fir trees and dragging them back to Pinewood Avenue to build the cubbies.

There were three boys, much older than me, whom we youngsters looked up to as cult figures. They were Derek Archbold (or Archbald), the main ringleader, and Jacky Greenwood and Ken Butcher.

We would think nothing of jumping on our bicycles and charging to the Fire Station in the High Street, after hearing the siren, asking where the fire was – mostly on heathlands, forests, or there was a chimney alight – and then try and beat the fire engine there. For some reason (I have not found out why to this day) our village fire engine was painted grey* and not the usual red.

---

*The grey fire engines were auxilliary ones, known as 'grey riders', and used sometimes during the war, whereas the red ones were known as 'red riders' – Crowthorne Fire Service.

My Memories of Crowthorne Yesteryear and other accounts

I also remember cutting across the Forestry Commission land, that is now where the Road Research Laboratories are situated, with my friends, to have picnics by an old oak tree affectionately called "the swinging branch", because of a low-hanging branch the tree had. We also carved our names into the trunk. I believe the tree is still standing, having avoided the bulldozers and the buildings going up.

My school chum and leisure time friend was David Allen, who sadly came to be killed in a mishap while riding his motorcycle. Mr and Mrs Allen, David's parents, had a smallholding in Pinewood Avenue, not far from my family home and on the opposite side of the road. Their detached house was on a comparatively large plot and in the smallholding they kept pigs. I believe the Allens were the first family in Pinewood Avenue to have television.

As with other lads in the village, I did a paper round in the mornings, earning me my first chance of buying a racing cycle. The paper shop concerned was that of Mrs Nora Lawrence (where A and A Car Spares in the High Street is now), before Mr V. B. Elston took it over. I purchased the racing cycle from Hatfield's, next door to the newsagent's, then owned by Tommy Hatfield, that is still trading and run by Keith, his son.

I spent the last two terms of my schooldays at St. Crispin's secondary school, Wokingham, which were not very fruitful I must add! Most of us concerned did not want this move so late in our school lives (resulting from permanent changes that had taken place at Crowthorne C. of E. School, with all pupils having reached a certain age being sent to the secondary school), and I am afraid that ultimately not much was taken in!

After leaving school I started work at Cadby's Garage (now Gowring's) at the junction of Finchampstead and Sandhurst Roads. I carried out my national service in the RASC, from 1958 to 1960, and was the penultimate intake to do national service. After carrying out my basic training at Aldershot and trade training at Blandford (Dorset), I saw parts of the world that I would never have seen had it not been for army life.

During my national service I travelled to Malaya on the troopship Navasa, stopping off at Gibraltar, Aden, Ceylon (now Sri Lanka) and Singapore. I also did six months service in Borneo before returning home on the troopship Kittiwake.

Just after arriving home and continuing my career, I met my future wife, Jillian Nightingale, who lived in Waterloo Road, Crowthorne, though she was born and lived for a time in Sandhurst. We had our engagement party in a room behind the Crowthorne Inn pub, the

My Memories of Crowthorne Yesteryear and other accounts

landlord being Jim Cronin.

On the second of June 1962 we married at Crowthorne C. of E. Church. The Rev. Michael Campling took the service. Our reception was held in the now Parish Hall, Heath Hill Road.

We were later blessed with a daughter, Sandra, and a son, Anthony. Sandra and her husband Shaun have a daughter, Samantha, aged 9. Anthony and his wife Karen have three children: Gary, eleven, Kelly, 9, and Mitchell, eighteen months.

Footnote: I have had two 'close calls' in my life. The first was, while playing and swimming in Palmer's Lake (off Nine Mile Ride). I slipped off a drainage pipe my friends and I used to dive from, and while struggling for breath I was pulled to the surface by Alan Douglas, who at the time had his arm in plaster.

The second was, while riding a motorcycle, just after being demobbed, I collided with a car on Lower Wokingham Road, then took ten feet of privet hedge down with my body, before landing on someone's lawn, looking up at the stars and wondering where the hell I was!

Ken Parker lives with his wife, Jillian, in Winnersh.

Some members of the Parker family, at Southsea – 1955 or '56. L. to r. Arthur (Pake) Parker, his wife Beatrice, their son Dennis, and daughters, Sylvia, Anne and Kathy.   (Photo - Ken Parker.)

318

My Memories of Crowthorne Yesteryear and other accounts

Above, Jillian Nightingale and Ken Parker at their engagement party in the room behind 'The Crow' (the Crowthorne Inn), in 1959. Below, guests at the engagement party. L. to r. Arthur (Pake) Parker; Margaret (sister of Ken) and her husband, Bill; Beatrice Parker and Sylvia Parker. Standing, l. to r. Dennis Parker; Derek Clacey; 'Son' Reason, and standing by the table, Kathy Parker.
(Photo courtesy of Ken Parker.)

My Memories of Crowthorne Yesteryear and other accounts

Ken Parker, standing by a Land Rover, "without the stretchers attached", said Ken, at Tenjong Aru Beach, Jesselton, N. Borneo, in 1960. (Photo courtesy of Ken Parker.)

Jillian (née Nightingale) and Ken Parker, in the British Legion Hall, Crowthorne, New Year's Eve 1994/'95.
(Photo courtesy of Ken Parker.)

My Memories of Crowthorne Yesteryear and other accounts
PETER TICKNER

I was born in October 1935, the younger son of Harry and Dorothy Tickner, and, with my brother John, we lived in Woolston, Southampton.

When the war started we lived only a few hundred yards from the Supermarine works in Woolston and as this became a target for Hitler's bombs, we moved temporarily to an aunt's of mine for safety.

As my aunt's house was also in Southampton it was not long before Adolf's bombs followed us there. During one air raid our house was hit by a bomb blast and all the windows were blown in. My brother received cuts from the flying glass.

I remember then being carried by Mum and, with the rest of the family, she made a mad dash with me for the air-raid shelter. The shelter, unfortunately, was flooded with about two feet of water, which meant Dad, Mum and John had to stand for the remainder of the raid in the cold and dirty water. I spent the rest of the raid, also, in Mum's arms, being only four years old and not very big. If I had stood, most of me would have been under water.

Because of the bomb damage to the house, we had to move on again. Finally we were given sanctuary by a Mr and Mrs Greenough, living in Pinewood Avenue (in the semi-detached house now known as No.67), next door to the then Marder's grocery shop. And so we had arrived in Crowthorne! (Part of Mrs Greenough's one-time home appears in the background of the photo on Page 312, concerning Derek Marder's account – Editor.)

The year was 1941. My father started work at Broadmoor, as an attendant, staying there until his retirement in 1966. He also had a part-time job with George Donnelly, the local coalman in Pinewood Avenue. Sadly my father is now deceased.

John and I started at Crowthorne C. of E. School. My earliest memories of there are of dancing around the May Pole with Ann Durling and with Ian Robertson, both of Pinewood Avenue. I also recall Ian and I being chased out of Mr Lewington's orchard, at the top of Pinewood Avenue, by what was called 'The Valley' (the woodland area we went through to get to school), and getting the cane from teacher Miss Gladys Burton with her sawn-off golf club.

I became a choir-boy at St John the Baptist Church, Crowthorne and was asked to read a lesson one Christmas. However, I was never asked to *sing* solo. Rev. Nugee knew what he was doing!

At the age of thirteen I delivered newspapers for Elston's news-agent's before school and groceries for Thame's Stores afterwards, my combined wages being 17/6 (87½ p).

My Memories of Crowthorne Yesteryear and other accounts

On leaving school, in December 1950, Ted Noakes, the sub-postmaster of Crowthorne, asked me if I would deliver telegrams for the Christmas period. I agreed and this was to be my introduction to the Post Office.

After Christmas I was employed as a junior postman at Wokingham Post Office, a position I held until my national service in 1954. It was my experiences during this period that have left me with fondest memories of the village, when I played football for Crowthorne Reserves. But as my job meant working most Saturdays I could only play a few games.

We had a very active Youth Club run by Mr Len Wheeler. The club stood where the Morgan Centre is now (in Wellington Road). We, the club members, used to organise our own games and entertainment. This included a trip to Margate one year and many dances. It was at one of the dances that Ted Rowe and Vic Wheeler (the youngest son of Len) talked me into doing a solo dance to the record 'Hootin' Blues'. This went down quite well until I put my backside through the interior wall of the club, much to the amusement of all the members present.

On completion of my national service I returned to the Post Office in Wokingham, until my transfer to Crowthorne Post Office in 1976.

After delivering mail to the Duke's Ride and Heathermount Drive area for two years, I finally finished up with the High Street/King's Road round, together totalling 17 years of being so employed in the village. Many shops and houses have gone during this time, to be replaced by larger properties. Manhattan House, where my school chum Ted Rowe lived, was one of them, which was at one end of the terrace of houses, Manhattan Place. Ted's house was demolished, but the fir tree standing at the bottom of his garden remained. We never could climb it, Ted's father having removed all the lower branches.

There are, of course, some shops still remaining in the village from my school days, and I hope for many years to come, such as C.T. Bell's, Newman's and Hatfield's.

Peter Tickner, who retired from the Post Office in October 1995, lives in Church Road in the village, with his mother, Dorothy.

My Memories of Crowthorne Yesteryear and other accounts

Above, yes, it's Peter Tickner in far off days. But who would have guessed? Below, Peter Tickner, in his Crowthorne postman role. February 1992. Picture taken in King's Road in the village. *(See also picture on Page 337.)* (Photo's courtesy of Peter Tickner.)

My Memories of Crowthorne Yesteryear and other accounts

Crowthorne Youth Club float in celebrations at Crowthorne for the Coronation of Queen Elizabeth the II, in 1952. (L. to r.) Wendy Long (now Mrs Wheeler); Hilary Benham (now Mrs Arnold); Ann Buckner (now Mrs Danes); Jean Collins; Dorothy Grinstead (now Mrs Brown); and tramps for the occasion, Peter Tickner and Eric Davis (known as "Tiny").
(Photo - Elena Moran, courtesy of Peter Tickner.)

My Memories of Crowthorne Yesteryear and other accounts

A group of customers outside the Crowthorne Inn, waiting to go to a Cup Final match in the 1950s.
(Photo - Bracknell Times, courtesy of Peter Tickner.)

1. Peter Tickner; 2. George Robertson; 3. Peter Gater; 4. Ken Butcher; 5. Don Hunt; 6. Bob Hull; 7. Bert Butcher (father of Ken); 8. Don Street; 9. ? ; 10. Malcolm Farminer; 11. Ted Hunt; 12. Ian Robertson (son of George); 13. Albert Fidler; 14. Nick Carter; 15. Bert Parker; 16. Tom Pepper; 17. Len Davis; 18. Bert Simpson; 19. Des Reay; 20. 'Drummer' Hawkes; 21. Terry Kelly; 22. ? Hussey; 23. Pat Sullivan; 24. Bill Duncan; 25. ? ; 26. Harry Tickner (father of Peter); 27. Doug Stonebridge.

My Memories of Crowthorne Yesteryear and other accounts
MICHAEL ABBOTT

My parents, John and Constance Abbott, came to Crowthorne in September 1945 from a dairy farm in West Meon, Hampshire, to take over the dairy, The Hygienic Dairy, in the High Street. They had bought it from people named Southern, from Lancashire, who only a few months beforehand had bought it from Furlong.

Milk was collected daily from Lord Brockett's Farm and Parson's Farm at Eversley, before being delivered locally by my parents.

The dairy and original shop were all in the same building (Talbot House), which now houses The Flower Shop and the Mayfair Cards shop. Our new Health Food shop (once the dairy shop) is in that of the former Co-op. They are all joined by the building which was originally the entrance from the High Street into the dairy yard, which we built over. Mack, the bookmaker, rented it for several years.

My parents lived on the premises and had a small grocery shop in the front of the house originally. The five children of the family were Keith (born in 1930); Don (1932); Dorothy (1933); Michael – myself (1935); and Geoff (1939). Don, Dorothy and I went on the rounds before going to school and on Saturdays and Sundays carried out bottle washing and milk bottling. Don and I worked in the business from leaving school.

Mum and Dad had a horse and cart, also a van, in their early days in Crowthorne. These were kept in our back garden, with its entrance from Wellington Road. At this time there were about eighteen dairymen in the area.

After their years of successful trading in the village, Mum died, sadly, in 1961. The dairy continued to grow and in 1963 Don and I formed Abbotts Dairy Ltd.. We also bought out Bill Gear, of Birchin Inhams Farm near Wokingham, the last remaining local dairyman.

Dad remarried and retired to Finchampstead, after which, in 1965, he too sadly died.

In 1972 we bought the Co-op and opened a freezer shop, running it along with the dairy, until we sold it to Clifford's Dairies, of Bracknell, in 1986.

We gradually made the shop smaller and now just run our Health Food shop. The remaining property was turned into offices.

Don, Dorothy and I all went to Crowthorne C. of E. School. Keith went to Ranelagh Grammar School at Bracknell, where he was Head Boy, and then to Reading University.

Geoff, whom many will remember from his working with Dad on his rounds – and who has Down's syndrome – now attends an Adult Training Centre in Wokingham. He is 56 and keeps very well.

My Memories of Crowthorne Yesteryear and other accounts
Michael Abbott lives in Lyon Road in the village, with his wife Hilary.

John Abbott, left, owner of The Hygienic Dairy, in Crowthorne High Street, from 1945 for many years (now Abbotts Health Food Store), relaxing with his son, Geoff, a sufferer of Down's syndrome, behind the dairy, in 1958. (Photo courtesy of Michael Abbott.)

My Memories of Crowthorne Yesteryear and other accounts

Abbotts Health Food Store, 1995 (once Abbotts Hygienic Dairy), forming part of Talbot House, on the corner of the High Street and Wellington Road, Crowthorne.
(Photo - Michael Abbott.)

My Memories of Crowthorne Yesteryear and other accounts
E. C. (TED) DRAY

I came to Crowthorne in February 1947, after leaving the forces, with my parents, Percy William and Jessie Beatrice Dray. We took over the Senior Supply Stores, then and for many years a small grocer's shop in the middle of the High Street near what was the Co-op grocery store, now Abbotts Health Food shop. We had come from Betchworth, near Dorking and Reigate, in Surrey (where my parents had a baker's business), and had seen details of the shop and flat above it, in Crowthorne, advertised in an estate agent's in Guildford.

I married Joyce in 1939. We had a daughter, Jacqueline, and my marriage was subsequently dissolved. Jacqueline married and has three sons and a daughter. Joyce and Jacqueline and family now live in Australia. I was called up into the army in 1943 and went over to France just after D-Day in 1944, where I was taken prisoner of war and finished up in Odessa in Russia. I came home from there in 1945, but still had time to do in the forces, till the end of 1946, when I came out.

I took the Senior Supply Stores over on the day my leave expired, February 24th 1947, from people named Blomer. I think they were there for just over eighteen months. Before then a Mr Read had the shop, and prior to him a Mr Philpott had it.

When my parents and I arrived in Crowthorne there were deep snow conditions, during the severe winter, that went on till the Easter Bank Holiday. From our initial day in the village we lived above our shop, where there was no bathroom.

The takings when we first took over the shop were £85-0s-0d a week. In a few months I had got them to £200-0s-0d a week. Food rationing (fats and sugar) and overheads came to affect the trade and the business was losing money in the end. However, I loved the place and when the lease ran out, after I had been in Crowthorne for 36 years, I retired. This was on January 17th 1983, when I had reached the age of sixty-seven.

I enjoyed Crowthorne itself in a way and would deliver goods locally to my customers by bike, or by car, the furthest distance being to New Wokingham Road. This was at lunch-times, or after my day's work in the shop. I only needed to have one week out of the shop through illness in all my time there. Sadly, my mother Jessie, a diabetic, passed away in December 1960, aged seventy-four, and my father Percy died in April 1969, aged eighty-four.

The Senior Supply Stores was taken over after my retirement by Mr Roy Riley of the Berkshire Cycle Company, who still has it as his cycle shop.

Before the war, and my time in Crowthorne, I was a keen cyclist

My Memories of Crowthorne Yesteryear and other accounts

and member of a cyclists' touring club. Consequently I did a lot of cycling, including to Wales, touring and back in two weeks.

I am a member of the Crowthorne British Legion Club where I regularly attend several times a week.

Ted Dray lives in Sandhurst.

Footnote:- Mr George Daniel, of Crowthorne, and a Mr Lee took over the shop concerned in the above account, from new in the mid-1920s and subsequently sold it to a Mr Douglas, who, said my informer, *probably* sold it to the Mr Philpott mentioned by Mr Dray – Editor.

E. C. (Ted) Dray in his grocery shop, Senior Supply Stores, High Street, Crowthorne, Christmas Eve 1980.
(Photo - Michael Arthy.)

My Memories of Crowthorne Yesteryear and other accounts
TOM PEPPER

Crowthorne has not changed all that much since I came to the village in 1955 from Reading, where I worked for Colebrooks, the large meat and fish retailers with eighteen branches mainly throughout the south of the country. I saw an advert placed in the Fish Trades Gazette by F. J. Talmage of the village for a 'fishmonger/poulterer'. He was the well-known butcher whose shop was in the centre of the High Street, now Larby's.

A house went with the job. This was at Cambridge Terrace, a block of four houses (the one at one end, nearest to Napier Road, had once, before my time in the village, incorporated a fish and chip shop). Cambridge Terrace was situated between where at one time Sid and May Townsend's sweet and ice-cream shop, and his garage at the back, were, and the combined building of I. V. Scott's house and his ironmonger's shop, now Bob's DIY. Both Townsend's and Scott's premises were also there before I came to the village.

At the age of 4 years I moved from London to Hastings in Sussex to live with an aunt, as my parents had died of TB. I stayed there till 1944 or '45, when my aunt had died. My uncle remarried and I was not welcome. I then moved to Bexhill to work and met my now late wife, Dorothy. After marrying, we moved to Reading.

From my getting the job at Talmage's, Dorothy and I then had only one day to move into Cambridge Terrace before I started work, for a Bank Holiday was involved.

I found my job interesting, which included selling fish, dressing and selling crabs, preparing and selling poultry and game, etc.

Frank Talmage did not impress me very much and was a difficult man to work for. The staff of the shop in happy contrast were very nice to work with and I got on very well with them all. As for the customers, mostly they were fine but a few were awkward.

I was at the shop for ten years, approximately. From September 1959 I worked there for R.H. Larby, who bought the shop after Frank Talmage retired.

Sometime after the death of Dorothy, in 1974, I left Cambridge Terrace, which had been condemned, and moved to Rothwell House in Wellington Road where I lived for some thirteen years. I have now lived in Carlysle Court, King's Road (where I moved to from Rothwell House), for eight years.

My overall view nowadays of Crowthorne is that there has been a vast improvement in it from when I first moved to the village. Someone mentioned that it was like a "cemetery with lights" when I first came, but shops were small and friendly and one could buy almost

My Memories of Crowthorne Yesteryear and other accounts

all types of clothing for ladies and gents in Armitage's, Macey's or Long's, also household fabrics, curtaining, towels, etc.

Now there are two supermarkets and three banks (while there used to be only two), but I'm sorry to say the small shops like Bill (Edwin) Dray's (grocer), hairdresser John A. Bennett, both in the High Street; the small outfitter's, Macey's, of Church Street, are gone; and a few yards further along from there (on the opposite side of the road) was a fried fish and chip shop, though we now have another fish and chip shop in the High Street.

There are still the same three pubs in the High Street that have always been there: the Prince Alfred, the Crowthorne Inn and the Iron Duke.

I only went into the old sweet shop (a cafe or snack bar selling sweets) in the High Street twice, that was once owned by Mr T. Mitchell and is now a secondhand goods shop run by C.O.A.T.S. (Crowthorne Old Age to Teens Society) charity shop. They do a very good trade all the week, with the proceeds going to the old people of Crowthorne.

The improvement of the village is still going on. Recently, for example, by great demand, six bus stops were given bus shelters, supplied by Crowthorne Parish Council.

Tom Pepper lives in King's Road, in the village.

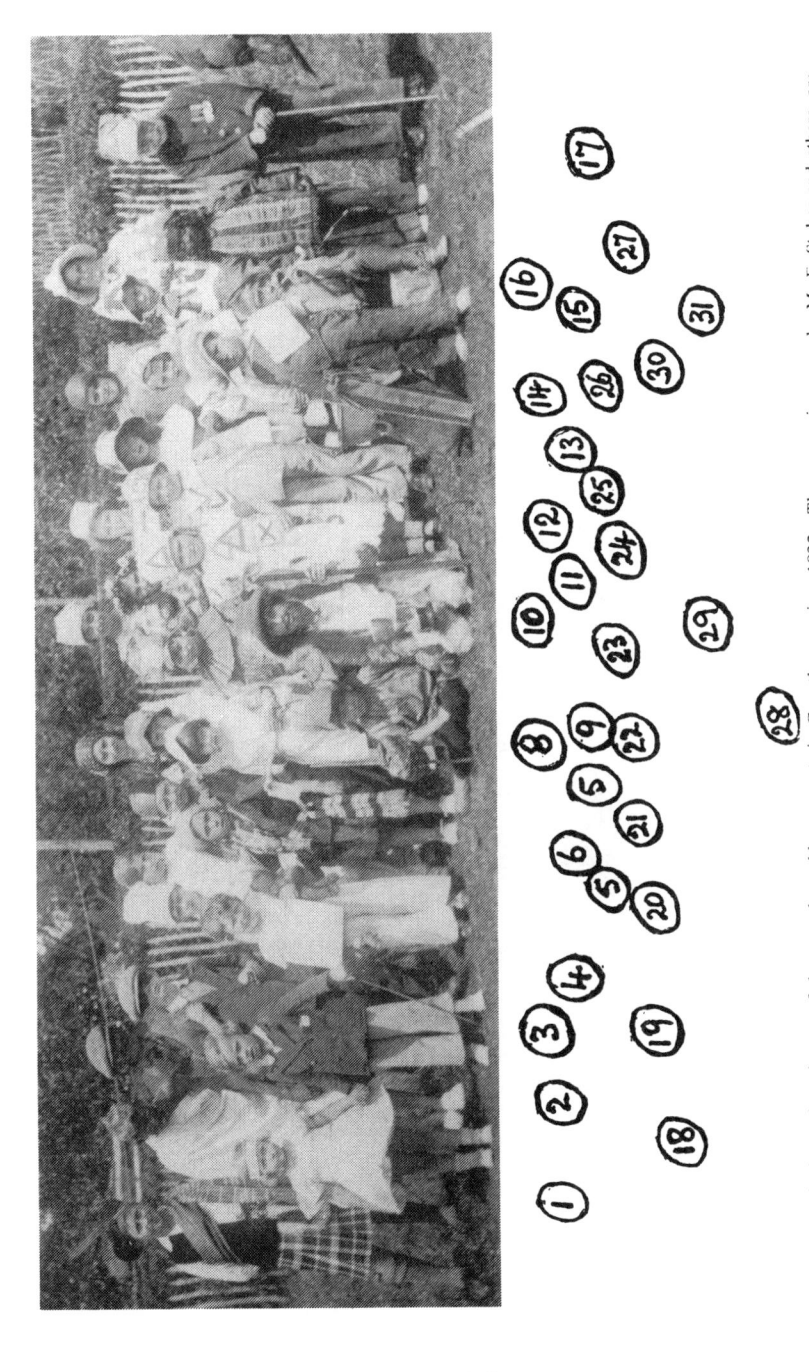

My Memories of Crowthorne Yesteryear and other accounts

Children in fancy dress in one of the annual gymkhana events in Crowthorne, circa 1932. These occasions, run by Mr E. Stokes and others, are detailed fully in *Our Memories of Crowthorne Yesteryear*. Participants:- 1. ? ; 2., 3. and 4. three Justice boys; 5. ? ; 6. Vera Ankerson; 7. ? ; 8. Maisie Manktilow; 9. Avis Webber; 10. Winnie Watkins; 11. and 12. ? ; 13. Joan Kingston; 14. Marjorie Dale; 15. and 16. ? ; 17. Ernie Milam; 18. ? ; 19. José Daniel (now Mrs Stonebridge); 20. Maurice Honeybell; 21. Beryl Daniel (now Mrs Day); 22., 23. and 24. ? ; 25. John Clacey; 26. Winnie Milam; 27., 28. and 29. ? ; 30. ? Bird; 31. ? .   Several of the unidentified children were from Sandhurst. (Photo courtesy of Beryl Day.)

My Memories of Crowthorne Yesteryear and other accounts

Open-top charabanc outing to Southsea, of the Methodist Church, Crowthorne, circa 1928. A notice on the vehicle, 'Speed 12 M.P.H.' meant (if obeyed) the trip would have taken some five hours each way! Passengers:- 1. Granny Kingston; 2. Mr Read; 3. Mrs Waite; 4. 'Granny' Waite; 5., 6. & 7. ?; 8. Wilf Nans; 9. Bert Woodage; 10. Colin Vaughan; 11. Ray Barber; 12. Mona Edwards; 13. & 14. ?; 15. Ivy Justice; 16. Ray Slattery; 17. Jack Slattery; 18. Mrs Slattery; 19. Victor Hale; 20. Alan Hale; 21. 'Granny' Hale; 22. Charlie Torkington; 23. Mrs Read; 24. Milly Welman; Beryl Daniel (now Mrs Day), baby; 25. Emily Cook; 26. Betty Waite; 27. John Daniel; 28., 29. & 30. ?; 31. Avis Daniel; 32. Milly Welman; Beryl 33. Mrs Redshaw; 34. Mrs Wheeler; 35. Eric Sewell; 36. ?.

(Photo courtesy of Beryl Day.)

334

My Memories of Crowthorne Yesteryear and other accounts

Crowthorne C. of E. School top classroom picture, 1949. Back row, l. to r., Muriel Saunders, Shirley Woodason, Colleen Sullivan, Alice Butler, Esther Bernard, Margaret Wyles, Clare Price, Janet Dorrell. Middle row, l. to r., Peter Clarke, Edward (Ted) Cane, Ken Butcher, Michael Pratt, John Woods, Richard Varden, Maurice Woodason, Robert Bowler. Front row, Wendy Scrivens (?), Jeanne Gange, new teacher at the school, Mr Webb, teacher Mrs L. Mohr, Josephine Hughes, Jean Hayward.   (Photo courtesy of Josephine Hughes.)

My Memories of Crowthorne Yesteryear and other accounts

Her Majesty the Queen being driven along Duke's Ride, close to Albert Road and Wiltshire Avenue, towards the village. Date uncertain, but possibly in 1974 when she visited Wellington College to open 'Queen's Court', a complex of classrooms, lecture rooms and a theatre (information supplied by the college).
(Photo courtesy of Mary Watts.)

My Memories of Crowthorne Yesteryear and other accounts

The main entrance-exit of Broadmoor Hospital today, from major constructional alterations that took place at the hospital in the latter part of the 1980s. (Photo courtesy of Mary Lane.)

Peter Tickner, Crowthorne postman for nineteen years, soon after his retirement in October 1995. Picture shows him proudly holding a camcorder, he was presented with, from the Crowthorne Traders' Association in the village, in recognition of his work for them. *(See also pages 321 - 324.)* (Photo - The Wokingham Times.)

MY MEMORIES OF THE TYPHOID FEVER OUTBREAK IN CROWTHORNE.   by Shirley E. Peckham.

While my memories tell me that I was working at Talmage's the butcher's at the time of the epidemic, I could not have been because the event was in the spring of 1949, apparently, when I was in my last months at school. This, therefore, points to a flaw or distortion in my recollections of the incident.

Like Win Rixon (you will have read, in her account in this book), I recall cars or vans going about the village issuing messages from loud-speaker systems to householders, particularly: "Boil all drinking water." This went on for days.

The typhoid outbreak was said to have been caused by, or attributed to, tinned corned beef (from a 6lbs tin) sold from Swain's, the butcher's in the village High Street, all those affected bought and ate. I never heard that this was officially confirmed. However, a number of people contracted the disease, twenty or more very likely, some of them whom died. Thirteen were taken to an isolation hospital in Winchester (as detailed fully in *Our Memories of Crowthorne Yesteryear*).

Several homes in Pinewood Avenue were among those hit, really bringing the situation home to me! And up to three people in each of those homes suffered the illness, some of whom died. Two people in one house (possibly a husband and wife) applied in some cases.

I do not remember the names of those in Pinewood Avenue concerned, except – if my memory serves me right – the Norton family, who lived near to the Avenue's crossroads with Ellis Road.

All the time the trouble was going on everyone talked about it in alarming, though some in frivolous (bravado-like), style. Anyone with a sore-throat became over-anxious as to, have I got the disease now?

It was a great relief, of course, when we had the 'all clear' that the disease had finally (excuse the expression) died out in the area.

FINALLY

Many, particularly Crowthorne, residents were disappointed in not being able (weren't in time, or heard about it too late) to buy a copy of *Our Memories of Crowthorne Yesteryear*, published in November 1994, and all 300 copies sold out in 3½ months. If, reader, you were one of these people and would like a copy, I am considering a reprint and therefore ask that you contact me at the publisher's address in the preliminary pages of this book. If I have sufficient demand I will arrange a reprint of the book as soon as possible. The cost per book was and likely *will* be £13.95, plus £1 p & p. Please do not send payment when you let me know you would like to buy one. I will advise you about this in correspondence after hearing from you.

CROWTHORNE
Sketch Maps

On the following four pages are sketch maps of Crowthorne, viz:-

Map 1 - West Crowthorne
Map 2 - Central Crowthorne
Map 3 - East Crowthorne
Map 4 - Crowthorne and surrounding areas.

All sketch maps are approximate.

LEGEND

══════	Road (Maps 1 - 3)
▬▬▬▬▬▬	Road (Map 4)
──┼──┼──	Railway
■	Building
⬭	Lake/Pond
🌲 🌳	Trees
─ · ─	Civil Parish Boundary (CP)

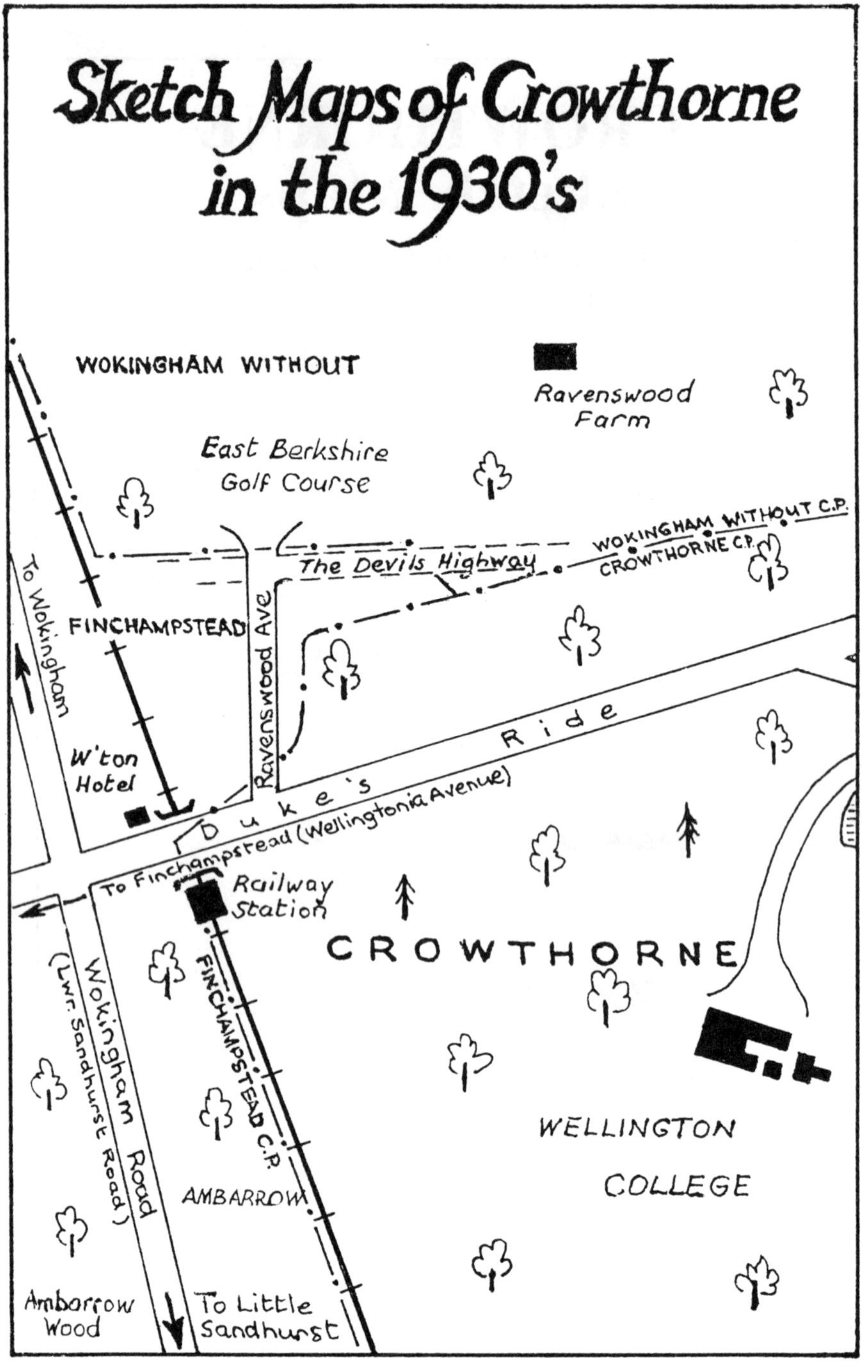

My Memories of Crowthorne Yesteryear and other accounts

Sketch Maps of Crowthorne in the 1930's

MAP 1

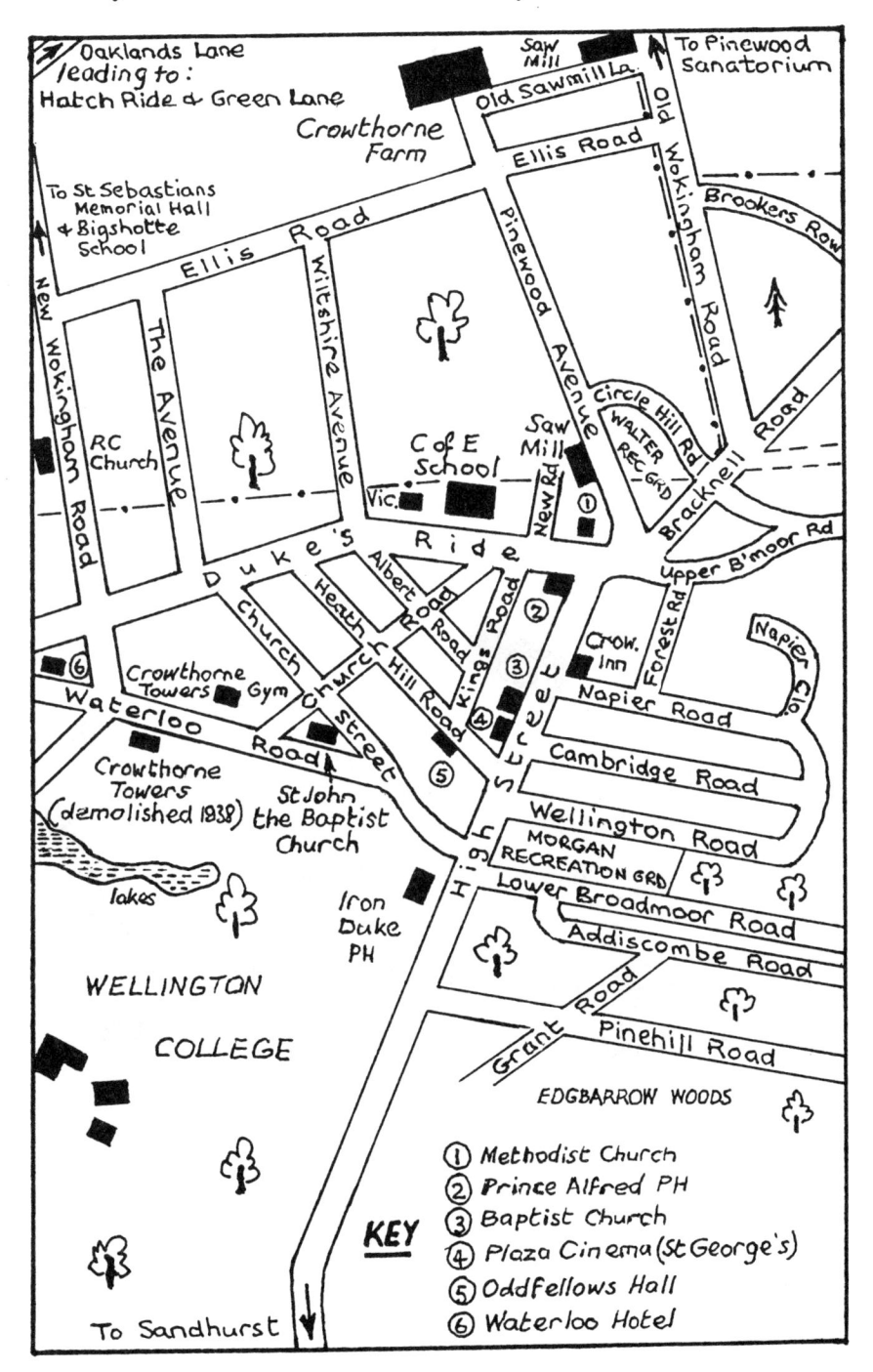

My Memories of Crowthorne Yesteryear and other accounts

KEY
① Methodist Church
② Prince Alfred PH
③ Baptist Church
④ Plaza Cinema (St George's)
⑤ Oddfellows Hall
⑥ Waterloo Hotel

MAP 2

Page 341

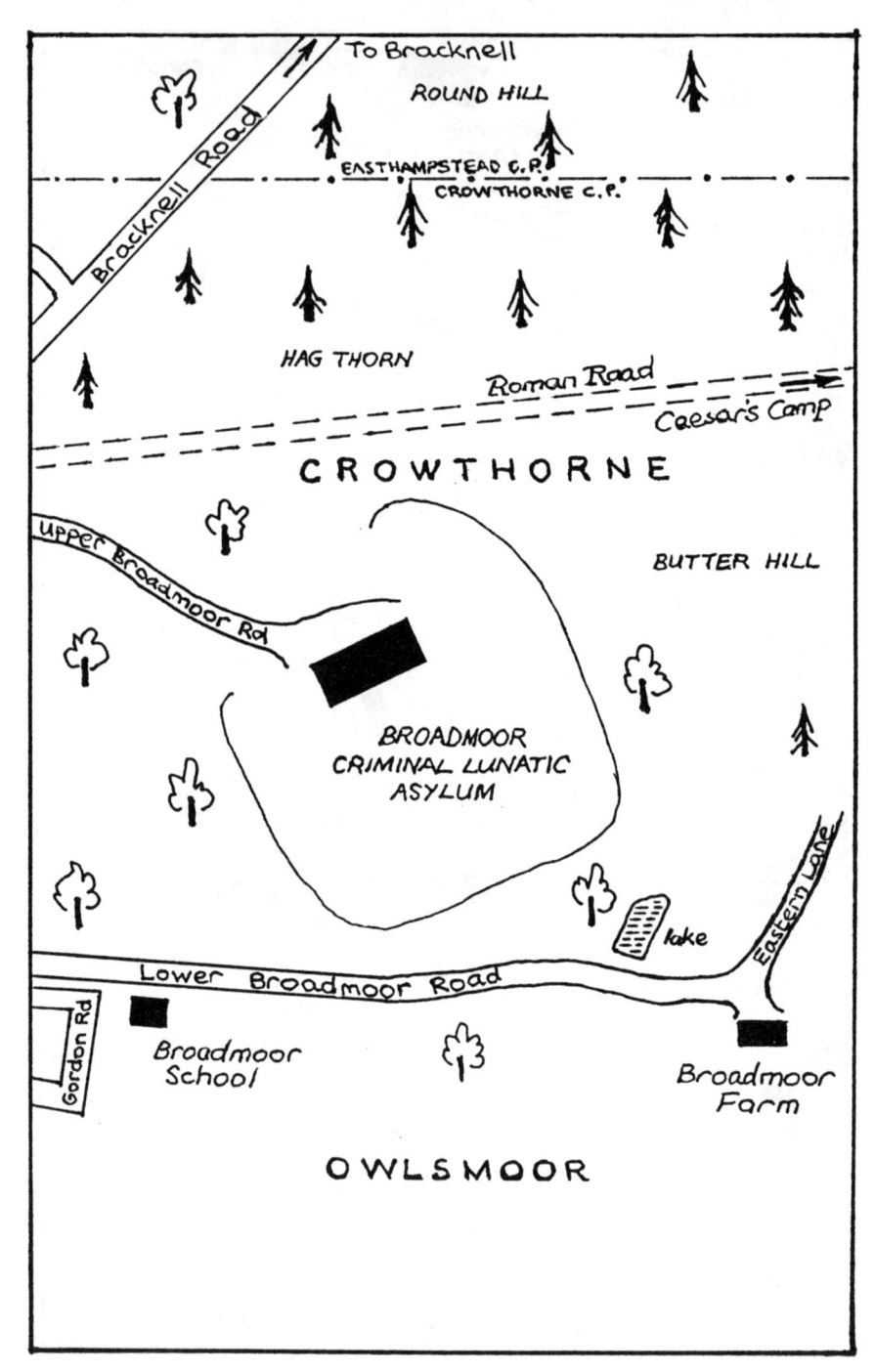

My Memories of Crowthorne Yesteryear and other accounts

To Bracknell

ROUND HILL

EASTHAMPSTEAD C.P.
CROWTHORNE C.P.

Bracknell Road

HAG THORN

Roman Road

Caesar's Camp

CROWTHORNE

Upper Broadmoor Rd

BUTTER HILL

BROADMOOR CRIMINAL LUNATIC ASYLUM

lake

Eastern Lane

Lower Broadmoor Road

Gordon Rd

Broadmoor School

Broadmoor Farm

OWLSMOOR

MAP 3

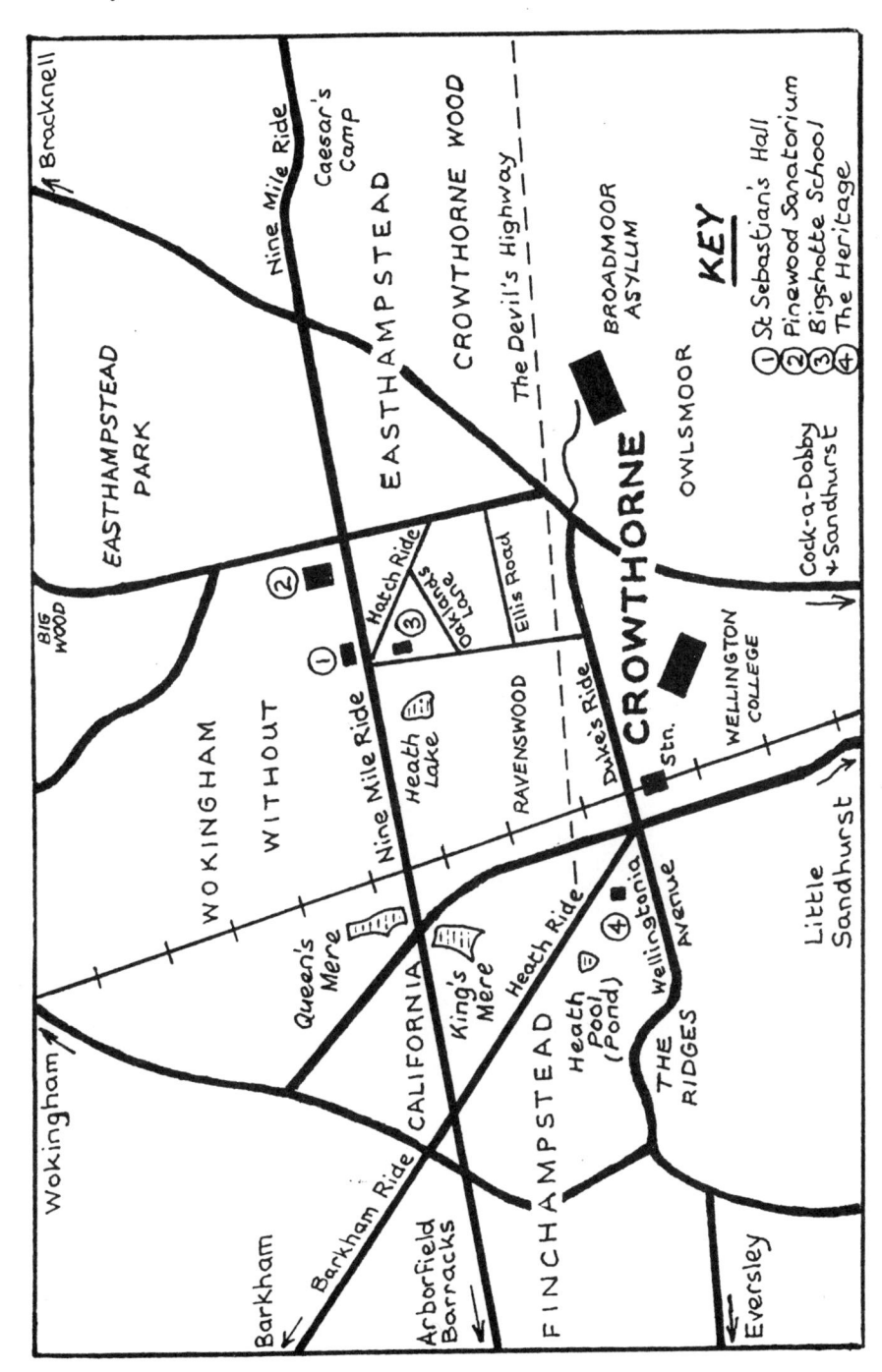

My Memories of Crowthorne Yesteryear and other accounts

MAP 4